AN APPRAISAL OF THE NEGRO IN COLONIAL SOUTH CAROLINA, A STUDY IN AMERICANIZATION

An Appraisal of the Negro In Colonial South Carolina

A STUDY IN AMERICANIZATION

BY

FRANK J. KLINGBERG, Ph.D.

Professor of History
University of California at Los Angeles

THE ASSOCIATED PUBLISHERS
WASHINGTON, D.C.
1941

To

DR. CARTER GODWIN WOODSON

*Founder of the Association for the Study
of Negro Life and History. Author, Editor,
and Publisher of Significant Work, Establishing that American History is One Story
of All Its Peoples*

TABLE OF CONTENTS

PREFACE

THE function of the historian is to present the long view of events and to analyze the present by going upstream to the origins of our own times. A main contemporary current is frequently made up not of the downstream additions, of the recent decades, but is first to be found for from the lower broad reaches. The Nile and the Colorado are not fed in their last stretches but from remote lakes or upland streams.

The study of the South Carolina plantation is to be linked with similar developments in the Americas and it has an importance not confined to South Carolina in the colonial period. Capitalistic farming, in the form of the plantation, is not the product of this century, but has been an American phenomenon wherever large scale operations and investments were necessary, as in the West Indies, in South Carolina, or in California. It is not, moreover, necessarily a phenomenon involving slave labor but appears in certain areas with white native, Mexican, or other immigrant labor.

Inherent in the plantation regime are many of the characteristics of capitalistic enterprise, especially the large unit of production which makes the farm colonist a losing competitor and calls either for his absorption or his expulsion. This phenomenon, it should be pointed out, is the effect of the spread of the plantation, and not the intention of the persons within the system.

The transformation from farm to plantation may even take place with a social unawareness on the part of all parties concerned. It is of interest that the S.P.G. missionary in South Carolina was a pioneer observer and reporter of this all but inexorable change, and foretold its consequences, good and bad, noting particularly the loss of his family unit, the small farm or yeoman parishioner, as he was pushed to new ground farther west. Legislation in Parliament, in colonial legislatures, as in the case of Jamaica, seemed unavailing to arrest or prevent this drainage even when the plantation owner himself used his utmost power to stem the flight of men who, if they could remain, would strengthen the white community, fill the militia, preserve order in case of insurrection, maintain schools, and in general help build a new society.

In the West Indies, in South Carolina, in California, and elsewhere, the plantation developed. In one case a rector and his entire
parish moved from an island to Carolina, and there helped build
the identical economy from which they had fled, with its ever-recur-
rent catastrophe. In California, the large Spanish land grants probably predisposed this development, and it was later intensified by the
gold rush, the first nonagrarian migration in our history, which
made California economy capitalistic almost at a blow. In the United
States the plantation has always lived side by side with the farm, and
the ebb and flow can be seen today in California where the small
farmer, growing vegetables, fruits, and grains, is often concealed
by the high-sounding term, "ranch."

The continuity of historic events is illustrated by Federal and other
legislation of recent years which attempts, as did the British legislative bodies, to prevent the destruction of the farmer by aiding his
threatened community, or re-establishing him in new agricultural
enterprises. The folk story, too, runs through cycles of repetition:
thousands of Americans of eighteenth century stock have lately arrived in the West, dispossessed, as were the colonial refugees, by tra-
ditional manifestations of plantation expulsion, together with twen-
tieth century machinery, the cotton picker, for example, and the
hazards of climate, the dust bowl.

The founding of the colony of South Carolina, as here told,
is cheerful reading, for it is a success story. So closely interwoven
into the plot is the Negro, that it is impossible to separate him or to
treat him as a race apart. With the particular genius which has always made him more than an impersonal unit of production, he was
to impress himself so fundamentally into the creative pattern of the
community that the white master often spoke of him as one of the
family, and recognized him as the teacher of his own race, a fact
clearly demonstrated in the account of the Charleston Negro School.

In telling the Negro's story, that of all the builders of South
Carolina for three quarters of a century, must necessarily be told.
These fresh accounts give glimpses of all the peoples active in the
founding of a colony. Here were the "honest Switzers" and Germans, brought in to produce food and household materials so that
the wealth of the plantations need not be paid out to New York
and Pennsylvania. Here were skilled mechanics, white and black,
to make the community self-sufficient in its necessary crafts. Here

were proud French Huguenots and Britons, experimenting with new crops, building beautiful homes, drawing upon the homeland for literature and the luxuries of an expanding economy. All was adventure and daring. The account of the successful introduction of indigo culture, despite a West Indian *saboteur,* by Eliza Lucas Pinckney, mother of two signers of the Declaration of Independence, reminds the reader of colonial rivalry and of the many ties between the Caribbean Islands and the American continent. In the search for marketable crops, silk and wine were failures, but indigo and rice made the port of Charleston equal in importance to that of New York in the colonial period. Tar, turpentine, and other products of the forest, sent out in large amounts, brought wealth, settlers, and therefore new developments.

The Indian was there, the Yamassee, the Cherokee, and the Creek, fighting a valiant but confused rear-guard action. By means of the fur trade, he was the link between the colony and points west to the Mississippi. He had only a continent to lose, while Negro and white were backed by Africa and Europe, with endless resources of men and skills. Disease appeared in every report, drove families from coast to uplands, back to the cities, back to England, or into the northern colonies. The missionaries, seized by illness due to the hostility of an environment utterly different from that of Great Britain and Ireland, went home to recover, sometimes several times.

Reporting from as many as fourteeen areas, each with five or six men in succession, the missionary was the sounding board of the community. Riding thirty or forty miles to cover his parish, he saw the planter on the tidewater, the poor man on the frontier, the Indian, and always the Negro, and noted every change of a mobile community. Through seventy-five continuous years the story of the founding of a new virile society was recorded upon his eighteenth century film. On the reels of the S.P.G. is preserved Americanization in living process.

To Dr. St. George Leakin Sioussat, Chief of the Division of Manuscripts, Library of Congress, for continual access to manuscripts; to the staff of the Huntington Library; to the staff of the University of California at Los Angeles Library; to the University of California for annual research grants; to Helen E. Livingston for assistance in the collection and study of documents; and to Dr.

Carter G. Woodson for his generosity in making possible the publication of this and other work: to all of these I acknowledge indebtedness over a long period of time.

                              FRANK J. KLINGBERG

University of California,
Los Angeles
August, 1941

CHAPTER I

THE FOUNDERS

AN analysis of the American population instantly reveals the fact that, of the many racial and nationalistic elements which have fed the main stream of United States history, one of the oldest and largest is that of the Negro, who, according to all available estimates of colonial population, arrived early and in such numbers as to equal, and in many cases, far exceed, the white population. As an involuntary immigrant, living and working in communities where he represented a suppressed majority, his full part in the building of America needs to be brought to light. Indeed, the fact that his contribution has been so largely overlooked by scholars, as compared with European groups: Irish, German, Italian, Greek, Polish, Russian, etc., suggests a tacit acceptance of his status as an original settler and founder.[1] Equally indispensable to the mastery of the continent, and fundamentally analogous to other immigrant groups in the problems confronting him, the story of the Negro, when laid bare from the beginning, presents clearly the successive stages of Americanization and adaptation to the New World environment.

No other area on the American continent is more rewarding for the study of relationship between the Negro and white man, than that embraced under the term, colonial South Carolina, covering as it did areas not clearly defined. Here the Negro came early, from the West Indies and from Africa, in such numbers that the conflicting estimates show only one constant feature: the Negro in excess of the white man. Of these estimates, that of 1715 seems fairly accurate. In this year the population of South Carolina was given as 6,250 whites and 10,500 Negroes. A generation later, in 1749, 25,000 white inhabitants and 39,000 Negroes were reported. The 1775 figures of approximately 100,000 Negroes to 60,000 whites shows a ratio of ten Negroes to six whites.[2]

[1] For a tacit acceptance of the English and Scotch and the Negroes as the founders of America and all others as immigrants, see the excellent recent study by Carl Wittke, *We Who Built America* (New York, 1939).

[2] For the amazingly different quotas of population statistics see Evarts B. Greene and Virginia D. Harrington, *American Population Before the Federal Census of 1790* (New York: 1932), pp. 172-176. Due to the lack of any organized

In any event, these figures indicate the important part played by the Negro race in the development of the Americas. Reginald Coupland puts the matter boldly in his conclusion that as a productive economic unit, "America was saved by Africa."[3] An even more arresting suggestion is that in the eighteenth century, at least, the relationship between the British colonies and Africa was closer than that between these colonies and South America. Connecting commercial lines ran from Liverpool, Bristol, London, to Africa, across the Atlantic, to the West Indies, up the Continental coast and back to British ports, thus forming one of the heaviest of all trade routes with business running into millions of pounds annually. While exact figures are not available for the migration either of Negroes from Africa or Whites from Europe, a reasonable deduction is that before 1800 the stream of Negroes was much the larger.[4] Obviously no such human bridge of contact existed between North America and South America. The fact that the colonial South drew so heavily on this Negro immigration has caused one recent writer to comment that the stock of the South is, in origin, "pure British or pure African,"[5] omitting for emphasis the Huguenots, Germans, Swiss, Spaniards, and the French of Louisiana.

Under the conditions of his economic and social life, the first written record of the Negro was made, not by himself, but by the white man. More recently, as with other peoples, he is becoming more aware of his own history, and giving his own emphasis and points of view. Busy in the unearthing of new or more complete records are Negro

effort toward accurate population figures before the first census, various sources have been used by the authors. The figures quoted for 1715 are from George Chalmer's *Revolt,* II, 7, and George Bancroft, *History of the United States* (6 vols.), II, p. 238; those for 1749 from the *Journal* of the Board of Trade; for 1775 from *Correspondence of Henry Laurens.* Slightly earlier figures for 1773 and 1774 show the same Negro preponderance, but the census of 1790 shows a ratio of seven whites to five Negroes, revealing either a striking change or the unreliability of earlier calculations. For comparison see in *ibid.* the population statistics for 1787 (p. 8). For example, Virginia had 300,000 black men and 300,000 whites; Maryland 174,000 whites, 80,000 Negroes.

[3] Reginald Coupland, *The British Anti-Slavery Movement* (London: 1933), p. 18.

[4] W. E. B. Du Bois, *Black Folk Then and Now* (New York: 1939), p. 142. Du Bois estimates "that 25,000 Negroes a year arrived in America between 1698 and 1707. After the Asiento of 1713 this number rose to 30,000 annually, and before the Revolutionary War it had reached at least 40,000 and perhaps 100,000 slaves a year. . . . The total number of slaves imported is not known. Dunbar estimates that nearly 900,000 came to America in the sixteenth century, 2,750,000 in the seventeenth, 7,000,000 in the eighteenth, and over 4,000,000 in the nineteenth, perhaps 15,000,000 in all. . . ."

[5] Green Peyton, "Call me a Confederate," in *The Southern Literary Messenger,* I, No. 7 (July 1939), pp. 435-436.

scholars and institutions.[6] The background of the Negro as a business man is, for instance, quite different from what the white man might assume it to be. His history as a laborer likewise needs telling by himself. So, too, his rise into the professions must be told by his own historians to get the full picture.[7] But the story of his beginnings in this country, so often seen only through fiction or legend, can best be told by such contemporary agencies as the Society for the Propagation of the Gospel in Foreign Parts,[8] which, by its very nature, was intimately associated with both the Negro and the white man in the colonies. Even in its early days, the structure of colonial society in America was complex and the tie of relationship with the mother country many-stranded. In this variegated scene, the missionaries of the Society served in the double capacity as creators or transformers of this new society and as reporters of the changing social scene.

The activities of the S.P.G. in South Carolina, both in Christianization and education of the Negro, in addition to their immediate interests in the history of the Commonwealth, are also of wider significance with an element of timelessness inherent. The community in Great Britain, beginning with the S.P.G., acted as an intermediary between the white man and the Negro in the Empire and is doing so today. This function, as interventionist, has repeatedly aroused the hostility of the slave owner, and the employer of Negro labor. The objection to similar interference was one of the remote causes of the Boer War. In the West Indies, the white man was so overwhelmingly in the minority that he could not openly resist British humanitarian intervention, because he was dependent on British protection for his sheer existence. When such European protection became temporarily confused, as in the case of France during the French Revolution, the Negro drove the white man out of Haiti.

Early South Carolina is particularly interesting because here, during the eighteenth century, a more friendly race relationship between white man and Negro was worked out by Christian leaders and the

---

[6] Valuable work is being accomplished by The Association for the Study of Negro Life and History, Incorporated, of Washington, D.C. The Association publishes *The Journal of Negro History;* and *The Negro History Bulletin.*

[7] See *The Negro History Bulletin,* edited by Carter G. Woodson, III, No. 4 (January, 1940), pp. 49-50, 62, for an article entitled "The Background of the Negro as a Business Man," also in *ibid.,* III, No. 5 (February 1940), see articles "Negro History Week Features Labor," pp. 65, 72; "The Negro as a Laboring Man in the New World," pp. 66, 72-73, 74; "Gains and Losses of Negro Labor Summarized," pp. 68, 70-72.

[8] Hereinafter referred to as the Society or the S.P.G.

Negro in time became a Christian. Notwithstanding Secession, Civil War, and Reconstruction, these ideals have animated humane men not only in South Carolina but everywhere in the South.[9]

The S.P.G. based its program on the fundamental assumption that the Negro's future would be identified with the white man's fortune which thesis was pre-visioned in the crucial early decades of the eighteenth century. From 1702,[10] when the Society's missionaries first entered South Carolina,[11] they recorded their progress in the informative reports now to be presented. Working side by side with the other clergy who were maintained by the colony of South Carolina, the missionaries of the Society, particularly charged to instruct the Negroes as well as whites,[12] had a double duty, whereas the dissenting

[9] For an illuminating statement of the reasons leading to southern secession, and the terms which the southern whites had worked out as a scheme by which two unlike races could live together, see Ralph H. Gabriel, *The Course of American Democratic Thought* (New York, 1940), Ch. 10. For the re-emergence of this scheme after the Civil War, when the fundamentals of this discipline had been adapted to the new order see Ch. 12. The withdrawal of the northern armies by President Hayes and the decision of the United States Supreme Court of 1883 virtually nullifying the Civil Rights Act of 1875 ended northern intervention on a large scale in the race relationships between white men and the Negro. With the tacit consent of the North, the Southern states assumed control of their own internal affairs as had been the ardent demand of John C. Calhoun, before 1850. Freed from the tension of northern intervention, the South, under its own leaders, Thomas Nelson Page and others, set itself to the task of educating the Negro and protecting him from violence. As time passed, more and more Negro leaders spoke for their race in many diverse fields.

[10] Samuel Thomas to [Secretary], South Carolina, January 29, 1703, in *Journal of the Society for the Propagation of the Gospel in Foreign Parts* (Library of Congress Transcripts), I, June 18, 1703. Cited hereafter as *Journal of S.P.G.* (L.C. Trans.).

[11] The worship of the Church of England in South Carolina was established by law on November 30, 1706. Article One of the Church Act was "An Act for the Establishment of Religious Worship in this Province, according to the Church of England; and for the Erecting of Churches for the public Worship of God; and also, for the Maintenance of Ministers, and the building convenient houses for them." Part of it read, "That the Book of Common Prayer, and Administration of the Sacraments, and other Rites and Ceremonies of the Church, according to the use of the Church of England, the Psalter or Psalms of David, and Morning and Evening Prayer therein contained, be solemnly read by all and every Minister or Reader in every Church which now is, or hereafter shall be settled, and by Law established within this Province; and that all Congregations and Places for the Public Worship, according to the Usage of the Church of England, within this Province, for the Maintenance of whose Ministers and the Persons officiating therein, any certain Income or Revenue is, or shall by the Laws of this Province be established and enjoined to be raised or paid, shall be deemed Settled and Established Churches." See Frederick Dalcho, *Historical Account of the Protestant Episcopal Church in South-Carolina* (Charleston, 1820), Appendix 1. "The Laws Relating to Religious Worship in South Carolina," pp. 437-438.

[12] See the Extracts from the "Instructions for the Clergy Employed by the Society . . ." and "Directions to the Catechists for Instructing Indians, Negroes, etc." in Frederick Dalcho, *Historical Account of the Protestant Episcopal Church in South Carolina,* pp. 43-51.

ministers devoted themselves largely to the white colonists. The educational, inseparable from the Christianization program, was the first break in the dyke, and the beginning of the whole enterprise which made it possible for Negroes in the United States to be Christianized, to become readers and, passing out of slavery, to have their own churches, bishops, colleges, and institutions.

In order to teach the essentials of Christian doctrines, the missionaries developed skilful techniques. Some, without much use of books, depended upon sermons, conversations, and oral instructions; others upon reading and writing as preliminary measures. The latter scheme was preferred by the majority of missionaries. Dr. Francis Le Jau, one of the founders, was apparently among those who wished to select candidates for instruction with care. Plans for education met with opposition from many of the planters, but, with a few masters cooperating, progress, at first on a laboratory basis, soon included larger groups. The opponents of instruction held to the tradition that education was useless; that it was unnecessary; that it took too much time away from manual work; that it made the slaves lazy and proud; and that the slave could not interpret what he read.[13] It may be noted here that these same objections were raised in England when book learning was proposed for white illiterates, and that objectors to the extension of schooling to new groups used the same phrases in describing the pride, and untoward conduct of the newly schooled.[14]

[13] Original interpretations of the dramas and poetry of the Bible were given by the Negroes, after they learned to read. The Negroes had a tendency to dramatize their reading and would spread their own interpretations of Christianity to others. One report that often found its way to England was that the Negroes, after instructions, would think themselves better than the average slave. The Rev. Charles Martyn said, ". . . they become lazy and proud, entertaining too high an opinion of themselves, and neglecting their daily labour." See Charles Martyn to Philip Bearcroft, St. Andrews, South Carolina, June 25, 1752, in *S.P.G. MSS.* (L.C. Trans.), B 20, No. 137; same letter in *Journal of S.P.G.* (L.C. Trans.), Vol. XII, November 17, 1752.

[14] Bernard Mandeville's *Essay on Charity and the Charity Schools* which appeared in 1723 is typical of the bitter attacks on general education. "The more a shepherd and ploughman know of the world, the less fitted he'll be to go through the fatigue and hardship of it with cheerfulness . . ." he maintained, and further, that education which proposed "to divert children from useful labour until they are 14 or 15 years old is a wrong way to qualify them for it when they are grown up." In the same year "Cato" in *The British Journal* demanded, "What benefit can accrue to the public by taking the dregs of the people out of the kennels and driving their betters into them?" For a discussion of this opposition see M.G. Jones, *The Charity School Movement* (Cambridge: University Press, 1938), pp. 85-96. Du Bois offers a provocative discussion of the problem of the slave as allied to the contemporary struggle of free white labor to gain the rights of education and political expression, pointing out the close connection between "significant dates in the emancipation of Negro slaves and the enfranchisement of white workers." See W. E. B. Du Bois, *Black Folk Then and Now*, Ch. 9 "Emancipation and Enfranchisement," pp. 177-195.

No better summary of slave life and of the impediments to missionary work can be found than the letter presented to the Society by the Clergy of South Carolina in 1713. This document is worth quoting at length:

. . . The conversion of slaves which is the second article, is, considering the present circumstances of things, scarcely possible. 'Tis true, indeed, that an odd slave here and there may be converted when a minister has leisure and opportunity for so doing, but this seldom happens. Nevertheless it must be said to Dr. Le Jau's advantage, that his endeavours have been very great this way, and not altogether unsuccessful tho' some unreasonable malicious people can give him no thanks for his service. When I say this of the Doctor I exclude not the rest of the clergy from their just share of praise in this respect, since there is none of [them] who have been for any time in that Province that have not distinguished themselves by a commendable zeal and diligence in this matter. But alas! as the opportunities are neither great nor frequent for carrying on so good a work so the success must be little and inconsiderable in comparison of what might be expected because there are so many rules and impediments that lie in the way.

1st. The slaves have not time to be instructed by the minister but on the Lord's Day; and then he has work enough from the white folk on his hands; nor is it possible or can it be expected from him, that he should follow them at their work on week days.

2ndly. The plantations are so many and so remote and distant from one another that the slaves can't be well assembled together for their instruction; and if they could there would be a great deal of hazard in the experiment, because they would thereby have a opportunity of knowing their own strength and superiority in point of number; and perhaps may be tempted to recover their liberty, though it were the slaughter and destruction of the whole colony.

3rdly. The masters of slaves are generally of opinion that a slave grows worse by being a Christian; and therefore instead of instructing them in the principles of Christianity which is undoubtedly their duty, they malign and traduce those that attempt it. This I say is the case of most masters. However, I must not forget to do justice to some who have distinguished themselves by a contrary practice; and are very eminent for the care they take about their slaves in matters of religion.

4thly. The legislature does not countenance or encourage a work of this importance as much as it should or could. The conversion of slaves is thought inconsistent with the planters' secular interest and advantage; and it is they that make up the bulk of our assembly. For besides the general notion that they have their slaves being worse for being Christians, they know that if they would encourage their conversion, they must allow them some reasonable time for their instruction; and this would consequently be a hindrance to their work and an abatement of the master's profit. And tho' this is not openly owned and avowed to be the true cause of that lukewarmness or rather unwillingness, they express on this occasion, yet I may venture to say 'tis so at the bottom. Nor can some of them forbear to speak out their minds, though they endeavour to justify and excuse themselves by pretending that the slaves (the negroes especially) are a wicked stubborn race of men, and can never be true converts, tho' to gull and deceive their masters they may put on an air and appearance of religion; and hence they conclude that it is not only a sensible loss to them, but likewise so much time and pains thrown away to no purpose.

5thly. There are many planters who, to free themselves from the trouble of feeding and clothing their slaves allow them one day in the week to clear ground, and plant for themselves as much as will clothe and subsist them and their families. In order to do this, some Masters give their slaves Saturday, some half that day, and others Sunday only; which they endeavour to justify saying, that if they were not obliged to work that day, they would be employed in that which is worse. 'Tis needless to show the weakness of this excuse, and, therefore, I will only observe, that those who have Saturday given them seldom fail of working more or less on the Lord's Day too; for which they will always have this to say for themselves, that what cannot be perfected one day must be done another and that it is not just to debar a poor slave from that which is no loss or injury to his master, and upon which his food and raiment and the support of his family and all that is dear to him in this world, does so absolutely depend.

Thus I have given a short account of those more obvious impediments that lie in the way to the slaves conversion, nor indeed do I see any likelihood, humanly speaking, how this necessary work, so shamefully and scandalously neglected hitherto can be carried on with any great hope of success if the legislature does not promote and encourage it by proper laws to be enacted for that purpose.

If anyone should think that the clergy can do this of themselves without the Government's countenance and the help of itinerant catechists he is greatly mistaken, for with equal grief and truth I speak it, they have a worse generation of infidels than those poor heathen slaves to deal with; who though they are children in one respect have made themselves worse than dogs in another sense and are scarce worthy to feed upon the crumbs that fall from their father's table. The ignorance, therefore, of those poor slaves in the principles of Christianity in a Christian country and under a Christian government is not so much their fault as their unhappiness in falling into the hands of such ill masters who not only neglect to instruct them but scoff at those who attempt it and give them likewise strange ideas of Christianity from the scandalous lives they lead.[15]

[15] "Instructions of the Clergy of South Carolina given to Mr. [Gideon] Johnston on his coming away for England, enlarged and explained by the said Mr. Johnston, and humbly presented to . . . the Society," in *S.P.G. MSS.* (L.C. Trans.), A 8, pp. 427-430. The Clergy wrote the instructions, March 4, 1712-

This early demand for the "Government's countenance"[16] was repeated many times by the missionaries and by others. A scheme for compulsory education for every tenth Negro is discussed later.

The first worker for the Society was at once beset by numerous difficulties. When the Rev. Samuel Thomas arrived in Charleston on Christmas day, 1702,[17] his mission was to convert the Yamassee Indians. However, on arrival, he found that the Negro and Indian slaves around the Cooper River and Goose Creek needed instruction, so he settled in that district.[18] For this decision, Thomas brought down upon himself the wrath of Mr. Thomas Nairne, agent among the Indians who said in a letter of August 20, 1705:

By a private paper I received in Charlestown containing an account of the Society's transactions. I perceive their good . . . intentions . . . are quite perverted under the notion of converting the Goose Creek negroes as a work good and necessary . . . All Carolina laughs

1713 at Charlestown, and they were presented no doubt in the fall of 1713, see William Taylor to Dr. Le Jau, November 30, 1713, in *S.P.G. MSS.* (L.C. Trans.), A 8, p. 452, in which Mr. Taylor states that Commissary Johnston had arrived and laid before the Society what the missionaries in South Carolina had asked him to present.

[16] In the Civil War, efforts to give aid to the Negroes on the part of the government began early. Private organizations cooperated with the government in helping them and in September, 1861, at Fortress Monroe, the first freedmen's school was opened. On March 3, 1865, a Freedman's Bureau Act was passed which created a "Bureau of Refugees, Freedmen, and Abandoned Lands." Major General O. O. Howard was put at the head of the field. See P. S. Peirce, *The Freedmen's Bureau* (University of Iowa Studies, III, No. 1, Iowa City, 1904.)

[17] Frederick Dalcho, *Historical Account of the Protestant Episcopal Church of South Carolina*, p. 42, states, "The Society . . . had resolved not to obtrude the Episcopal Service upon the Colonists against their wishes. They did not, therefore, appoint Missionaries, until applications were made by the Colonists, for Ministers of the Church of England; nor until they were assured that adequate means would be provided for their comfort and support. As soon as the formation of the Society was known, applications for Missionaries were received from various parts of America. It became then their duty, to send Episcopal Clergymen to the Colonies."

[18] Samuel Thomas was also influenced by the Governor, Sir Nathaniel Johnson, who declared that the Yamassees had revolted from the Spaniards and were unwilling to embrace Christianity, therefore they would leave the English to unite with hostile tribes unless efforts at friendship were made. See Frederick Dalcho, *op. cit.* p. 51. For an account of S.P.G. contact with the Indians in South Carolina, see Frank J. Klingberg, "The Indian Frontier in South Carolina as seen by the S.P.G. Missionary," in *Journal of Southern History*, V, No. 4, November, 1939, pp. 479-500. It is interesting to note that the decision of Mr. Thomas brought about a Standing Order of the Society, "The Report of the Com[tee] about M[r] Edward Marston's Letter to D[r] Bray relating to M[r] Thomas, one of the Society's Missionaries to South Carolina having been read Resolved that it be a Standing Order of this Society that if any Minister sent over to the Plantations with an Allowance from this Society be any particular place, shall fix himself in any other place by the direction of the respective Governor, or other wise this Society will not continue the allowance to the s[d] Minister until the said Change shall be approved by the Society." See *Journal of S.P.G.* (L.C. Photo.), I, p. 105, April 16, 1703.

at that untruth . . . which . . . is an action highly base and dishonor-
able for people who have the best estates in this country and such
numerous families of negroes to employ that men and money designed
for the poor Indians, [is used] to instruct their slaves.[19]

In addition to Captain Nairne, the Rev. Robert Stevens, of Goose
Creek, said he had heard

. . . that Mr. Thomas is instructing the negroes of Goose Creek. I
live at Goose Creek, but know no negroes that he . . . instructed any
other way than by his now and then preaching . . . where there might
be 5 or 6 Christian negroes . . . for I know of no more in Goose
Creek . . . Three or four of those negroes may read, yet it is but
sorrily, and I am informed they have books.[20]

Moreover, Stevens declared that the slaves probably belonged to
the late Governor Moore and "Surely he doth not desire your Honors'
charity to present his Christian slaves with Bibles and Common
Prayer Books, but if they had none, would buy them himself."[21] Although Mr. Thomas had only five communicants at first, the number
soon increased to thirty-two.[22] Mr. Thomas took Negroes for instruction, and taught twenty of them to read.[23] This was a notable beginning and settled the matter permanently for the Society, as to the
Negro's ability to learn quickly.

In 1705, Mr. Thomas took a trip to England and submitted to the
Society ". . . a very full and satisfactory account of the state of the
Church in South Carolina."[24] The Society was acquainted with the
great abuse of employing Negro slaves in their usual labors on Sun-
day; the Secretary of the Society was directed to ask the Bishop of
London[25] for aid in remedying this circumstance. The energetic be-

[19] Thomas Nairne to the Rev. Edward Marston, St. Helena, South Carolina,
August 20, 1705 inclosed in Robert Stevens to the Society P. G., Goose Creek,
n.d. [November 1705] in *S.P.G. MSS.* (L.C. Trans.), A 2, No. clvi.
[20] Robert Stevens to the Society for Propagating the Gospel, n.d. [Novem-
ber, 1705] Goose Creek, South Carolina, in *S.P.G. MSS.* (L.C. Trans.), A 2,
No. clvi.
[21] *Ibid.*
[22] David Humphreys, *Historical Account of the Incorporated Society for the
Propagation of the Gospel in Foreign Parts* (London: 1730), p. 82.
[23] *Ibid.*
[24] Report presented before the Society in 1705, by Samuel Thomas, in
Journal of S.P.G. (L.C. Trans.), Vol. I, January 18, 1705-1706.
[25] The origin of the jurisdiction of the Bishop of London in sending over
ministers to the plantations can be found in *An Account of the Society for the
Propagation of the Gospel* (London, 1706), pp. 11-12. (Huntington Library).
Extremely rare third Report "An Order of King and Council is said to have
been made to commit unto the Bishop of London, for the time being, the
Care and Pastoral Charge of sending over ministers into our Foreign Plantations, and having the Jurisdiction of them; but when the present Lord Bishop

ginnings made by Thomas were ended by his early death in 1706, but he had laid a foundation for his successors. The astonishment of Captain Nairne that the missionary should decide to teach Negroes to read seems to have been genuine and unbounded. His further point that the S.P.G. funds were to be used for the Indians, and that, if Negroes were to be taught, it should be at the planter's expense, was perhaps a natural consideration to a commissioner of Indian affairs.

The man who followed Thomas was one of the most capable and famous missionaries ever sent to the Colonies. Dr. Francis Le Jau, a native of Angiers, France, who had been a missionary to St. Christopher in the West Indies, from 1700-1701, arrived in Goose Creek in 1706.[26] Overcome at first, by the problem of his huge parish, Dr. Le Jau, wrote:

---

of London was advanc'd to that See in 1675, his Lordship found the title so defective, that little or no Good had come of it. For it being left to such as were concern'd in those parts to provide for the transporting of such ministers as should be appointed or allowed by the Bishop; there was so little done, that when his Lordship enquired how the several colonies were provided, he found there were scarce four ministers of the Church of England in all the vast Tract of *America*, and not above one or two of them at most, regularly sent over. To supply this sad Defect, his Lordship made his Proposals to several of these Places to furnish them with Chaplains, and had generally an Encouragement from them to do so. And for the better effecting of it, his Lordship prevailed with his Majesty King Charles II to allow to each minister, or School-master that should go over, the Sum of twenty Pounds for his Passage; which Royal Bounty hath been ever since continued. Instructions were given to each Governor to admit none authoritatively to serve any cure of Souls, or to teach School in such only as brought over the Bishop of London's License with them. And as a farther great Favor, it was ordered that from that time, every minister should be one of the vestry of his respective Parish and all ecclesiastical jurisdiction was to devolve upon the ministers except Inductions, Marriages, Probates of Wills and administrations left to the Governors for revenue." See also Simeon E. Baldwin, "The American Jurisdiction of the Bishop of London in Colonial Times," in the *Proceedings of the American Antiquarian Society,* XIII, Pt. 2, October 21, 1899, pp. 179-221. In 1709, the Bishop of London recommended to the Society that, until some arrangement could be made about sending a Bishop to govern the Church in plantations, a commissary be sent over to superintend the clergy there. See *Journal of S.P.G.* (L.C. Trans.), I, June 3, 1709. For an extended account of the relation of the Bishops of London to the Colonial Church, see A. L. Cross, *The Anglican Episcopate and the American Colonies* (Cambridge, Mass., 1924), pp. 1-240 *passim* and Norman Sykes, *Edmund Gibson, Bishop of London, 1669-1748* (London, 1926), pp. 333-375.

[26] "There is no evidence of the Huguenots having had a minister of their own nativity prior to 1706, when Francis Le Jau, born and reared a Huguenot in France and Episcopally ordained in London, came to Carolina to officiate in the Anglican Church of Goose Creek. . . . Le Jau had been a canon in St. Paul's Cathedral and had been honored with the degree of Doctor of Divinity by his alma mater, Trinity College, Dublin. He was sent to the Goose Creek congregation in conformity with the policy of the English government to cater to the desire of the French portion of the population in the province. . . . Doctor Le Jau was a constructive religious statesman, fearless in his convictions, a builder and organizer of rare skill and insight. He was a thoroughly Anglicized

I have been now six months here and can give some account of the place . . . the negroes are generally very bad men, chiefly those that are scholars. I will baptise none but such as lead a Christian life and of whom I have good testimony. My parish reaches about 30 miles in length and near as many in breadth up between Ashley and Cooper rivers, a vast number of children were not baptised because their parents had no money.[27]

However, three months later, he had taken stock and had begun systematic organization.

I design with God's blessing to have a day in the week for the instruction of the poor . . . negroes, their masters like it well most of them; they are well used in this place, better than in the islands [West Indies] ; but I can hardly do anything till I have a house of my own.[28]

The development of Le Jau's program for the Negroes can best be told in his own words which reveal, with a contemporary flavor, not only his own sagacity and firm intentions in the matter, but also show the Negro as eager to avail himself of the opportunity for instruction. More than a year after his arrival, he wrote on November 15, 1708:

Several Negroes have asked me for the Holy Baptism, as I see no necessity to be too hasty, I stay till I have proof of their good life by the Testimony of their Masters. There is I bless God a visible reformation of the Lives of some Persons, but in those things belonging to Conscience I don't perceive any willingness in them to be known and I want some further directions about it, as well as the opinion of the Honorable Society for the case of many tender souls concerning some matters I proposed in my last Letters, how we shall behave ourselves that we answer not before God for the Wars promoted by some of our Traders to get Slaves for their Profit; how we shall prevent the promiscuous Cohabitation of Slaves, which is horrid.[29]

In February, 1709, Le Jau declared:

I have often advised them [the planters] to Labour to prevent several Enormities committed by the Slaves; I am answered that such a thing cannot be helped. I have urged the Dutys of Christian love

Frenchman, . . ." from Arthur Henry Hirsch, *The Huguenots of Colonial South Carolina* (Durham: 1928), pp. 68-72. See also Edgar Legare Pennington, "The Reverend Francis Le Jau's Work Among Indians and Negro Slaves," in *Journal of Southern History*, I, No. 4 (November 1935), pp. 442-458.
    [27] Francis Le Jau to Mr. [Philip] Stubbs, St. James, Goose Creek, South Carolina, April 15, 1707, in *S.P.G. MSS.* (L.C. Trans.), A 3, No. cxli.
    [28] Francis Le Jau to John Chamberlayne, St. James, Goose Creek, South Carolina, June 30, 1707, in *S.P.G. MSS.* (L.C. Trans.), A 3, No. 142.
    [29] Francis Le Jau to Secretary, St. James, Goose Creek, South Carolina, November 15, 1708, in *S.P.G. MSS.* (L.C. Trans.), A 4, No. 91.

and humanity. I cannot to this day prevail upon some to make a difference between Slaves and free Indians, and Beasts, yet there are worthy persons of another Mind in this Parish, else I should have little comfort in my spiritual endeavours.[30]

Dr. Le Jau continued his instructions once a week, but he began to question the wisdom of teaching the slaves under existing conditions, and to present clearly the ills of slavery as seen in practice:

. . . the children of this parish are well acquainted with their catechism; but as I feared the negros and Indian slaves should not be sent to be instructed. I must give the melancholy account that it has so happened; yet I will take all opportunities and will use all means as God pleases to enable me to secure those poor souls. Their working upon Sunday for their maintenance, and having wives or husbands at a great distance from their plantations, in my humble judgment does much harm and hinders much good.
. . . Several sensible and sober slaves have asked me also to be baptised and married according to the form of our Holy Church. I could not comply with their desire without the consent of their Masters, but I have exhorted them to perseverance and patience. I also humbly desire to be directed therein: the masters are willing, most of them.[31]

Five months later he expressed the same caution. "I could easily multiply the number of slaves proselyted to Christianity but I put off their baptism and the receiving some persons to the holy table till we have a good testimony and proof of their life and conversation."[32] Dr. Le Jau often kept the Negroes on trial for two years. For example, in October, 1709, he gave the following account of his endeavors to secure cooperation from masters and slaves:

As for the spiritual state of my parish . . . constant communicants every two months near 30, among whom are two negroes.
On Sunday next I design, God willing, to baptize two very sensible and honest negro men whom I have kept upon trial these two years. Several others have spoken to me also; I do nothing too hastily in that respect. I instruct them and must have consent of their masters with a good testimony and proof of their honest life and sober conversation. Some masters in my parish are very well pleased with my proceedings in that respect; others do not seem to be so; yet they have given over opposing my design openly. It is to be hoped the good example of the one will have an influence over the others. . . .

[30] Francis Le Jau to John Chamberlayne, Parish of St. James, near Goose Creek, South Carolina, March 22, 1709, in *S.P.G. MSS.* (L.C. Trans.), A 4, No. 92.
[31] Francis Le Jau to John Chamberlayne, South Carolina, St. James near Goose Creek, South Carolina, March 22, 1709, in *S.P.G. MSS.* (L.C. Trans.), A 4, No. cxlii.
[32] Francis Le Jau to John Chamberlayne, St. James, Goose Creek, South Carolina, August 5, 1709, in *S.P.G. MSS.* (L.C. Trans.), A 5, No. 48.

To remove all pretence from the adult slaves I shall baptise of their being free upon that account, I have thought fit to require first their consent to this following declaration: You declare in the presence of God and before this Congregation that you do not ask for the Holy Baptism out of any design to free yourself from the duty and obedience you owe to your master while you live, but merely for the good of your soul and to partake of the graces and blessings promised to the members of the Church of Jesus Christ. One of the most scandalous and common crimes of our slaves, is their perpetual changing of wives and husbands, which occasions great disorders: I also tell them whom I baptize: "The Christian religion does not allow plurality of wives, nor any changing of them; you promise truly to keep to the wife you now have till death doth part you." I[t] has been customary among them to have their feasts, dances, and merry meetings upon the Lord's day, that practise is pretty well over in this parish, but not absolutely. I tell them that present themselves to be admitted to baptism they must promise they'l spend no more the Lord's day in idleness, and if they do I'l cut them off from the Communion.

These I most humbly submit to the judgement of my Superiors whose commands and instructions I will follow while I live. I see with an incredible joy the fervor of several of those poor slaves.[33]

It was the practice of the missionaries not only in South Carolina but in New York and elsewhere to secure the permission of the master and thus enlist his interest and cooperation in the slave's instruction for the rites of the church. The formal statement required of the slave that it was not his intention to set himself free by baptism is remarkable and significant.[34] This declaration was a direct answer to the

[33] Francis Le Jau to John Chamberlayne, St. James, Goose Creek, South Carolina, October 20, 1709, in *S.P.G. MSS.* (L.C. Trans.), A 5, No. 49.

[34] The question of whether or not baptism made slaves free was often a decisive factor in the masters' attitude toward slave education and Christianization. For example, Mr. Elias Neau, catechist in New York City, wrote to the Society that he was resolved ". . . to obtain an act of assembly to confirm the right of the inhabitants over their slaves after baptism in the same manner that they had it before, for without that, they will not suffer them to be instructed, for fear they should be baptised without their knowledge." See translation of Elias Neau to John Chamberlayne, New York, April 30, 1706, in *S.P.G. MSS.* (L.C. Trans.), A 2, No. CLXVII. This controversy was often mentioned in the Annual Sermons. For examples, see William Fleetwood, Bishop of St. Asaph, *Sermon* preached before the S.P.G. in St. Mary Le Bow, London, February, 1711 (Huntington Library), p. 21, in which he said, "If therefore it be lawful in our Country, to have or keep any slaves at all it is, equally lawful to have or keep them so, tho' they are Christians." Martin Benson, Bishop of Gloucester, *Sermon* preached before S.P.G., 1740 (Huntington Library), p. 19, stated that to baptise a Negro made no alteration in the "outward state of these poor creatures." Robert Drummond, Bishop of St. Asaph, in *Sermon* before S.P.G., 1754 (Huntington Library), p. 18, maintained, "The common error that Christianity makes them (Negroes) free has been so often obviated by the plantation laws, by the justest reasoning upon the laws of the realm and the laws of the Gospel that this objection is probably either worn out or insincerely made use of."

opposition of the master to Christianization of the slave, which
hostility arose in every area where the S.P.G. program was set up.
The missionaries were so determined on the Christianization and education of the Negro that they constantly aided in securing legal
acknowledgement that baptism was not emancipation. Nevertheless,
the gain of religious rights had important economic and legal implications, however intangible the forward steps might be. The missionaries were moreover fully aware of the ironies of slavery as incom-
patible with Christian doctrines, particularly the circumstances which
separated wives and husbands, children and parents.[35]

A long letter from Dr. Le Jau to the society in early 1710 is interesting not alone for its account of the state of his parish and the
sensation created by one Negro scholar, but as a record of Indian
and Negro life in the same parish. Implicit in his observations, is
comparison of these two native peoples: the first long resident, the
other newly brought to the continent.

I find myself mightly comforted and encouraged to hear that my
small endeavors are not disagreeable to the Honorable Society my
most worthy superiors, . . .

[35] This clerical problem was well put by the missionaries at Westchester and
Rye, New York, who spoke for the exasperated clergy in South Carolina as
well. See John Bartow to David Humphreys, Westchester, New York, November 15, 1725, in *S.P.G. MSS.* (L.C. Trans.), B 1, No. 81. ". . . I cannot
be very zealous to baptize slaves because I know they will not or cannot live
up to the Christian covenant in one notorious instant at least, viz. matrimony,
for they marry after their heathen way and divorce and take others as often
as they please, and Christian baptism cannot [be consistent] with adultery, and
should we marry them I fear they would do the same unless there were a law
to restrain. But against our marrying them the masters will object and say it is
not lawful to part man and wife, and how can we sell one of them? This will
be a hard obligation upon us to sell both to our detriment. I never knew but one
couple that were married by the Society's missionary, Mr. Brooks, and afterward their master George Willocks of Amboy, had occasion to sell one and because he would not part man and wife, he sent both to be sold at York, and
soon after the man ran away and forever forsook his wife."
Again the Rev. Robert Jenney, in a letter to David Humphreys, Rye, N.Y.,
November 19, 1725, in *S.P.G. MSS.* (L.C. Trans.), B 1, No. 78, states the case:
"If Christian persons live together as man and wife without marriage, they live
in fornication, and if they are married they must not be parted. . . . Hence
it will follow that if both parties are in the same family the Master lies under an
obligation either to keep both or sell both, let his necessities be ever so press-
ing. . . . And if they are in different families . . . then the removal of one of the
family to a different part of the country at some considerable distance is a
parting of man and wife. . . . I find it a very difficult thing . . . to keep them
faithful at any considerable distance from one another."
For the great mass of legal complications arising from the marriage of slaves,
see Helen Tunnicliff Catterall, (Ed.) *Judicial Cases Concerning American Slavery and the Negro* (Washington, D.C.: 1929), II, "Cases from the Courts of
North Carolina, South Carolina, and Tennessee." See also Ulrich Bonnell
Phillips, *American Negro Slavery* (New York: 1918), Ch. XV, "Plantation
Labor," and XVI, "Plantation Life."

Mr. Marston did not see yet our present Governor. He keeps as I am told in the remotest of our parishes near the Yamousee Indians. It was to those parts I had the honor to tell you I had an inclination to go, hearing of the great desire of those Indians to have a clergyman among them. But I never went, finding many occasions to employ me in this parish. I take all the opportunities I can to instruct our slaves, but for whole months together we are confined at home the weather is so bad, hot or cold, for the seasons are not long moderate in this place. I see our free Indians, and several come to see me, when they fix their abode near me, for they are perpetually changing places to get food, having no provisions laid up. Could we make them capable to understand what is meant by words commonly used by us when we speak of religion, we would find them other than we imagine; or could we understand their meaning. As they grow acquainted and familiar and trust to one, they disclose surprising things. What I had the honor to tell you of something practised among some Indian like to circumcision, I had from a friend, an ancient gentlewoman Mrs. Bird by name that came these many years past to this country from Barbadoes and had that observation from travellers. I will tell more particulars about that when I have seen her again. Three weeks ago my Indian neighbors that live upon and near our glebe land had a dance which they keep yearly from time immemorial for three days together, in the daytime the men dance by themselves, the women for that time are absent and never come near till the three days are over; but those women keep their dance among themselves by night. As I asked one of the men the reason of that separation, he told me 'twas to remember a time wherein Man was made alone and there was no woman; but after, God took somewhat out of man and made the woman. Asking what it was that God took, the man put his hand upon his breast and somewhat there, and then called it a bone. My wife presently named a rib, the Indian smiled and said Yes. I heard also of some other Indians not far from us who at a certain time yearly take the largest deer they can get among many, for all go hunting that day on purpose, and hang it upon a long post to the Lord and leave it consume there. Our Indian neighbors call their nation Ittiwan. When any of them dies they anoint him all over with oil, either of bear or hickory nuts, for they have no other, that's a constant practise and women's employment. The Savannah language is so called by corruption and ill habit from our European pronouncing. It should be called Saönah as I am informed, which is the name of the most considerable town and nation among the Indians northwest of us. They came originally from Albany and settled near this province. Even before the nation of the Westos were destroyed and to this day they keep about the places where the Westos lived, but perhaps are not so numerous; but I am still told by several traders that it is understood in this northern continent, though not spoken by a great many nations who have all of them different dialects; but they affirm to me that if any person speaks the Saönah language he may travel and be understood from hence to

Canada inclusively. The Crick Indians language, nations that border
near Florida is also understood in the southern parts. I have a
promise of some speciments of both languages with many observations which I hope will afford some satisfaction. I take notice that
the young Indians born since we inhabited these parts and that converse with us are pretty tractable and speak good English, though
their old parents bring them up in their wild fashion. I believe they
will in time like better things. Some lads are free enough to discourse
with us, I encourage them as much as I can.

The spiritual state of my parish is much the same. I have baptized
two sensible and honest negroe slaves as I had the honor to tell you
in my last; several come constantly to Church and are instructed and
I hope in time do well. I have in this parish a few negroe slaves
and were born and baptized among the Portuguese, but speak very
good English. They come to church and are well instructed so as to
express a great desire to receive the communion amongst us. I proposed to them to declare openly their abjuring the errors of the
Romish Church without which declaration I could not receive them.
I bid them consider of it against Easter. On the first Sunday in Lent
next we design and prepare to communicate. Our constant number
is near 30 at a time and about 50 in all. At Easter some who never
did receive intend to prepare themselves for that sacred duty after
which time I will give a regular full account of all. . . .

We want a schoolmaster in my parish for our white peoples children,
but as for the negroes or Indians with all submission I would desire
that such a thing should be taken into consideration as the importance
of the matter and the consequences which may follow do deserve.
The best scholar of all the negroes in my parish and a very sober
and honest liver, through his learning was like to create some confusion among all the negroes in this country. He had a book wherein
he read some description of the several judgements that chastise men
because of their sins in these latter days, that description made an
impression upon his spirit, and he told his master abruptly there
would be a dismal time and the moon would be turned into blood,
and there would be dearth of darkness and went away. When I heard
of that I sent for the negro who ingeniously told me he had read
so in a book. I advised him and charged him not to put his own
constructions upon his reading after that manner, and to be cautious
not to speak so, which he promised to me but yet would never show
me the book; but when he spoke those few words to his master, some
negro overheard a part, and it was publicly blazed abroad that an
angel came and spake to the man. He had seen a hand that gave him
a book; he had heard voices, seen fires etc. As I had opportunities
I took care to undeceive those who asked me about it; now it is over,
I fear that those men have not judgement enough to make good use
of their learning and I have thought most convenient not to urge too
far that Indians and negroes should be indifferently admitted to learn
to read, but I leave it to the discretion of their masters whom I exhort

to examine well their inclinations. I have often observed and lately
hear that it had been better if persons of a melancholy constitution
or those that run into the search after curious matter had never seen
a book.[36]

Dr. Le Jau had evidently observed not only some of the characteristics of the Negro race, but had noted, too, the individuality of its
separate members. He suggested that masters help him choose men
of intelligence and of stability to become the readers of books and
leaders of their fellows. His strategy in attempts to free the Negro's
time on Sundays for instruction, or in proposals to prevent separation
of married slaves, both Indians and Negroes, and also his remarkable
scholarship, were shown in a letter of June 13, 1710.

The number of our families the same 87. Since the 20th Oct. 1709,
I baptized 19 among whom 3 negro men; the constant number of
communicants 30 or 36, among whom 4 negro men, all the communicants together are still about 50 because some went to live in
other places; marriages 3, burials 2 children; the number of our
negro slaves may be near 500 but above 1/3 part of them are children.

Since it has pleased Almighty God to bless me with health I have
upon Sundays, after our divine service, invited the negroes and
Indian slaves to stay for half an hour. The invitation, to my great
comfort has been joyfully received by about 50 of them; we begin
and end our particular assembly with the Collect *Prevent us O Lord*
etc. I teach them the Creed, the Lord's Prayer, and the Commandments. I explain some portion of the catechism. I give them an entire
liberty to ask questions. I endeavor to proportion my answers and all
my instructions to their want and capacity. I must acknowledge that
the hand of God does visibly appear on this particular occasion. I
had often attempted and proposed a time, a method and a means
easy, as I thought, for the instruction of these poor souls, but all in
vain till this last was put in my mind by special mercy. The most
pious among their masters stay also and hear. Others not so zealous
would find fault, if possible. Their murmurings sometimes reach my
ears, but I am not discouraged. The caution I have taken and which
the Society is pleased to approve of, viz. to do nothing without
the masters good testimony and consent, is a sufficient answer to
them that oppose most the happiness of their slaves, but the good
examples of some truly religious masters is a check upon the others.
The alteration is so considerable of late that in general very few
masters excepted, the slaves shall be fed and provided for by the
masters and whole time of the slaves shall be their masters. This is
what I have continually urged, knowing how idly and criminally the

[36] Francis Le Jau to John Chamberlayne, St. James, Goose Creek, South
Carolina, February 1, 1709-1710, in *S.P.G. MSS.* (L.C. Trans.), A 5, No.
XCVIII.

slaves spent the time given to them to work for themselves. I bless God for having at last rendered the masters sensible of their own advantage in that respect. Four or 6 shall be soon baptized by the consent of their masters, and the others with the children in time, except in danger of death. Those slaves behave themselves very well, and do better for their masters profit than formerly, for they are taught to serve out of Christian love and duty. They tell me openly that they will ever bless God for their knowing good things which they knew not before. The Lord's Day is no more profaned by their dancings at least about me. I asked once a pretty ancient and very fine slave whether he could read. His answer was he would rather choose hereafter to practise the good he could remember. As I had the honor to represent in one of my last letters the inconveniences which I perceive and often did perceive to arise from the bad use some slaves make of their reading, so as to discompose their heads, and do some harm to their fellow slaves. I forbear urging too far the exercise of reading among them, leaving to the discretion of their masters to choose the fittest persons to learn till I receive further instructions about that point.

Here Dr. Le Jau raised the point of student selection. In his mind, too, evidently was the idea that some slaves might devote themselves to book learning, while others, perhaps, might best be left to their craftsmanships and manual skills. Even when in recent decades, the matter of Negro education is being determined by the Negroes themselves, opinions vary as to the most desirable form of training, a subject debated between Booker T. Washington and W. E. Burghardt Du Bois. In Africa, too, the authorities in the educational field are now conducting a variety of experiments and comparing results.[37] Le Jau's letter continued:

. . . There are 3 or 4 Portuguese slaves in this parish very desirous to receive the communion amongst us. I framed a short model of submission grounded upon some Popish tenets which they told me of their own accord, without troubling them with things they know not. I require of them their renouncing of those particular points, the chief of which is praying to the saints and that they must not return to the Popish worship in case they should be sent to Madeira again. I gave them that form of submission in writing and left it to their consideration. They come constantly to church and are very sensible. I have proposed to some masters a thing that seems to me to be very easy to be done and will prevent horrid crimes and

[37] For a study of education as applied to the contemporary east African problem see Julian Huxley, *Africa View* (New York: 1931), pp. 50-62; 100-105; 213-227. Which language to use, by what methods to transfer ideas, and what kinds of education to encourage are some problems considered. See also Lord Hailey, *An African Survey* (London: 1938), Ch. XVIII, "Education." Further reading may be suggested by F. J. Klingberg, "A Survey of Recent Books on British Africa, with Special Reference to the Native Problem," in *The Journal of Modern History*, X, 1 (March, 1938), pp. 77-93.

confusions amongst negroes and Indian slaves for the future, that
none of those that are not yet married presume to do it without his
masters consent and likewise those that are now married do not part
without the like consent (I know some will transgress) but I hope
'twill do good to many, especially in time to come. This thought of
mine I most humbly submit to the Judgement of the Society to which
I ever yield the utmost respect. . . .
I discoursed lately with some of our free Indians. They ingeniously
own they have forgot most of their traditions since the establishment
of this colony. They keep their festivals and can tell but little of the
reasons. Their old men are dead. Many are gone farther up in the
country through bad usage they received from some of our people,
and daily complaints come of the cruelty and injustice of our Indian
traders. No longer than three months ago, one of those traders caused
a poor Indian woman a slave of his to be scalloped within two miles
of my house. She lived two or three days in that miserable condition
and was found dead in the woods. The history is as true as dreadful.
It is to be wished by the credit of the Society those enormities could
be prevented. I had the honor to inform you 2 years ago, or 18 months
rather of the cruel burning alive of a poor negro woman which all
of us thought to be innocent of a crime she was accused of. It has
pleased God to judge that injustice, the master and the evidence are
perished miserably of late, both being drowned. . . .
Our Indian traders will be in the settlement in some short time. I'll
get what information I can and will transmit the whole to you: The
right name for the Saönah nation is Chawonock and by corruption
we pronounce Savannah. That Chawonock nation is mentioned in
Purchas Pilgrim T. 4, L. 9, c. 3, p. 1694 to be on the south of Virginia
which is the right place. The American circumcision is also mentioned by Purchas in his abstract from J. Acosta T. 3, L. 5, c. 5,
page 1044. My Purchas is of 1625. Brother Maule has an Indian lad
which he thinks to be circumcised. I will endeavor to see that rarity.
That singular tradition among the Indians of a time wherein there
was no woman has been confirmed to me by some more Indians but
somewhat imperfectly. They don't know themselves at this time why
they do such and such things, and we and they want words to express
our thoughts. The Indian children of our neighborhood speak English! There is hope that in process of time they may be instructed.
Amidst their wild ways of living we may perceive a great deal of
patience, sobriety justice and modesty. Their eatables are in common. Their head man whom we ignorantly call king has the power
over them as that of a father in his family, but he labors and fares
with the rest.[38]

[38] Francis Le Jau to John Chamberlayne, St. James, Goose Creek, South
Carolina, June 13, 1710, in *S.P.G. MSS.* (L.C. Trans.), A 5, No. CXX. It may
be noted that the slaves of South Carolina were chosen for racial fitness. The
preference was for Angolas (Gullah) from the old Portuguese west coast
to the South of the Congo. Good looking, intelligent, amiable, some were de-
scendents of African Kings. In general, aristocrats themselves, they preferred the
aristocrat as master.

The insight into Indian and Negro character shown by Le Jau may have been influenced by the possibility that from the Indian there was little response and because of his aloofness, there was, consequently, no certain means of measuring the penetration of new ideas. The Negro made a more ready response, and with his sense of melody and of the dramatic, seized upon Bible drama and poetry and knowing his own Negro audience as no white man could, utilized these new literary sources in reciting to his fellows. The racial imagination, sensitive to nature and to human tragedy, had full expression in the gift for rhetorical language,[39] derived from the long heritage of musical African tongues. Modern writers in apt words have described that mysticism of the Negro world which so impressed Dr. Le Jau that he considered an alteration of his methods.[40] His "psychic power, the beauty of his recognition of mystery and the dark poesy of his sayings" have impressed those who knew him from the earliest times to the present.[41]

Throughout his service in South Carolina, the idea of gaining the confidence of the master, and of obtaining his consent for the baptism of the Negroes, was the basis of the success of Le Jau's labors. He

[39] For a description of the rhythmic Gullah, the oldest Anglo-American dialect, sometimes said to be a derivative of the Bantu dialects themselves more musical than Italian, but mixed 16th century pidgin English, and later inventions, see Samuel Gaillard Stoney, *Charleston, Azaleas and Old Bricks* (Boston: 1939), p. 7. It has been impossible in this study to discuss even briefly the current arguments regarding the migration of African customs to the New World. Suffice it to say that the view that all African lore was lost is being modified. The fact that the Negro himself does not know the source of some of his mores does not prove them non-African. For a discussion of the loss of social heritage of Negroes brought to America, see a review of Franklin Frazier, *The Negro Family in the United States,* by M. J. Herskovits in *The Nation,* January 27, 1940, p. 104.

[40] Julia Peterkin, in *Roll, Jordan, Roll* (New York, 1933), p. 146. "In a world where no printed words are read except from the Bible, and newspapers are useful only when pasted over the walls of rooms to keep wind and cold from coming through cracks, opinions are very different from the world where beliefs are shaped by writers and editors.

"Inanimate things take on far greater importance and are endowed with emotions, intentions. The moon rules the tides, and the tides rule birth and death. The flood tide brings human creatures into the world and the ebb tide takes their spirits away. Frailer, weaker things than tides can work their wills on men. Wise old trees have deliberately reached out limbs and smitten those who came to cut them down; other trees less gentle have fallen on their destroyers and crushed them. Rivers drown experienced fishermen who catch too many fish in their waters; cotton gins cut off fingers and arms of people who make them work when they are weary; lightning strikes proudful trees that strive to outdo their fellows and stretch their heads up into the sky."

[41] For a description of the Negro's gifts of imagination and perception see Archibald Rutledge "Insight. The Negro's Power of Perception," *The Atlantic Monthly* (September 1938), Vol. 162, No. 3, pp. 366-373.

worked tirelessly for the abolition of brutal or severe legislation concerning the Negroes.[42]

In the missionary record are many vignettes that sharply record the early pioneer scene. Throughout are noted vivid impressions of the sturdy character of the Negro. His racial vigor survived capture by the Arab slave trader, "gang" transportation to the African coast, the horrors of the Middle Passage, the hard apprenticeship of the "seasoning" in a new country. He took root in his new home, retained his racial vitality and with robust interest joined in the white

[42] In 1712, the legislature of South Carolina passed an act stating that conversion did not interfere with the legal right to Negroes' labor. Part of the law read as follows:
"That it shall be, and is hereby declared, lawful for any negro or Indian slave . . . to receive and profess the Christian faith, and be thereunto baptised. But . . . they shall not thereby be manumitted or set free, or his or their owner . . . lose his or their civil right, property and authority over such . . . slaves, but that the . . . slaves, with respect to . . . servitude, shall remain and continue in the same state and condition, . . . (as) before the making of this Act." See Section XXXIV of the Act passed on June 7, 1712 by the Legislature of South Carolina, quoted in Frederick Dalcho, *An Historical Account of the Protestant Episcopal Church in South Carolina*, pp. 94-95. Even though the legislators passed this Act, some other legislative acts were harsh. One of these was in relation to runaway Negroes. "By law . . . such a Negro must be mutilated by amputation of the testicles if it is a man, and of ears if it be a woman. I have openly declared against such punishment grounded on the law of God, which sets a slave at liberty if he should lose an eye or a tooth when he is corrected. Exodus 21., some good planters are of my opinion." See Francis Le Jau to [Secretary] St. James, Goose Creek, South Carolina, February 20, 1711-1712, in *S.P.G. MSS.* (L.C. Trans.), A 7, p. 395. Another severe act was passed in 1712, which punished runaway slaves. The slaves were to be mutilated or if they absented themselves for the fourth time in fourteen days, they were to be put to death. He wrote, "I have taken the liberty to say mutilation and death are too great punishments . . . but what I most complain of is that upon Sundays they are confined at home by the letter of the Act." Dr. Le Jau urged the magistrates to allow the slaves liberty to go to church, and he was answered that it was implied in their Master's leave, therefore Dr. Le Jau feared ". . . the greatest part of the masters . . . [will] take . . . advantage of the tenor of the act." See Francis Le Jau to [Secretary] St. James Parish, Goose Creek, August 30, 1712, in *S.P.G. MSS.* (L.C. Trans.), A 7, p. 436 ff. In practice these acts were modified, due in some measure to the value of the slave as capital. Ulrich Bonnell Phillips in *American Negro Slavery* (New York: 1918), has pointed out that "planters must guard their slaves' health and life as among the most vital of their own interests; for while crops were merely income, slaves were capital. The tendency appears to have been common, indeed, to employ free immigrant labor when available for such work as would involve strain and exposure." He cites the prevalent use of free Irish labor for the more perilous jobs and quotes, among other sources, a Virginia planter who explained that he had "an Irish gang draining for him by contract. . . . [because] 'It's dangerous work . . . and a negro's life is too valuable to be risked at it. If a negro dies, it is a considerable loss you know.'" (p. 301) The further discussion in Ch. XIX, "Business Aspects of Slavery" develops the point that it was to the owner's economic advantage to keep his slaves healthy, happy, and contented, thus circumventing as much as possible the difficulties involved with runaway slaves.

man's enterprises. The mastery of the continent, therefore, made room not only for the white man, but for thousands of Negroes whereas this same process of settlement extinguished by rapid degrees the tribal life and domain of the Indian who could not quickly identify himself with the white man. With his forests and fields still to lose, the Indian had a special motive for resistance, while the Negro had lost his African homeland. Illustrative of the Negro's ability to find his place in a community is Dr. Le Jau's note to the Society in July, 1710:

The great heat has thrown several persons and families into fevers. I was also sick and very weak which accident interrupted my duty of catechizing the poor slaves. That interruption has afforded to me the comfort of seeing that those slaves are sincerely desirous to do well, for they come constantly all of them near and about the windows of our church, which cannot contain them when the parishioners are met, and behave themselves very devoutly. I hope by the blessing of God to begin again that beloved work in a short time. Some masters are come to me of their own accord to signify their consent and desire about the baptism of some of their slaves. Some other masters find difficulties which I endeavor to answer as I have opportunities.[43]

In 1711, Dr. Le Jau began once more to catechize the Negro slaves and commented happily upon conditions in a letter to the Society, February 9, 1711,

Upon the 1st Sunday in Advent I baptized 4 adult negroes two men and two women with the caution of which I had the honor to give an account to the Society. The ceremony was done after our divine service to the satisfaction of some pious masters. Some others did not like it so well at first. Their chief argument was from the impossibility of bringing the slaves into a right order. I have exhorted them to begin and try, and I thank God we see some good success, and an appearance of better in God's own time. They come sometimes 40 or more to Church. I intend to catechise them again when I have done instructing our white children. I believe 'tis best to wait a little, except in case of danger. I endeavor always to act by the consent of the masters. The spiritual state of my parish 30th June 1710 to February the 1st instant is 17 children baptized, an adult white and sensible man and 4 adult negroes, 3 marriages and 8 burials. Concerning the communicants I have admitted five that had not received the Holy Communion before. Our constant number is 30 among whom five negroes. In all I believe I have 50 and more communicants. . . .
Give me leave before I end my letter to beg of you whether I

[43] Francis Le Jau to John Chamberlayne, Goose Creek, South Carolina, July 14, 1710, in *S.P.G. MSS.* (L.C. Trans.), A 5, No. CLXI; same letter in *Journal of S.P.G.* (L.C. Trans.), Vol. 1, October 20, 1710.

might presume to ask of the Society a little present of 2 or 3 yards of ordinary linen for the negroes who are baptized by me and continue to live in an edifying manner. I humbly think such an encouragement would do good among them and others, . . .[44]

Le Jau wrote a few months later that the catechizing ". . . work produces some good, and the most stubborn masters that opposed me are now forced to say little or nothing against it."[45] However, his parishioners provided such incidents as these noted by Dr. Le Jau :

. . . A few days ago I heard of some strange reasoning of my neighbors. What, said a lady considerable enough in any other respect but in that of sound knowledge, Is it possible that any of my slaves could go to Heaven, and must I see them there? A young gentleman had said sometime before that he is resolved never to come to the Holy Table while slaves are received there. I really believe they speak so unwisely through ignorance, and will [not] fail to take proper opportunities to instruct them. There are two poor negro slaves, born and brought up among the Portuguese, that are very desirous to abjure the popish heresies and be received to the Communion among us. I have them above two years upon trial, as to their life and behaviour and have taught them as diligently as I could. One of them has an admirable sense and is a pattern of faithfulness and sobriety to all the slaves in the parish ; the other has not so much wit, but is very honest. I intend, God willing, to receive them both in some short time, and to do it in public in the best and most solemn manner I can contrive.[46]

Le Jau made a practise of receiving into the Church any slave children who were presented by their masters. The adult Christian Negroes could have their children baptized if both parents had been admitted ; the Christian slaves in the same plantation would be ". . . received as sureties because of the difficulties of prevailing upon the white people to be so charitable."[47] The advice of the Society was given in reply to the question as to whether or not a child could be received who had but one of his parents baptized,

As to the difficulty with you with respect to the baptizing a child who has but one of his parents baptised, it is apprehended, that, that

[44] Francis Le Jau to John Chamberlayne, Goose Creek, South Carolina, February 9, 1711, in *S.P.G. MSS.* (L.C. Trans.), A 6, No. LVIII.
[45] Francis Le Jau to the Secretary, Parish of St. James, Goose Creek South Carolina, September 5, 1711, in *S.P.G. MSS.* (L.C. Trans.), A 6, No. CXLI.
[46] Francis Le Jau to the Secretary, St. James, Goose Creek, South Carolina, September 18, 1711, in *S.P.G. MSS.* (L.C. Trans.), A 6, No. CXLII. C. F. Pascoe in *Two Hundred Years of the S.P.G.* (London, 1901), Vol. 1, p. 15, gives the date of this letter as August 18, 1711.
[47] Francis Le Jau to the Secretary, St. James, Goose Creek, South Carolina May 26, 1712, in *S.P.G. MSS.* (L.C. Trans.), A 7, p. 405.

matter is resolved by St. Paul in the 7th Chapter of his Epistle to the Corinthians where he says, the children are holy when one of the parents only is a believer.[48]

At Easter, 1712, there were thirty-seven actual communicants, among whom were five Negroes.[49] During the last six months of 1712, five more Negroes were allowed to attend communion.[50] The next year, between January and April of 1713, one Negro woman received the communion and three were baptized.[51] By August, Le Jau's communicants had increased to sixty, among whom were five Negro men and two Negro women, and the missionary reported that in a short time he expected to baptize two Negro men, ". . . and receive the abjuration of a negro woman that had been bred in Guadalope, but now expresses a great desire to serve God according to his Word."[52]

The continued reports noted that the number of baptisms increased yearly,[53] and Dr. Le Jau rejoiced in the good conduct of his charges,

It is a singular comfort to me to see that while so many professed Christians appear but lukewarm, it pleases God to raise himself faith-

[48] William Taylor to Dr. Le Jau, November 6, 1712, in *S.P.G. MSS.* (L.C. Trans.), A 7, p. 478. A French minister, James Gignillat, who had a high regard for the Society, said that the Roman Catholic Priests Christened all the Negroes that went into their midst. He reported to John Chamberlayne that he was willing to do the same, and offered to instruct the slaves in order to prepare them for baptism and communion. "All the objection they have against it is this, that they observed that those that had been made Christians were the worst of their slaves, and that all other slaves do laugh at them and render 'em worse and worse. Now the quick and present remedy . . . is . . . an order sent by you to all . . . families that they ought to send all their slaves to their ministers to be instructed and Christened, and that they ought also to bring them to church along with them and not permit them to work on Sunday. . . ." See James Gignillat to John Chamberlayne, Santee, South Carolina, May 28, 1710, in *S.P.G. MSS.* (L.C. Trans.), A 5, No. CXIX.
[49] Francis Le Jau to [Secretary], St. James parish, Goose Creek, August 30, 1712, in *S.P.G. MSS.* (L.C. Trans.), A 7, p. 436.
[50] Francis Le Jau to William Taylor, St. James near Goose Creek, South Carolina, February 23, 1712-13, in *S.P.G. MSS.* (L.C. Trans.), A 8, p. 346. The complete spiritual state of the Parish from July 1, 1712 to December 31, 1712, was as follows:
Baptized 8 among whom 3 adults.
Marriages 4.
Burials 2.
Actual communicants on Christmas day 36 among whom 3 new communicants and five negroes.
Communicants in whole Parish about 55.
[51] Francis Le Jau to William Taylor, Charleston, South Carolina, April 11. 1713, in *S.P.G. MSS.* (L.C. Trans.), A 8, p. 361.
[52] Francis Le Jau to William Taylor, St. James near Goose Creek, August 10, 1713, in *S.P.G. MSS.* (L.C. Trans.), A 8, p. 363; same in *Journal of S.P.G.* (L.C. Trans.), Vol. II, June 1, 1714.
[53] In December, 1714, the Society increased the salary of Dr. Le Jau from £50 to £60 per annum, in acknowledgement of his hard work. William Taylor to Francis Le Jau, London, December 17, 1714, in *S.P.G. MSS.* (L.C. Trans.).

ful and devout servants from among the heathen, who are very zealous in the practice of our Christian duties. I hear no complaining of
our proselytes. Their masters commend them for their faithfulness. . . .[54]

To demonstrate that the designs of the Society were "not fruitless
as irreligious men would insinuate," he related an incident of considerable interest:

About Christmas last past there was a rumour spread of an intended conspiracy of the negroes against us all, like that of New
York. I was told that the plot had been formed in Goose Creek where
there is a good number of fine negroes. This news made me enquire
and observe being resolved to find out how true the thing might be.
The matter has been examined very diligently by our Government
this week. Twelve or fifteen negroes living on the north side of
Cooper River, having been apprehended under suspicion it has appeared upon good evidence that a negro fellow brought hither some
years ago from Martinaco, and of a very stubborn temper, had enticed
some slaves to join him that they might get their liberty by force.
The thing being proved against him he has been put to death for it.
Two more slaves have been severely chastised for hearkening to him,
but there is not any sufficient proof to take their life and all denied
the crime. The other prisoners have been acquited. But what I consider as a singular providence there has not been so much as one of
our Goose Creek negroes accused for having knowledge of the plot,
far from having consented to so great a crime. The most sensible
of our slaves, whom I have admitted to Holy Sacrament have solemnly protested to me that if ever they hear of any ill design of the
slaves, I shall know it from them that it may be prevented, and I
can't but depend upon the truth of their words, knowing them to be
exemplary and honest.[55]

Convinced that the program thus launched should be carried
through more thoroughly, Dr. Le Jau advised the sending of additional workers to the Colony. He had recommended to the Society that
it send a schoolmaster to Goose Creek for the white children.[56] Consequently, in 1710, Mr. Benjamin Dennis was appointed. Soon after
his arrival, he met with the misfortune of breaking his thigh bone
and became very ill. Therefore, in February, 1712, the sufferer reported to the Society that nothing had been

[54] Francis Le Jau to William Taylor, St. James near Goose Creek, January
22, 1713-1714, in *S.P.G. MSS.* (L.C. Trans.), A 9, p. 258.
[55] Francis Le Jau to William Taylor, St. James near Goose Creek, January
22, 1713-1714, in *S.P.G. MSS.* (L.C. Trans.), A 9, p. 258-259. For an account
of the 1712 Negro uprising in New York, see Frank J. Klingberg, "The S.P.G.
Program for Negroes in Colonial New York," in *The Historical Magazine of
the Protestant Episcopal Church*, VIII, No. 4 (December, 1939), pp. 306-371.
[56] Francis Le Jau to John Chamberlayne, St. James, Goose Creek, South
Carolina, February 1, 1709/10, in *S.P.G. MSS.* (L.C. Trans.), A 5, No. XCVIII.

... done as to fixing a school as yet . . . it will be a tedious work . . .
as health will permit me, [I] have taught such as have been sent . . .
I have at present 18 scholars, four of which are blacks. Two of them
being children of one man who was born in Portugal and there baptized, but now goes to Church and is desirous of learning arithmetic
etc. . . .[57]

Mr. Dennis had taken in Negroes and Indians in addition to the
whites, securing a fair number of scholars until the Indian War
which broke out in 1715, dispersed the people.[58] In July, 1712, the number in school had totalled twenty-nine, including two Negroes;[59] the
next year thirty, with one Negro;[60] and in 1714 twenty-three, including
one Negro.[61] The books used by Mr. Dennis for teaching were the
Testaments, Prayer Books, Primmers, Grammars, by Lilly and the
Christian Schoolmaster by Dr. Talbot.[62]

Dr. Le Jau's death on September 10, 1717, was an irreparable
loss.[63]

[57] Benjamin Dennis to [Secretary], Boochaw near Goose Creek, South Caro-
lina, February 26, 1711/12, in *S.P.G. MSS.* (L.C. Trans.), A 7, pp. 402-403.
[58] For the unsettled condition of the southern frontier see Herbert E. Bolton's
"Introduction," entitled "The Debatable Land, a Sketch of the Anglo-Spanish
Contest for the Georgia Country," in *Arredondo's Historical Proof of Spain's
Title to Georgia* (Berkeley: 1925), pp. 1-110; see also, Verner W. Crane "The
Southern Frontier in Queen Anne's War," in *American Historical Review,*
XXIV (April 1919), pp. 379-395; by the same author, *The Southern Frontier,
1670-1732* (Durham, 1928), especially Ch. X "The Carolina Florida Border,
1721-1730," and Chapter XI "International Rivalries in the Old Southwest, 1715-
1730."
[59] Benjamin Dennis to John Chamberlain, Boochaw, near Goose Creek,
South Carolina, July 24, 1712, in *S.P.G. MSS.* (L.C. Trans.), A 7, p. 427. The
pupils were: 25 whites, 2 blacks, 2 Indians.
[60] Benjamin Dennis to William Taylor, Boochaw, near Goose Creek, March
20, 1712-1713, in *S.P.G. MSS.* (L.C. Trans.), A 8, p. 349. The pupils were 27
whites, 1 black, 2 Indians.
[61] Benjamin Dennis to William Taylor, Boochaw near Goose Creek, South
Carolina, April 22, 1714, in *S.P.G. MSS.* (L.C. Trans.), A 9, p. 267. The
students were 20 whites, 2 mustees (half Indians), 1 Negro.
[62] *Journal of S.P.G.* (L.C. Trans.), Vol. II, December 21, 1711.
[63] Thomas Hasell to David Humphreys, St. Thomas, South Carolina, September 20, 1717, in *S.P.G. MSS.* (L.C. Trans.), B 4, No. 95. The family was
left in dire circumstances and a debt of nearly £100 was charged by the attending physician. A distinguished church historian, Dr. Edgar Legare Pennington, says of Dr. Le Jau, "His life had been strenuous, and he seems never
to have been free from malaria. He continued his labors, being zealous for
the welfare of the Negro slaves until the last. He was offered St. Philip's parish,
Charles Town, where he would be assured of a better benefice and sufficient
support; and the Society took pains to express commendation of his splendid
service. But the recognition came too late. . . . He had been sick for several
months before his death, and had lost the use of his limbs and also his
speech. His body was interred at the foot of the altar of the Goose Creek
church." See E. L. Pennington, "The Reverend Francis Le Jau's Work
Among Indians and Negro Slaves," in *Journal of Southern History,* I (November 1935), pp. 448-449.

CHAPTER II

THE GROWTH OF A PROGRAM

MEANWHILE in other parishes, the Society's education of Negroes was progressing. Its technique was to proceed with due caution, in the hope that small units of work would serve not only to show that the slave could profit by his schooling, but also to help form liberal opinion and enlist the interest and support of the whites. It might be conversely stated that the first duty of the missionary was not to cause opposition, leading to his dismissal, but to secure co-operation of the community in the program. The missionary must first be asked for by the local residents.[1] Upon arrival he began his distribution of the Society's literature, the Pastoral letters to masters and mistresses of plantations, and the copies of the Annual Sermons, of which as many as 10,000 copies would be printed by the Society and sent to the colonies each year.[2] He saw that his own slaves, if any, were instructed, the while visiting and inviting the planters to follow his example.

With these general plans and procedures of the Society in mind, review of the work in the several parishes is in order.[3] Attention may

---

[1] On March 21, 1706-1707, the Society "Resolved that if any place in the plantations desired a Minister the Society would not send one until it knew that the place was willing and able to contribute to the Maintenance of the Minister. If the place be willing and able the Society will supply them with Ministers before the places which are not willing to contribute to such maintenance." In *Journal of S.P.G.* (L.C. Trans.), I, March 21, 1706-1707.

[2] By 1761 Richard Newcome, Lord Bishop of Llandaff, in his Annual Sermon could say that "more than One Hundred and thirty thousand Volumes of Bibles and Common Prayer Books, with other Books of Devotion and Instruction, together with an innumerable Quantity of pious small Tracts, have been dispersed in Foreign Parts; . . ." See *A Sermon* preached before the S.P.G. Friday, February 20, 1761 (London: 1761), pp. 22-23. (Huntington Library). Bishop Gibson's *Three Addresses on the Instruction of the Negroes,* written in 1727 (including an address to the Christians in England on Negro Instruction, one to the Masters and Mistresses in the Plantations, and one to the Society's missionaries), were widely distributed. *The Knowledge and Practice of Christianity made easy to the meanest capacities: or an Essay towards an Instruction for the Indians* (London: 1741), by Thomas Wilson, Bishop of Sodor and Man, was familiar to every missionary. In addition, copies of the Annual Sermons, Catechisms, Bibles, Prayer Books, and Hornbooks were frequently requested by the missionaries, and furnished by the Society.

[3] The parishes clustered along the Atlantic coastline, extending approximately 100 miles in each direction from Charleston harbor which determined the population as well as the geographic center of early South Carolina. Spread-

be turned first to the Rev. Robert Maule who settled in St. John's parish in 1707. St. John's was

. . . on the *Western* Branch of *Cooper* River; it is a pleasant and healthful part of the Country, and the Planters there, were generally good, sober, and teachable People; but settled at a great Distance from each other, in scattered Plantations. . . . Upon his [Maule's] Preaching at his first coming, to a good Number of Churchmen, he had several *Independents* and *Anabaptists* who came to hear him, . . . and upon Account of the Distance between the Settlements, was obliged to ride very often, which was exceeding fatiguing (especially during the sultry Season in that Country) as well as expensive to him. . . . Upon his first Settling here, the *English* had no Church to perform Divine Worship in, but about 10 French Families had Built them a small Church, and their Minister Mr. *Tuilliard* offered Mr. *Maule* the Use of his Church, which he accepted, and Preached often there; and such of the *French* as understood *English,* came to hear him. At other times, he Preached up and down among the Plantations, as the Houses lay most convenient for the People to meet at. . . .[4]

In a long letter dated October 20, 1710, Maule explained to the Society the arguments he had used with the planters.

At Easter last I baptized a negro woman publicly in the church. I had had her a considerable time before under instruction till she was able to give a very good account of the Christian faith. And here I cannot but take notice how strangely unwilling the Planters generally are to have their slaves made Christians out of a mistaken

---

ing fanwise from the harbor, where tiny St. Philip's, containing Charleston, projected into the bay, were the parishes of St. Paul's, St. George's, St. Andrew's, St. James (Goose Creek). St. John's, St. Thomas 'and Christ church. To the north, in the French Settlements, was St. James Santee, and above it Prince George's, sparsely populated and large enough to hold all the Charleston harbor parishes within its borders. On the south the large frontier parishes of St. Bartholomew's and St. Helen's extended to the Savannah river, and included the Yamassee settlements. See David Humphreys, *An Historical Account of the Incorporated Society for the Propagation of the Gospel in Foreign Parts,* map between pp. 80-81. For a map covering the entire Southern Frontier in this period see Verner W. Crane, *The Southern Frontier, 1670-1732,* p. 326.

[4] David Humphreys, *An Historical Account of the Incorporated Society for the Propagation of the Gospel in Foreign Parts,* pp. 88-89. St. John's parish ". . . was laid off in Berkley County, by Act of Assembly, November 30, 1706, and its Boundaries defined by an Act Dec. 18, 1708, as follows: 'to the North-East by the bounds of Craven County, to the South by the bounds of the Parishes of St. Thomas and St. Dennis, and by the Eastern branch of Cooper River, then down Cooper River to the Mouth of the Back River to the South-west, partly by the said Back River, to the Plantation of David Durham inclusive, and partly by a North-west line from the West part of the said Durham's Plantation, to the North-West bound of Berkley County, and to the North-East by the said bounds of the said County.'" See Frederick Dalcho, *Historical Account of the Protestant Episcopal Church in South Carolina,* p. 264.

notion that they are free after they are baptized. I have therefore frequently made it my business among them to represent the Groundlessness of such an opinion, plainly declaring that as far as I can apprehend, baptism makes no great alteration as to the outward circumstances of their slaves in this world, that it is merely out of Compassion and Charity to these poor creatures that we are so forward and earnest in teaching them the knowledge of the Christian religion, and that since they are by the Providence of God, placed in such mean and oftentimes uncomfortable circumstances in this world, it would be the very highest degree of Cruelty in any one to deny them the use of those means which might advance them to a state of Happiness in the other. Nay, I have further told some of them that they do not consult even their own Temporal Interest if they deny their slaves baptism when duly qualified for it, because whilst they continue ignorant heathens, they can expect at best but an eye service from them and such a obedience as proceeds purely from fear, whereas were they sufficiently instructed in the doctrine of Christianity, that would in all probability teach them obedience to their masters out of a Principle of Conscience and render them much more true and faithful to their interests than now they can reasonably be expected to be. . . .

The phrase "eye service" is arresting. The Negro might not raise his hand to his master, on penalty of death, but sabotage was easy, particularly in the cultivation of rice. Raising a water gate at the wrong moment would destroy the crop and possibly ruin the planter, by a total loss of his profits. The Negro might also reserve his powers, work slowly, strike, run away, or play truant temporarily.[5] Mr. Maule continued:

. . . I have at length prevailed with several to consent to the having their negroes Baptized and have at this present time 5 or 6 under instruction for that purpose. Nay, so far have I gained upon one man particularly, that he has promised me, not only to admit me as occasion serves to instruct his slaves but that he will himself set apart some particular times for the teaching them in my absence, that so he may hasten their being qualified for Holy Baptism. After all I must confess that my labors have been chiefly employed about the

[5] For conditions as to food, slave strikes, and holidays among the Negroes see U. B. Phillips, *American Negro Slavery,* Ch. XV, "Plantation Labor." Said this author, "Virtually all the plantations whose records are available suffered more or less from truancy, and the abundance of newspaper advertisements for fugitives reinforces the impression that the need of deterrence was vital. Whippings, instead of proving a cure, might bring revenge in the form of sabotage, arson, or murder. Adequacy in food, clothing and shelter might prove of no avail, for contentment must be mental as well as physical. The preventatives mainly relied upon were holidays, gifts and festivities . . . overtime and overtask payments . . . kindliness and care to call forth loyalty in return; and the special device of crop patches to give every hand a stake in the plantation." (p. 305)

white man in my parish since I came hither, partly imagining my Mission to have been more immediately to such, partly concluding that if they can at once be persuaded to lead truly Christian lives, it would very much facilitate the conversion both of our negroes and free Indians. It is a melancholy reflection to consider how very much the wicked lives and scandalous behavior of many professing Christianity have hitherto retarded this in These Parts of the world, for not a few of these as I am credibly informed have sometimes been guilty of such gross enormities, as even the more modest heathens themselves have been ashamed of. I wish I could not say that the white men now trading at a Distance amongst our neighboring Indians were not still notoriously faulty in this particular, being generally by report, Persons of very Lewd and Debauched practices. It were much to be desired that some effectual Method could be fallen upon to hinder any from being engaged in that trade who were not men of sober and virtuous lives. This I conceive would be an excellent means to hasten the conversion of these poor infidels, to make them in love with our Religion and dispose them readily and heartily to embrace it. I am afraid I should tire your patience too much, did I pursue these reflections any further at present, for they would naturally lead me to give you some account of the Temperament and Manners of these Indians, and of some other things I cannot possibly crowd into so little room; this therefore I shall defer till some other opportunity. . . .[6]

In 1709 the missionary for St. Thomas', the Rev. Thomas Hasell,[7] arrived in his parish. An early historian describes the two chapels, the glebe, and the appointment of Mr. Hasell:

He had been formerly employed by the Society, as Catechist in Charles-Town; which Office he discharged with Diligence: The first Church Built here, (now used for a Chapel of Ease) was called *Pomkinhill* Church, from a rising Hill of that Name, on which it was Built; it is situate near the River Side, made of *Cypress* Wood, 30 Foot square, Erected about the Year 1703, at the Charge of the Neighbourhood, and by the particular Assistance of Sir *Nathaniel*

---

[6] Robert Maule to John Chamberlayne, n.d. [June 3, 1710], St. John's South Carolina, in *S.P.G. MSS.* (L.C. Trans.), A 5, No. CXXXIII; same in *Journal of S.P.G.* (L.C. Trans.), Vol. I, October 20, 1710. Maule served for ten years from 1707 to 1717, died of dysentery in 1717, and bequeathed £750 to the S.P.G.

[7] Hasell served at St. Thomas' from 1709-1743, having previously been at Charleston from 1705-1708. His term of service 35 years at St. Thomas', was longest of that of any missionary in one charge. An account of his death appears in *An Abstract of the Proceedings of the S.P.G.* (London: 1733), p. 52, Printed with Bearcroft Sermon (Huntington Library), as follows: ". . . The Reverend Mr. *Hassell,* the Society's Missionary at St. *Thomas's* Parish, having been disabled thro' Age and Infirmities for some time . . . died there on the 9th of *November* last, . . . Mr. Hassell had been for 35 years the diligent and worthy Pastor of this Parish, and we hope now rests from his Labours among *the Dead which dye in the Lord, and their Works follow them.*"

Johnson. But the Parish-Church of St. *Thomas* was Built of Brick, situate on a Neck of Land, on the *North-West* of *Wandoe* River, and *South-West* of *Cooper* River; in Pursuance of an Act of Assembly made in 1706. The Foundation of this Church was laid in 1707, and the Building finished the next Year; Mr. *Hasell* was the first Minister of this Church, elected by Virtue of the above-mentioned Act. There are in this Parish upwards of 600 Acres of *Glebe* Land, 200 of which adjoin to the Church; and 420 to the Chapel of Ease.[8]

Hasell himself, in his first reports, described his arrival in South Carolina, and commented that as soon as he was settled he expected to distribute the books sent over with him by the Society to such persons, whether slave or free, as he should find best inclined to make use of them. He was resolved to instruct ". . . the youth . . . and among them such negro . . . slaves as I shall find capable of it, and can be procured by the consent of their master. . . ."[9] His report of the baptism of a Negro child, both of whose parents were Christians, contained the information that the master and mistress not only stood as sureties for it but would, he believed, instruct the child as soon as it was able to learn.

. . . I hope to persuade several other masters and mistresses . . . to imitate these good people, and instruct their negro children . . . the young may be easily instructed if masters and mistresses would be prevailed upon to take a little pains. There are some in this parish have promised me to do this and for their encouragement and assistance, I propose . . . to set apart one day in the week for the instruction of negroes, . . .[10]

Hasell further concluded that the Negroes born and brought up in South Carolina, were civilized and spoke English as well as himself, whereas those newly brought from their own country seldom had attained good command of English.

In 1711, Hasell baptized two Negro slaves, and in 1712 he had between twenty and thirty Negro men and women who constantly attended his Chapel of Ease, one of whom was free and two were baptized.[11] However, from the time of the outbreak of the Indian War in 1715 to about 1720 disturbance and delay occurred, and very

[8] David Humphreys, *Historical Account of the Incorporated Society for the Propagation of the Gospel,* pp. 103-104.
[9] Thomas Hasell to John Chamberlayne, St. Thomas' Parish, South Carolina, April 25, 1710, in *S.P.G. MSS.* (L.C. Trans.), A 5, No. CX.
[10] Thomas Hasell to [Secretary], St. Thomas' Parish, South Carolina, March 12, 1712 [1712-1713], in *S.P.G. MSS.* (L.C. Trans.), A 7, pp. 401-402.
[11] Thomas Hasell to the Secretary, William Taylor, St. Thomas' Parish, South Carolina, August 18, 1712, in *S.P.G. MSS.* (L.C. Trans.), A 7, p. 435.

few baptisms were made.[12] In 1720 Hasell could report only eight
or nine baptized Negroes in the parish although there were about 110
families in St. Thomas' with more than 800 Negro and 90 Indian
slaves.[13] By 1724, only twelve of 950 Negroes in his parish were
baptized,[14] and this ratio of baptisms to the mass of Negroes remained the same for two years.[15] However, Hasell was convinced
that this slow progress was not due to a lack of inclination on the
part of the Negro for in 1726 he declared:

The native negros and Indians among us are undoubtedly capable
of instruction in Christianity, but few masters and mistresses will
be convinced that it is their duty to instruct them or have them instructed, nor will they be persuaded to take the necessary care and
pain in order to do it.

By the Blessing of God, I have some negro slaves of my own.
Among them I have several young ones born in the country, two of
which are instructed, one of them is baptized, and can read . . . I
shall take [care] of the others as they come to age, capable of instruction.[16]

In 1727, Hasell reported the state of his parish was ". . . much
the same. . . . I have . . . married a couple of negroes Christian, the
man a slave, the woman free."[17]

The many legal complications of marriages between free and slave
Negroes filled the Southern courts with cases, the records of which

[12] The Rev. John Whitehead of Charlestown wrote on Sept. 16, 1715, that
it was not in his power ". . . to prevail with any more than one single negro
to embrace Christianity," although he had tried both publicly and privately. See
John Whitehead to [Secretary], Charlestown, South Carolina, September 26,
1715, in *Journal of S.P.G.* (L.C. Trans.), III, November 22, 1716.
[13] Thomas Hasell to David Humphreys, St. Thomas', South Carolina, February 16, 1720, in *S.P.G. MSS.* (L.C. Trans.), A 14, p. 70.
[14] Some of the baptized were free and some slave, the exact number of
each is not given, see "Notitia parochialis" of Thomas Hasell to David Humphreys, St. Thomas' Parish, South Carolina, April 15, 1724, in *S.P.G. MSS.*
(L.C. Trans.), B 4, No. 174. The number of whites is given at about 565, and
the Indians as 62 slaves.
[15] Thomas Hasell to David Humphreys, St. Thomas' Parish, South Carolina,
September 12, 1726, in *S.P.G. MSS.* (L.C. Trans.), B 4, No. 208.
[16] Thomas Hasell to David Humphreys, St. Thomas' Parish, South Carolina,
May 12, 1726, in *S.P.G. MSS.* (L.C. Trans.), B 4, No. 200. Hasell was constant in his instructions, and in 1731 he wrote that he was not only instructing
the Negro children owned by himself, but requiring the adults who could understand English to attend public service. See Thomas Hasell to David Humphreys,
St. Thomas', South Carolina, December 2, 1731, in *S.P.G. MSS.* (L.C. Trans.),
B 4, No. 257. The Negroes attended Mr. Hasell's "Chapel at Ease," a church
contiguous to his dwelling, where he officiated every other Sunday.
[17] Thomas Hasell to David Humphreys, St. Thomas' Parish, South Carolina, August 16, 1727, in *S.P.G. MSS.* (L.C. Trans.), A 20, p. 96. In 1728, the
number of Negro slaves had increased to 1000.

have been carefully compiled by an American scholar, who cites many instances of fair verdicts, decisions which varied however from state to state.[18] The problems of the free Negro both economic and legal were exceedingly difficult, and owners who set free their slaves found emancipation was but half the task. After observation of the disproportionate ratio of free negroes sentenced, or kidnaped and sold South, colonization societies of which Virginia had thirty-four, became active in the first quarter of the nineteenth century. Wills and legacies set aside funds for expenses of transportation to Africa together with a year's maintenance or grants of money on arrival there for such slaves as were willing to undertake emigration.[19] Virginia, intermittently forbade further manumission under pressure of experience.[20]

[18] Cases from the courts of South Carolina, as cited in Helen Tunnicliff Catterall (Ed.), *Judicial Cases Concerning American Slavery and the Negro.* See Vol. II, pp. 267-478 for South Carolina. Mrs. Catterall states that "The free negroes of South Carolina were accorded many of the privileges of white men." They were part of the militia, were permitted to own land, and even allowed seats in legislatures (p. 269). For an account of "Action of trover. . . . The plaintiff . . . a free mulatto woman descended from a white mother: she purchased John, (who was her husband) from Cato Gallman, a free negro. . . ." See case of *Cline v. Caldwell,* I Hill 423, December 1833, (p. 354) in *ibid.* See also *Mathews v. Mathews* (p. 383) and *Bowers v. Newman* (p. 383) where it is "Held: a free person of colour, by the laws of this State, may take and hold, convey by deed, dispose of by will, or transmit to his heir at law, both real and personal estate. . . ."

[19] Lincoln's interest in Ile La Vache, West Indies, as a place for colonization, and later in Texas or the Southwest, is discussed in Carl Sandburg, *Abraham Lincoln, the War Years,* Four Volumes (New York: 1939), I, (p. 564). On August 14, 1862, he appealed to a Committee of free Negroes for volunteers for settlement in Central America (pp. 574-576). "Could I get a hundred tolerably intelligent men, with their wives and children and able to 'cut their own fodder' so to speak? Can I have fifty? If I could find twenty-five able-bodied men, with a mixture of women and children—good things in the family relation, I think—I could make a successful commencement. I want you to let me know whether this can be done or not. This is the practical part of my wish to see you." For the provisions of the emancipation act of District of Columbia, offering steamship tickets to Liberia or Haiti for any freed Negroes willing to go, see p. 578.

[20] An account of these colonization societies, and the number of free blacks in Virginia is given in Theodore M. Whitfield, *Slavery Agitation in Virginia 1829-1832* (Baltimore: 1930), p. 7. "From less than 3000 at the close of the Revolution, they grew to 12,254 by 1790, and in 1800 numbered 19,981. Despite unfriendly legislation of 1806 again conditioning manumission upon removal, Virginia counted in 1810, 30,269; in 1820, 36,760, and in 1830, 46,729. The last was more than one-seventh of the free colored population of the United States." An interesting expedient to avoid banishment on manumission is given in *Virginia, A Guide to the Old Dominion,* American Guide Series (Oxford: 1940), p. 79: "Free Negroes would purchase their slave relatives for the nominal sum of five shillings each—an amount that was written into the deed of manumission but was seldom paid. By holding these relatives ostensibly as slaves, free Negroes evaded the legislative act of 1806, banishing from the State within 12 months all Negroes thereafter emancipated." See also U. B. Phillips, *American Negro Slavery,* Ch. XXI, "Free Negroes." On p. 426, Phillips stated, "Manumissions

Mr. Hasell's letter of 1728 included a brief census and embodied his considered reflections about education.

There are in this parish about 1,000 negro and 50 Indian slaves, including men and children, but few of them as yet instructed. Some few masters and mistresses take care to instruct. . . . But the generality of people wholly neglect this duty and will not be persuaded to take any pains about it.[21]

The "irreligious and wordly minded people" in his parish, Hasell declared, were in opposition to his opinions, and there seemed but little probability of making any advances in education "till the legislature shall think fit to pass a law to oblige masters and mistresses to the observation of some proper method for instructing them."[22] To influence the masters, he distributed the literature of the Society, reporting in 1731[23] that he had distributed Dr. Gibson's Pastoral Letter to neighboring missionaries and parishioners, but that it had so far had less effect than he had hoped for.[24]

This Pastoral letter was itself a recognition of such difficulties as Hasell was encountering. Letters from the missionaries to the home office complaining of the masters' negligence were received in great number from all the colonies. In 1727 Dr. Edmund Gibson, Lord Bishop of London, made clear the Society's position in the matter by sending the important Pastoral Letter "To the Masters and Mistresses of Families in the English Plantations abroad; Exhorting them to encourage and promote the Instruction of their Negroes in the Christian Faith." The S.P.G. had ten thousand copies published and dispersed throughout the colonies, including South Carolina. Sections of the Letter read as follows:

I am loath to think so hardly of any *Christian* Master as to suppose that he can *deliberately* hinder his Negroes from being instructed in the Christian Faith; or, which is the same Thing, that he can,

---

were in fact so common in the deeds and wills of the men of '76 that the number of colored freemen in the South exceeded thirty-five thousand in 1790 and was nearly doubled in each of the next two decades. The greater caution of their successors, reinforced by the rise of slave prices, then slackened the rate of increase to twenty-five and finally to ten per cent per decade. Documents in this later period, reverting to the colonial basis, commonly recited faithful service or self purchase rather than inherent rights as the grounds for manumission."

[21] Thomas Hasell to David Humphreys, St. Thomas' Parish, June 4, 1728, in *S.P.G. MSS.* (L.C. Trans.), A 21, p. 116.

[22] Thomas Hasell to David Humphreys, St. Thomas', South Carolina, February 12, 1730-1731, in *S.P.G. MSS.* (L.C. Trans.), A 23, p. 229.

[23] Thomas Hasell to David Humphreys, St. Thomas', South Carolina, December 2, 1731, in *S.P.G. MSS.* (L.C. Trans.), B 4, No. 257.

[24] A discussion of Bishop Gibson's interest in the plantation and of the importance of this Pastoral Letter appears later in this study.

upon sober and mature Consideration of the Case, finally resolve to deny them the *Means* and *Opportunities* of Instruction. . . .[25]

Dr. Gibson continued by saying that he hoped that all masters, especially those possessing great numbers of Negroes, would be willing to give contributions for the instruction of the slaves, and that other planters not owning so many would join in to support a common teacher for the Negroes. The Lord Bishop added:

The Society for Propagating the Gospel in Foreign Parts, are sufficiently sensible of the great Importance and Necessity of such an established and regular Provision for the Instruction of the Negroes, and earnestly wish and pray, that it may please God to put it into the hearts of good Christians, to enable them to assist in the work, by seasonable Contributions for that End. . . .[26]

In general the Society acted as a spur upon the missionary, both in ideology and in the techniques of setting out upon his task. Alone as perhaps the best educated man in the frontier community, he was usually backed by a few planters, willing to set aside an hour, or an afternoon, or to provide a place where the slaves might gather from the fields for their regular instruction. But these brief contacts suggested to the missionary again and again an act of compulsory education for the slaves.

The Annual Sermons, delivered at the Society's headquarters in London by a notable churchman, especially selected each year, furnished additional ammunition for the missionary in the field which was to be used to good account throughout the century. Each Sermon was printed and distributed by thousands of copies, the S.P.G.

[25] Frederick Dalcho, *An Historical Account of the Protestant Episcopal Church in South Carolina,* p. 107. The complete letter is quoted in this book, pp. 104-112, also in Humphreys, *Historical Account of the Incorporated Society for the Propagation of the Gospel,* pp. 257-271. One of the first Bishops to set forth the duty of instructing the Negroes in the Christian religion was William Fleetwood, Bishop of St. Asaph, in the annual *Sermon* preached before the S.P.G. in 1711 (Huntington Library). This sermon was widely distributed in 1711 and reprinted again in 1725 for distribution. Other Bishops also stressed Negro education, for example, Edward Chandler, Bishop of Coventry and Litchfield, in his *Sermon* preached before the S.P.G., 1718-1719 (Huntington Library), stated that the only way to make the slaves better servants and eliminate the false notions concerning the English, was to teach the Negroes Christianity; Samuel Bradford, Bishop of Carlisle, *Sermon* preached before the S.P.G., 1719-1720 (Huntington Library), stressed the duty of every Christian to have his Negroes instructed.
[26] Frederick Dalcho, *An Historical Account of the Protestant Episcopal Church in South Carolina,* p. 108. "Pastoral Letter" by Dr. Edmund Gibson, Bishop of London. See Norman Sykes, *Edmund Gibson* (London: 1926) pp. 363-367, for a discussion of the Bishop's stand on Negro education and its results in the Colonies.

workers in the West Indies alone receiving two thousand at one time for distribution.

Threshed out in the early sermons preached before the Society, were the philosophical theories of the time as to primitive man, and his "natural religion." The argument was portrayed by Bishop Williams in 1706, who put the question in the mouth of a noble savage; the savage reasoned,

I [a native] grant what you say, that the Christian religion doth propose many excellent advantages to those that believe and embrace it; but I have been otherwise educated, and cannot easily part with what all my progenitors have lived and died in, and must have very convincing reasons to oblige me to forsake it: . . . give me a plain and positive answer, whether a heathen, continuing so to be, may not be saved, if he take nature and reason to be his guide, and live soberly and virtuously? And why must all the world submit to you? And are all to be damned that believe not as you do believe? . . . Then saith the native, let the fault lie upon me, and if I may be saved in the religion of my own country, I shall need no further instructor, nor shall I desire any change.[27]

In like manner, Bishop Fleetwood's famous Sermon of 1711 argued that the Negro was not inferior to the white man, that slavery was not justified by low prices for tropical products, that the Negro would work for wages, that he was "equally the Workmanship of God, with themselves; [the planters] endued with the same Faculties and intellectual Powers; Bodies of the same Flesh and Blood, and Souls as certainly mortal. . . ."[28]

From the beginning many of the Bishops asked for contributions to the Society because of the remuneration received by the English through trade with the Colonies. Gilbert Burnet, Bishop of Sarum, in 1704, summed up the argument, which was repeated in many forms throughout the 18th century:

In a Word, while our Colonies are as so many Mines of Wealth to us, and while such vast Numbers of Seamen are imployed in so many hundreds of Ships . . . While we have so many Blessings coming home daily, shall we take no Care to secure those Blessings

[27] J. Williams, Bishop of Chichester, *Sermon* preached before S.P.G. in St. Mary le Bow, in *Twelve Anniversary Sermons Preached Before the Society for the Propagation of the Gospel in Foreign Parts* (London 1845), pp. 15-37. For an analysis of other Annual Sermons before 1710, such as those by R. Willis, Dean of Lincoln, 1702; Gilbert Burnet, Bishop of Sarum, 1704; William Beveridge, Bishop of St. Asaph, 1707; and Sir William Dawes, Bishop of Chester, 1709; see Frank J. Klingberg, *Anglican Humanitarianism in Colonial New York* (Philadelphia, 1940), pp. 11-48.
[28] William Fleetwood, Bishop of St. Asaph, *A Sermon* preached before the Society, February 1710-1711 (Huntington Library), pp. 15-16.

to us and to our Brethren in those Plantations? . . . Shall we export nothing for the good of their Souls, while we import so much for the raising our own Wealth from their Industry. . . .[29]

Again, Dr. George Stanhope, Dean of Canterbury, in 1714 said that Christian traders had an opportunity to incline infidels to Christianity in their intercourse with them, and the English, to repay their material profit should offer spiritual gain.[30] John Leng, Bishop of Norwich in 1726, pointed out that the merchants who had become wealthy through colonies should contribute to the work of the S.P.G. as a thank offering for their own success.[31] Martin Benson, Bishop of Gloucester, in 1740, urged that the English were obliged to propagate the Gospel "particularly with respect to our Colonies in America, both on account of the great benefit we receive from them and the great opportunities we have of making this recompense."[32] The following year, Thomas Secker, Bishop of Oxford, asking support for the Society said, "But they more especially who are now raising Fortunes by Commerce with our *American* Settlements . . . should think often of how much hath accrued to them from the Produce of these Colonies . . . and reflect very seriously what Returns . . . Justice . . . Gratitude . . . Prudence . . . Piety, direct them to make."[33] Many other similar references, particularly to the wealth of London, can be found in the annual sermons down to the time of the American Revolution.

Meantime there were courageous planters who from time to time emerged as men genuinely interested in their slaves' welfare. A letter written by Mr. John Norris, a citizen of South Carolina to John Chamberlayne in August, 1711, deplored the lack of interest in the instructions of slaves in South Carolina and proposed the use of an almanac to inform the masters of the S.P.G. plans and to persuade them to provide daily instructions.

I humbly take the freedom to acquaint you that whereas I have not known or heard of any care generally taken in Carolina by masters or owners of slaves to instruct or cause them to be instructed

[29] Gilbert Burnet, Bishop of Sarum, *Sermon* preached before S.P.G., 1704 (Huntington Library), p. 20.
[30] George Stanhope, Dean of Canterbury, *Sermon* preached before the S.P.G. in 1714 (Huntington Library), p. 23.
[31] John Leng, Bishop of Norwich, *Sermon* preached before S.P.G., 1726 (Huntington Library), pp. 1-32, *passim.*
[32] Martin Benson, Bishop of Gloucester, *Sermon* preached before S.P.G., 1740 (Huntington Library), p. 11.
[33] Thomas Secker, Bishop of Oxford, *Sermon* preached before S.P.G., 1741 (Huntington Library), p. 43.

. . . only in or near Goose Creek. The case of these poor people . . . is much to be pitied. I have heartily wished that masters in general could be prevailed with to instruct or cause them daily to receive some short instructions . . . for I think it almost impossible to be effectually done by ministers alone without the assistance of these that are their daily commanders. I have had thoughts and am desirous to procure some persuasive and prevailing arguments to induce the masters and others in command to take care and give them some daily instructions, in order to lay a foundation in their understandings whereby ministers' endeavors may afterwards make greater impressions on them; but considering when I had got it printed, how I should get it to be dispersed in their hands seeing men generally neglect procuring what they do not foresee to be temporal pleasure and profit. Then I thought of this expedient, whereas I ought to oblige the inhabitants in general what in me lies, and I have found very generally the use of an almanac there being none printed that I know of for that province. I also intended to get about 2500 or 3000 printed for them. The copy is already calculated for four years for that latitude. Then I thought it might be proper to print the aforesaid persuasive arguments with the almanac, thereby I supposed it would be dispersed for the sake of the almanac which I presume will be very serviceable and acceptable to them. But this may be a query whether it is proper to join it to a common almanac, lest the persuasions should be less esteemed thereby. But I hope 'twill not have the less effect with them in general, because the almanac itself will be so great a novelty to most families, as such advice to them. In this almanac I intended briefly to show the reasons why the several festivals and some particular Sundays so called and observed, which may probably be of some use to some people that are not yet satisfied with the reasonableness thereof. The copy of my weak argument or reasons to masters and others, although I cannot but know it's very imperfect, yet, sir, if you please to give yourself the trouble to read it and do afterwards suppose it's probable that these propositions may be useful to the purposes aforesaid, and if you think fit to acquaint the Society or Committee therewith and they approve of this method, I would be heartily glad if I should be honored with a copy of more convincing reasons and arguments to that purpose than I am capable to give, but do in a plain intelligible and familiar style to be comprehended by mean capacities, or mine carefully corrected and amended with additions, and I'll carefully procure it to be printed where it may not be taxed, for I am lately informed this Almanac must not be printed in England though it's useless here unless I pay the tax which is too heavy for me. Your answer, sir is desired by: . . .

P.S. Sir.

If it were recommended by the Society, I apprehend it might make the greater impression on them to observe and put in practise, and likewise to give the reader some short account of the Societies for the Propagating the Gospel, and Christian Knowledge and with all advertise them that what progress either of them shall make in converting the heathens either slaves or free, if they acquaint me in writing or some other proper person whom you appoint, from whom both Societies may be there with acquainted and their names and good success of their endeavors shall be sent you. . . .[34]

Mr. Norris appeared before the Society, received its approval of his almanac project, and was commended for his zeal in promoting Christianity.[35] This action was an early recognition of the tremendous advertising value of the almanac, found in many eighteenth century homes, and a subject of daily reading.[36]

Planters here and there ". . . were zealous in encouraging the instruction of their slaves such as Mr. John Norris (of St. Bartholomew's) [and] Lady Moore, Captain David Davis, Mrs. Sarah Baker, and several others at Goose Creek. . . ."[37] But especially notable was

[34] John Norris to John Chamberlayne [London] August 6, 1711, in *S.P.G. MSS.* (L.C. Trans.), A 6, No. c; also in *Journal of S.P.G.* (L.C. Trans.), Vol. II, August 17, 1711. Although before the Revolution there was only sporadic restriction on Negro education, after the war reaction followed and methods were devised to restrict the Negro in his quest for learning. See Carter G. Woodson, "Educating the Negro before General Emancipation," in *Negro History Bulletin,* III, No. 2 (November, 1939), pp. 17-18. "The result of this reaction . . . not only closed the schools for Negroes but provided that anyone teaching the Negroes even privately should be punished. . . . A little hope came from various sources. There were white planters who were a law unto themselves, and when it was necessary to teach a Negro to read, write, and cipher in order to make him a useful slave, they did so in violation of the law. For instance, Joseph Davis, the brother of Jefferson Davis, had Isaiah T. Montgomery trained as an accountant for his entire plantation. There were also sympathetic white persons of religious orders who were morally brave enough to violate the law in teaching the Negroes to read the Bible." See also "Snatching Learning in Forbidden Fields," in this *Bulletin,* p. 21, wherein it is stated, "A few Negroes educated themselves by observing what passed at schools to which they went as servants for their owner's children. Often in the private schools near home the Negro servant figured as a constant attendant, carrying books and the like, . . . Many of the boarding schools of the day provided special quarters for such servants."
[35] *Journal of S.P.G.* (L.C. Trans.), II, August 17, 1711. For more information on Mr. Norris, see Faith Vibert, "The Society for the Propagation of the Gospel in Foreign Parts: Its Work for the Negroes in North America before 1783," in *Journal of Negro History,* XVIII, No. 2 (April, 1933), pp. 171-212. Miss Vibert states (p. 188) "Mr. Norris, an enterprising citizen of South Carolina, who afterward took Holy Orders that he might become a missionary on the frontier of his native province, proposed to the Society in 1711 that he should include an exhortation to owners concerning their Christian duty to their slaves in a Carolina almanac. . . ."
[36] The first almanac in the United States was William Pierce's in 1639. Bradford's appeared about 1685, and the popular "Poor Richard's" of Franklin between 1732 and 1757. In England, "Moore's" and "Poor Robin's" had a wide public from 1663-1828.
[37] C. F. Pascoe, *Two Hundred Years of the S.P.G.,* I, p. 15. Mr. Pascoe also mentions, among others, Landgrave Joseph Morton and his wife (of St. Paul's) and the Governor of South Carolina.

the work done by members of the Alexander Skene family. In 1713, the Rev. Ebenezer Taylor of St. Andrew's commended them in his report to the Secretary:

Sir, I can't but honour Mr. Skaim's [Skene's] the Secretary of Barbadoes, sister, Madame Haigue, who is lately come to his plantation in my parish, to which belongs a very considerable number of negroes that were very loose and wicked and little inclined to Christianity before her coming among them. I can't but honour her so much, she so well deserves it, and it is such a rare thing hereaway, as to acquaint the most Christian Society for the Propagation of the Gospel in Foreign Parts, with the extraordinary pains this gentlewoman and one Madam Edwards, that came with her, have taken to instruct those negroes in principles of Christian religion, and to reclaim and reform them, and the wonderful success they have met with in about half a years time in this great and good work. Upon these gentlewomen lately desiring me to come and examine these negroes about their knowledge of the principles of the Christian religion. I went and among other things I asked them who Christ was. They readily answered, he is the son of God and the Saviour of the World, and told me that they embraced him with all their hearts as such, and I desired them to rehearse the Apostles Creed and the Ten Commandments and the Lord's Prayer which they did very distinctly and perfectly. Fourteen of them gave me so great satisfaction, and were so very desirous to be baptized, that I thought it my duty to baptize them; and therefore I baptized these 14 last Lord's day. And I doubt not but these gentlewomen will prepare the rest of them for baptism in a little time.[38]

The Society asked Mr. Taylor to give Mrs. Haigue and Mrs. Edwards its thanks for their good example. By December, 1714, thirteen more of Mr. Skene's Negroes were qualified for baptism for whom the two women stood as godmothers.[39] The news of the practical work of these women had rapidly spread to other parishes and in January, 1715, the Rev. William Tredwell Bull, of St. Paul's expressed the hope that their example would be followed in other parishes. He had tried, in his parish, to get the masters to allow the Negroes Saturday afternoons for religious studies, but this effort proved unsuccessful; then he went to the various houses and engaged some whites to teach the slaves the Lord's Prayer. This aroused so much interest that he could not accommodate all the Negro and Indian slaves who came to

[38] Ebenezer Taylor to William Taylor, St. Andrew's Parish, South Carolina, July 28, 1713, in S.P.G. MSS. (L.C. Trans.), A 8, p. 356-357; also letter dated July 8, 1713, in Journal of S.P.G. (L.C. Trans.), Vol. II, October 16, 1713.
[39] Ebenezer Taylor to [Secretary] St. Andrew's, South Carolina, December 31, 1714, in Journal of S.P.G. (L.C. Trans.), Vol. III, October 7, 1715.

church, and in the last few months of 1714, he baptized twenty-six adults and children, many of them Negroes.[40]

Not alone in parochial affairs, but in those of the colony as well, Alexander Skene and his family, played an important part during this crucial period in South Carolina history. The Indian wars,[41] beginning in 1715, had ravaged the country, halted the profitable Indian trade, and temporarily suspended the work of the S.P.G.[42] The continued threat of the Spanish plus the piracy which preyed upon the trade of the port of Charleston, all contributed to the harassment of the struggling settlement which found itself stripped of wealth,[43] unable to plant crops, and lacking adequate defense against further invasion. In this crisis, the Proprietary government[44] made itself

[40] William T. Bull to [Secretary], St. Paul's, South Carolina, January 20, 1715, in *Journal of S.P.G.* (L.C. Trans.), Vol. III, October 7, 1715.

[41] Called the Yamassee war, this Indian uprising, probably instigated by the Creeks, was finally subdued when the Cherokees sided with the English colonists. See Verner W. Crane, *The Southern Frontier, 1670-1732,* Ch. VII, "The Yamassee War, 1715-1716," 162-186 passim. This war, an episode "in the advance of the farming frontier . . ." was more particularly "a far-reaching revolt against the . . . tyrannies of the Charles Town traders. . . . In its results, leading as it did to the awakening of the English colonial authorities to the danger of French encirclement, to a constitutional revolution in South Carolina, to far-reaching migration of the southern tribes, and to a re-orientation of wilderness diplomacy in the South which altered seriously the prospects of English, French, and Spanish rivalry, it takes rank with the more famous Indian conspiracies of colonial times." (p. 162)

[42] Only the missions at Christ Church, St. George's, St. Paul's, and St. Thomas' remained intact during these wars. Goose Creek, St. Andrews, and St. John's all lost their missionaries by death in 1717 and the posts were not filled until after the wars had subsided. The frontier missions at St. Helen's and St. Bartholomew's were completely abandoned in 1715, and the ravages of St. Bartholomew's in particular were so severe that not until 1733 was the parish able to support a missionary.

[43] The Indian trade, which had formed so important a part of the revenue of early South Carolina was, of course, completely wiped out during this period. At the time of the uprising, the Indians were debtors of the colonists to the amount of £10,000 Sterling. They cancelled these debts "by murdering their creditors," in the words used in an early "Historical Account of South Carolina and Georgia" (originally published at London in 1726) reproduced in B. R. Carroll, *Historical Collections of South Carolina* (New York: 1836), II, 145. For a full description of the political and economic effect of the Indian trade see, Verner W. Crane, *The Southern Frontier 1670-1732,* Ch. V, "The Charles Town Indian Trade," pp. 108-136. Extending over 1000 miles into the continent, this trade was a chief source of revenue, in the colonies. Moreover, "only the excellence of the British trade counterbalanced the superior position and diplomacy of the Spanish and French." (p. 115)

[44] This Proprietary Government, conducted under a royal charter, had been designed in 1669 by John Locke, and consisted of a territorial aristocracy of landgraves, caciques, and barons. For a reproduction of the *Second Charter granted by King Charles II to the Proprietors of Carolina,* see B. R. Carroll, *Historical Collections of South Carolina* (New York: 1836), Vol. II, pp. 38-57. Also in *ibid., The First Set of the Fundamental Constitutions of South Carolina: as compiled by Mr. John Locke.* II, pp. 362-389.

vulnerable when the absentee Proprietors in England replied to an
appeal for help from the colonials, with an order that the popularly-
elected Assembly be immediately adjourned. Further, the Bills of
Credit, enacted by the Assembly to the amount of £80,000, in a des-
perate effort to reëstablish themselves, were abitrarily voided, together with all other legislative acts of the body. It was at this juncture that Alexander Skene, outraged by such high-handed methods,
became a spearhead in the plot to overthrow the Proprietary government and convert South Carolina into a royal colony. This successful
revolution, and Skene's part in it, is described by Dr. Hewit:

. . . Alexander Skene, formerly excluded from the council, was
elected a member of this new assembly, which was chosen on purpose
to oppose the civil officers, considering himself as ill used by the
proprietors, turned a zealous and active person for pulling down the
tottering fabric of their government. This man, together with several
other members of assembly, held frequent meetings, to consider of
all their grievances, and the encouragements they had received from
time to time from Britain, respecting the great end they now had
in view. They recalled to mind what had passed in the house of peers
during the reign of Queen Anne, how her majesty had then ordered
her attorney and solicitor-general to consider of the most effectual
methods of proceeding against the charter. They knew also, that a
bill had been brought into the house of commons, for reducing all
charter and proprietary governments into regal ones. They had been
informed that Lord Carteret, conscious of the inability of the proprietors to defend their province in the Yamassee war, had publicly
applied for assistance from the British government, and that the
lords of trade were of opinion, that the government of the province
should belong to that power which bore the expense of its protection.
They had considered all these things, and flattered themselves with
the hopes, that the king would take the colony under his care as soon
as they renounced allegiance to the proprietors. And as the time drew
nigh in which they expected an attack from a powerful nation, they
concluded that the province needed assistance of the crown at the
present, more than at any time past. They had convinced the people
of the manifold advantages of the British constitution, and the great
happiness of those colonies which were under the immediate care
and protection of the crown, insomuch that they now desired nothing
more upon earth, than to enjoy the same invaluable privileges.[45]

Skene's letter of protest, written November 28, 1719,[46] was the
spark which ignited the "revolution,"[47] and he participated actively in

[45] Carroll, *Historical Collections of South Carolina,* I, pp. 224-225.
[46] A pamphlet entitled, "A Narrative of the Proceedings of the People of
South Carolina in the year 1719," was published in London in 1726, and is reproduced in B. R. Carroll, *Historical Collections of South Carolina,* II, 141-192.
[47] A comparison of this Revolution with that of 1776, is given in *ibid.,* I (p.

the governmental reorganization of the next ten years[48] which saw a rise in the influence of the planter over the merchant in positions of influence in South Carolina.

Meanwhile the S.P.G. hastened to reëstablish itself. Posts vacated by death and devastation, were promptly filled and, despite the social disorders which, of course, had included the Negroes, and particularly in spite of opposition aroused by a slave insurrection in 1720,[49] the program for the education and baptism of the Negroes was carried forward. In 1721, for example, a representation of the inhabitants of St. James Santee sent a petition to General Nicholson saying in part, "We have likewise several sensible negroes who, by the means of a catechist may be illuminated with the light of God according to the true intent of that illustrious Society."[50]

It is notable that the interest of the Skene family on behalf of their

---

240) : "In both cases a well-intentioned people, alarmed for their rights, were roused to extraordinary exertions for securing them. They petitioned, in a legal channel, for a redress of their grievances; but that being refused, they proceeded to bolder measures. Before they took decisive steps from which there was no honorable retreat; they both cemented their union by an association generally signed by the inhabitants. . . . When they had bound themselves by the tie of an association they seized their arms—took the forts and magazines into possession—and assumed the direction of the militia. A new government, without confusion or violence, virtually superseded the existing authority of the proprietary governor in one case and of the king's representative in the other. The revolutioners in both respectfully asked their former governors to join them; but from principles of honour and delicacy they declined. On their refusal they became private persons, and the people proceeded without them to organize every department of government by their own authority. The popular leaders in one case called themselves a convention of the people, and in the other a provincial congress; but in both, when the revolution was completed, they voted themselves an assembly—passed laws in the usual manner—and by manifestoes, justified their conduct to the world. In these proceedings neither faction nor party had any hand. The general interests of the great body of the settlers, were the pole star by which public measures were regulated. The people, guided neither by private views nor selfish ends, and acting in unison, eventually found their labours crowned with success; and that each change of government produced for their country a melioration of its circumstances."

[48] The far-reaching implications of this act have been assessed by Verner Crane, who says, op. cit., p. 186, "By slow degrees, as control of the province passed to the Crown, there was impressed upon the Board of Trade and the Privy Council the point of view . . . that South Carolina was 'A Barrier and might be made a Bulwark to all his Majesties Collonys on the South West Part of the Continent.' (Colonial Office Papers, 5 :1265, Q 76)."

[49] In his chapter on "Slave crime," Ulrich Bonnell Phillips, American Negro Slavery, commented: "In South Carolina, although depredations by runaways gave acute uneasiness in 1711 and thereabouts, no conspiracy was discovered until 1720 when some of the participants were burnt, some hanged, and some banished. Matters were then quiet again until 1739. . . ." (p. 473). See ibid., pages 454-488 for a review of such difficulties in slave-holding colonies.

[50] Representation of the inhabitants of St. James Santee in South Carolina to General Nicholson, inclosed in General Francis Nicholson to David Humphreys, Charlestown, South Carolina, November 6, 1721, in S.P.G. MSS (L.C. Trans.), A 15, p. 65.

Negroes was continuous. In March, 1724, more than a decade after the first mention of their good work, the clergy of South Carolina wrote to the Society:

At the same time we cannot without injustice forbear mentioning with great esteem to the Honorable Society with what indefatigable diligence and pious care the Honorable Mr. Skeen and his Lady and Mrs. Hague, his sister, take to have their negroes baptized and instructed in the principles of Christian religion, whose example we hope will be prevailing with others to do the like.[51]

Far too little it may be said here has been brought to light concerning the part played by the mistress of the plantation.[52] The adverse criticism at a later time of a Fanny Kemble,[53] a Harriet Martineau, or other reformers did not usually take cognizance of some sound achievements in Negro training and education contributed by the mistress in fulfilling her part of the plantation scheme.[54] A

[51] Clergy of South Carolina to David Humphreys, Charlestown, South Carolina. March 10, 1724, in *S.P.G. MSS.* (L.C. Trans.), B 4, No. 141; See also Francis Varnod to Society, South Carolina, April 1, 1724, in *S.P.G. MSS.* (L.C. Trans.), B 4, No. 173.
[52] For the interest taken in Negro schools by Deborah Franklin on behalf of her servant, Othello, see Richard I. Shelling, "Benjamin Franklin and the Dr. Bray Associates," in *Pennsylvania Magazine of History and Biography* (July, 1939), pp. 282-293.
[53] Conditions 100 years later on a rundown plantation neglected by an absentee master, are described by Fannie Kemble in her *Journal of a Residence on a Georgian Plantation in 1838-1839* (New York: 1863). The Journal was a subject of controversy at the time of its belated release in 1863, and contains evidence that the author, who belonged to the Anti-Slavery circle in Philadelphia, had read Matthew Gregory Lewis' *Journal of a West Indian Proprietor.* It provides much factual information as to the regime in the Butler and adjoining plantations. She notes the divisions of slave labor to include skilled crafts, such as coopers, blacksmiths, bricklayers, carpenters, etc. The Butler slaves had made all the furniture of the house (p. 25-26) and under the task system which she discusses at length, two of the men had made in their spare time an excellent boat which they sold for $60.00. For an account of Mrs. Stowe's visit to England, see F. J. Klingberg, "Harriet Beecher Stowe and Social Reform in England," in *American Historical Review,* XLIII (April, 1938), No. 3, pp. 542-552. See also U. B. Phillips, *American Negro Slavery,* Ch. XVI, pp. 309-330, "Plantation Life," and also by the same author, *Life and Labor in the Old South* (Boston: 1930), especially pages 196-202. "The plantation was a school," says Phillips (p. 198), "An intelligent master would consult his own interest by affording every talented slave special instruction, and by inculcating into the commoner sort as much routine efficiency, regularity and responsibility as they would accept. Not only were many youths given training in the crafts, and many taught to read and write, even though the laws forbade it, but a goodly number of planters devised and applied plans to give their whole corps spontaneous incentive to relieve the need of detailed supervision."
[54] See Elizabeth Watris Pringle, *Woman Rice Planter* (New York: 1913) *passim,* for an account of a woman owner and plantation manager who, after emancipation, assumes as a matter of course the responsibility for the education of two orphaned Negro boys of her plantation. Chiefly concerned with the boys, "Rab and Dab," it is a lively account of Carolina plantation life at a later period.

participant in the religious life of the time and at times a reader of religious tracts, even though helpless in effecting major ameliorations in
the slave system, the mistress might, nevertheless, encourage the
slaves to read their Bibles, and take their part in the white man's
activities.[55] Furthermore, in the administration of the home, a self-
sustaining factory producing its own bread, soap, clothing, light
(candles), heat and power, and also in the care of the sick, both black
and white, she trained the Negroes. They, in turn, then made their
own contributions to the plantation economy more satisfactorily.

On every plantation there were intelligent Negroes, known among
both whites and blacks for qualities of leadership or skills of various
sorts. Wood carving, a craft brought from Africa, was the chief art
of the Negro, and skill in carving was almost universal among the
slaves.[56] The plantation economy of the early South Carolina frontier
might be said to have encouraged these arts among the Negroes: pre-
cluding as it did by its nature the poor but skilled artisan of central
Europe, who settled in the North, while at the same time producing
a wealth and leisure which offered scope in these fields. Masons and
woodworkers were sometimes sent to England to be trained for the
fine craftsmanship to be seen in the beautiful homes of the planters.[57]

[55] Well phrased, and significant of the consistent tradition of this interest on
the part of the mistress of the plantation is a report from the Greenville district
in South Carolina, dated 1845, which reads, "There are some mistresses who
instruct their servants at home, and, to their credit be it said, that they pay
more attention to the instruction of the Negroes than masters; and to their
efforts we are indebted for so many well-ordered Negroes." See *The Proceedings
of the Meeting in Charleston, South Carolina, May 13-15, 1845, on the Religious
Instruction of the Negroes* (Charleston: 1845), p. 21 (Huntington Library).
[56] A study of the evolution of Negro art is given in "The Negro in Art from
Africa to America," *The Negro History Bulletin*, II, No. 6 (March 1939), pp.
49-50, 55; in this same issue, pp. 51-52, see "Persons and Achievements to be
Remembered in March," including short sketches of Edmonia Lewis, Meta
Vaux, Warrick Fuller, Augusta Savage, Sargent Johnson, Elizabeth Prophet,
Richmond Barthe, all artists and sculptors. For a discussion of the vitality of
African Art as an embodiment of universal human experience see *Arts of West
Africa*, Michael Sadler, editor (London: 1935) reviewed in *London Times
Literary Supplement*, March 14, 1935, p. 154. The introduction, by Sir William
Rothenstein, points out the difficulty of preserving tribal arts under new en-
vironments, due to "the crumbling of the religious and tribal systems under
which the native arts grew up." Sadler speaks of the "deep affinity between a
submerged part of European thought and the thinking of primitive peoples."
The chapter on "Significance and Vitality of African Art," points to the "elements in the indigenous faiths of West Africa which . . . embody universal
human experience. . . . We too, like the Africans, have a sense of the mystery
of things. Like them we feel that there is a bond between one spirit and the
spirits of other living things. We are conscious of something present but hidden,
powerful but not unfriendly . . . the dim background of all knowledge and
insight and creative will." It is from such elemental sources that the peculiar
characteristics of the African artistic genius seems to flow.
[57] Many of the beautiful homes built very early in the history of the colony

They became the teachers of other Negroes. The Negro was not only the teacher of his own people, but of the white children in many crafts, and in some cases their instructor in the elementary subjects. Occasionally, even, a Negro preacher served a white congregation.[58]

To return to the immediate problems faced by the S.P.G. missionaries in the formative period which began with the revolt in 1720 their reports to London reveal not only the variety of responsibilities placed upon them by the Society, but draw an excellent picture of the changing social scene. The Rev. Richard Ludlam, who served at Goose Creek from 1723 to 1728, took much care in instructing a large number of Negroes, but apropos of the master's attitude toward education, he told in 1725 of the treacheries "by secret poisonings and bloody insurrection,"[59] of some slaves who had been instructed and brought over to Christianity. Again in 1725, he wrote of the fear the masters had of instructing their Negroes, because of ". . . the

have disappeared as a result of the Revolution, the Civil war, and the ravages of time. Harriette Kershaw Leiding, *Historic Houses of South Carolina* (Philadelphia: 1921), has collected material regarding the architectural styles and manners of such structures still standing or destroyed. Of particular interest are the pictures of St. George's church, Dorchester, built about 1719 after a design of Sir Christopher Wren (opposite p. 196); the church at St. James, Goose Creek, built about the same time (opposite p. 22); and the magnificence of Drayton Hall, built about 1740 (opposite p. 202). "Most of the fine brick houses were built between the years 1710 and 1760. . . . After 1760 the tradition of stone and brick houses faded, masons became scarce, and saw mills developed, then wooden houses on brick basements were built," p. 3. For Charleston architecture see Samuel G. Stoney and Bayard Wootten, Charleston: *Azaleas and Old Bricks* (Boston: 1939), *passim*. Book has 42 plates by Wootten.
[58] In the eighteenth century, especially among the Baptists and Methodists, it was not uncommon to find a Negro pastor for a white congregation. See "Negro Preachers Serving Whites" in *Negro History Bulletin*, III, No. 1 (October, 1939), p. 8, 15.
[59] Richard Ludlam to David Humphreys, St. James, Goose Creek, South Carolina, July 2, 1724, in *S.P.G. MSS.* (L.C. Trans.), B 4, No. 181. On the whole, the records of South Carolina courts, as collected by Helen Tunnicliff Catterall in *Judicial Cases concerning American Slavery and the Negro* seem remarkably free of cases concerning revolt, murder, or poisonings on the part of slaves. The case of the *State v. Hudnall,* Vol. II (p. 315), in May, 1820, exactly 100 years later, censures a group of whites: "John Hudnall and William Vaughn, acting as Justices, but without being so . . . and . . . others, acting as free-holders, but not being such, [who] tried a negro, named Manuel, the property of . . . Silliman, on a charge for administering poison to Roger Parish, and before whom the said negro was convicted and sentenced to be executed." The court charged that the Negro "had not been tried within [six days] . . . after being apprehended; that the master had not been notified of the accusation, and that on the trial of the slave the testimony of Roger Parish, the prosecutor, was admitted without his being sworn." The court held that "Every feeling of humanity and justice revolts at the idea, that any other mode of trial less formal . . . than what the act [of 1740] has prescribed, should be sanctioned . . . the defendants are still allowed to plead to the declaration . . . at the next Circuit, . . . And in the mean time, and until a final decision . . . the defendants are prohibited from all further proceedings on the trial had against negro Manuel."

ingratitude of some bloody villians who have returned them the greatest of evils for the greatest good. . . ."[60] The letter continues with an account of agricultural conditions and a pentrating forecast of the future of the plantation system:

. . . I here beg leave to acquaint the honorable Society that since the time I have been here I have administered the sacrament of baptism to 31 souls in number, whereof there were 4 adults, 2 negros, and 25 infants. It is something unaccountable that this province from the time it was first settled has made no greater improvements than at present are to be found in it where it a thing to be credited what a rich soil and how capable of manifold products are the natural blessings of it one would think it might be a sufficient motive to invite multitudes of poor helpless families to come and possess a land as temperate as that which flowed with milk and honey and by honest industry and length of time might raise numberless families from the lowest ebb to very plentiful fortunes. But it's a wrong policy we are here fond of which is to engross more lands than it is possible a tenth part of and yet to be greedy after more as though they should not have enough for posterity. Hence I fear in some measure we have some reason to believe that we rather decrease than increase in the small number of Christian white inhabitants. What the consequence of this is likely to be unless timely very timely prevented I have no list to mention but were we as industrious to put a stop to growing evils as we are careless to let them be ready at every critical juncture to overrun us, we might be a flourishing and happy people.[61] As matters stand with us we make use of a wile for our present security to make the Indians and negros a check upon each other lest by their vastly superior numbers we should be crushed by one or the other. This I imagine one cause that intimidates the planters from being willing that their sensible slaves should be converted to Christianity lest as they allege they should make such an ill use of meeting to do their duty to God as to take the opportunity at such times of seizing and destroying their owners. I hope if it please God to bless us with suffragan bishops some means will be found out whereby thousands may be happily brought over to the Christian faith that they may enjoy the benefits (in their masters plantations) of Christianity without endangering their own or their owners happiness, till we are as it were by some wonderful means assisted, for the ordinary means is not rightly relished here. I doubt we are in a worse way than is here sought to be remedied or at home likely to be much credited

[60] Richard Ludlam to David Humphreys, St. James, Goose Creek, South Carolina, March 22, 1725, in *S.P.G. MSS.* (L.C. Trans.), A 19, pp. 62-63.
[61] By 1850 this tendency had reached such extremes that "two-thirds of the white people of the South had no connection with slavery and received only a very small part of the returns of the community output. A thousand families received over $50,000,000 a year, while all the remaining 666,000 families received only about $60,000,000." William E. Dodd, *The Cotton Kingdom* (New Haven, 1920), Vol. 27, The Chronicles of America Series, p. 24.

unless his Excellency Governor Nicholson stands our friends (which I believe he will), though we are too base and ungrateful to deserve any such favor at his hands who has met with ill returns for not sparing neither his purse nor person to hold us up by the chin, who are in general so deeply indebted for negros and the Indian war that we should most of us in a fair way to have been at least perpetual bondsmen and bondswomen if not fugitives and vagabonds. What I here hint I hope in a short while his Excellency will explain to his credit and our advantage both civil and sacred. This with my bounden respects.[62]

The missionary, of course, was an observer, and often an analyst of economic phenomena. His humanitarian objectives naturally made him acutely aware of the rapid social transformations occurring before his eyes. His rounds took him not only to the great plantations, but into the poor man's clearing. In the history of agriculture the size of the most productive unit has fluctuated from time to time, and from crop to crop. Some products have been grown by farm colony methods, wheat for example; and others such as cotton, sugar, and rice, by a plantation economy. The importance of rice as the staple crop in South Carolina, implying as it did, the slave as the unit of work, and a wealthy planter class, was full of implications to Ludlam. The warm climate, low swampy lands, the excellent port at Charleston, and proximity to the West Indian slave trade, all were contributing to the development of a crop which was rapidly becoming "more an institution than a cereal."[63] Tradition has it that rice was first

[62] Richard Ludlam to David Humphreys, Goose Creek, South Carolina, [c. March], 1725, in *S.P.G. MSS.* (L.C. Trans.), A 19, pp. 66-67. Nicholson's cooperation with the S.P.G. is described in B. R. Carroll, *Historical Collections of South Carolina*, I, 259-260. "For though he was bred a soldier, and was profane, passionate, and headstrong himself, yet he was not insensible of the great advantage of religion to society, and contributed not a little to its interest in Carolina, both by public influence and private generosity."

[63] From Samuel G. Stoney, *Charleston: Azaleas and Old Bricks* (Boston: 1929), p. 11. See this work for the many ramifications of rice as part of the way of life for a century in South Carolina. A description of the part played by the expanding frontier in this economy is described in B. R. Carroll, *Historical Collections of South Carolina,* I, p. 436, which reads: ". . . the settlers of Carolina began to stretch backward, and occupied lands above a hundred and fifty miles from the shore. New emigrants from Ireland, Germany, and the northern colonies obtained grants in these interior parts, and introduced the cultivation of wheat, hemp, flax and tobacco, for which the soil answered better there than in the low lands nearer the sea. The cattle, sheep, hogs, and horses multiplied fast, and having a country of vast extent to range over, they found plenty of provisions in it through the whole year. From different parts new settlers were invited to those hilly and more healthy parts of Carolina, where they laboured with greater safety than among the swamps, and success crowned their industry. By degrees public roads were made, and they conveyed their produce in wagons to the capital where they found an excellent market for all their productions, but especially the provisions which they raised."

planted in South Carolina about 1700 "owing to a lucky accident and a private experiment."[64] By 1710, it was generally planted,[65] and at midcentury, had become "the only commodity of Consequence produced in South Carolina."[66]

Mr. Ludlam observed very early in the movement the signs of the victory of the plantation and its effects on the small farmer. Just as the small farmers had had to leave Barbados for the continent, so in South Carolina, the poor man was headed for the back country, or, as is usually stated, for the frontier.[67]

[64] The story of the brigantine from Madagascar, is found in the pamphlet "A Description of South Carolina:" printed in London, 1761, and reproduced in B. R. Carroll, *Historical Collections of South Carolina,* II, pp. 270-271. The brigantine "happened to put into that Colony: [South Carolina]—They had a little Seed Rice left, not exceeding a Peck . . . which the Captain offered and gave to a Gentleman by the name of Woodward:—from a Part of this he had a very good Crop, but was very ignorant for some years how to clean it:—it was soon dispersed over the Province, and by frequent experiments and observations, they found out ways of producing and manufacturing it, to so great Perfection, that it is said to exceed any other Rice in value:—The Writer of this hath seen the said Captain in Carolina where he received a handsome Gratuity . . . in acknowledgement of the Service he had done that Province. . . . It is likewise reported, that Mr. Du Bois, Treasurer of the East India Company did send to that Country a small Bag of Seed Rice, some short time after; from whence it is reasonable enough to suppose there might come those two sorts of that Commodity, the one called Red-Rice in Contradistinction to the White Rice, from the redness of the inner husk. . . ." The source of this quotation is not given.

[65] A description of Rice culture written about 1710, and appearing in *ibid.,* II, p. 251-252, reads: "Rice is sowed in furrows about Eighteen Inches distant: a peck usually sows an Acre, which yields seldom less than thirty bushels, or more than sixty bushels. . . . Rice is cleaned by mills turned by Horses or Oxen. The Planters in this Colony sow much Rice, not only because it is a vendable commodity, but thriving best in low moist lands, it inclines people to improve that sort of ground, which being planted a few years with Rice, and then laid fallow, it turns to the best Pasture."

[66] The growing importance of the rice trade between the years 1720 to 1739, is shown in *ibid.,* II, pp. 265-270, where it is reported that 44,081 tons of rice were exported from South Carolina between 1720 and 1729; and 99,905 tons in the following ten years from 1730 to 1739. Chief markets in this latter period were "Holland, Hamburgh and Bremen including about 7,000 barrels to Sweden and Denmark," 372,118 barrels; Portugal, 83,379 barrels; and Great Britain, Ireland, and the British Plantations, 30,000 barrels. The importance of this trade is further discussed in *ibid.,* I, p. 343, with the comment that ". . . of the vast quantities of rice thus exported, scarcely one fifteenth part is consumed either in Great Britain or in any part of the British dominions so that the produce of the other fourteen parts is clear gain to the nation; whereas almost all sugar, and one fourth part of tobacco, exported from British colonies, are consumed by the people of Great Britain, or by British subjects; from whence it is evident, that the national gain arising from rice is several times as great in proportion as the national gain arising either from sugar or tobacco."

[67] See U. B. Phillips, *American Negro Slavery,* p. 334, for a statement that about 1860 the "tendency toward engrossment of estates prevailed." He continues ". . . This widespread phenomenon did not escape the notice of contemporaries. Two members of the South Carolina legislature described it as early as 1805 . . . as follows 'As one man grows wealthy and thereby increases his stock of negroes, he wants more land to employ them on; and being fully

Ludlam's interest in economic conditions did not interfere with his parochial affairs, for in 1726, he baptized eleven Negroes,[68] and the next year he reported the number of slaves as 1,500 (Negroes and Indians), and the baptism of five more Negroes.[69] Ludlam died in October, 1728, and, in his will embodied his dream for the parish. To encourage instruction he bequeathed all his estate to the Society *"for Erecting and Maintaining a School for the instruction of Poor Children of that Parish."*[70] The legacy amounted to about £2000 "Carolina Money."[71]

A contemporary of Ludlam's, the Rev. Brian Hunt, served at St. John's for five years, beginning in 1723. Early in his ministry, Hunt reported that "A sober sensible negro who can read and comes to church is a catechumen under the probation for baptism which he desires,"[72] but none of the Negro slaves were yet baptized. In 1725 he asked the members of his parish to give him some additional Negroes for his own service,[73] and a year later reported that he was

---

able, he bids a large price for his less opulent neighbor's plantation, who by selling advantageously here can raise money enough to go into the back country, where he can be more on a level with the most forehanded, can get lands cheaper, and speculate or grow rich by industry as he pleases.' Some three decades afterward another South Carolinian spoke sadly 'on the incompatibleness of large plantations with neighboring farms, and their uniform tendency to destroy the yeoman.' Similarly Dr. Basil Manly, president of the University of Alabama, spoke in 1841 of the inveterate habit of Southern farmers to buy more land and slaves and plod on captive to the customs of their ancestors; and C. C. Clay Senator from Alabama, said in 1855, of his native county of Madison, which lay on the Tennessee border: 'I can show you . . . the sad memorials of the artless and exhausting culture of cotton. Our small planters, after taking the cream off their lands, unable to restore them by rest, manures or otherwise, are going further west and south in search of other virgin lands which they may and will despoil and impoverish in like manner. Our wealthier planters, with greater means and no more skill, are buying out their poorer neighbors, extending their plantations and adding to their slave force.' "

[68] Richard Ludlam to David Humphreys, St. James, Goose Creek, South Carolina, November 25, 1726, in *S.P.G. MSS.* (L.C. Trans.), B 4, No. 216.

[69] Richard Ludlam to David Humphreys, (Goose Creek), South Carolina, December 12, 1727, in *S.P.G. MSS.* (L.C. Trans.), A 20, p. 101.

[70] David Humphreys, *An Historical Account of the Society for the Propagation of the Gospel in Foreign Parts,* p. 87.

[71] This legacy formed the foundation for a charity school later established in the parish. "Mr. Harrison transmitted to the Society, May 2, 1765, the Accounts of the Rev. Mr. Ludlam's Legacy. He informed them that the Parishioners had signed a subscription to the amount of £200 Stg. which they had bound themselves to pay, towards the building of a School-House." See Frederick Dalcho, *Historical Account of the Protestant Episcopal Church in South Carolina,* p. 260.

[72] Brian Hunt to David Humphreys, St. John's, South Carolina, October 30, 1723, in *S.P.G. MSS.* (L.C. Trans.), B 4, No. 167.

[73] Brian Hunt to David Humphreys, Charleston, South Carolina, May 12, 1725, in *S.P.G. MSS.* (L.C. Trans.), B 4, No. 192.

instructing these slaves (who were very young), as early as they were able to learn the Christian Religion.[74] At the same time Hunt was convinced, as were many of his fellow workers, that Christianity could not move forward unless the Society would ask the Governor, Council, and Assembly ". . . to pass a law that every planter who has ten slaves shall be obliged under . . . a penalty to have one of them taught to read the Bible and learn the Catechism . . . that these may learn the rest especially the youth."[75]

Mr. Hunt's plan of having every tenth Negro instructed suggests the certainty of the writer that in this manner, the remainder would also learn the rudiments of reading. It is to be noted that in the mass of letters from South Carolina as compared with those from New York and elsewhere there occur few complaints of stupidity or slowness in learning. The complaints are of a different character —of the difficulty in getting access to the slaves to teach them.

Hunt's experience at St. John's is a valuable commentary on the policy of the Society which, as has been seen, was conciliatory rather than contentious. His plan of government intervention and compulsion on behalf of Negro education strikes a modern note, and is testimony of his zeal in that direction. But the fact that the immediate results in his parish seem to have been negligible, due in part to the fact that the parishioners found him of a "contentious disposition,"[76] suggests the significance of the time factor in such movements. Throughout the records of the S.P.G. appears the suggestion that state intervention on behalf of Negro education was the ultimate end in view. To the harassed and thwarted missionary on the scene, immediate action by the state must, at times, have seemed the only means of advancing the program. The Society's position advocating not only gradual education for the slaves, but persuasion of the masters as well, called for more resourcefulness on the part of the missionary, but suggested more permanent results in the long run.

Certainly, in Hunt's case, zeal for the program, without adaptability, was not enough. By 1727, the difficulties in his parish, added to personal and household problems, had reached the point of desperation:

[74] Brian Hunt to David Humphreys, St. John's, South Carolina, October 3, 1726, in *S.P.G. MSS.* (L.C. Trans.), B 4, No. 210.
[75] Brian Hunt to David Humphreys, Charlestown, South Carolina, November 5, 1725, in *S.P.G. MSS.* (L.C. Trans.), A 19, p. 80.
[76] Frederick Dalcho, *Historical Account of the Protestant Episcopal Church in South Carolina*, p. 268.

he was ill, had spent twenty pounds on doctors, had a large family, and he asked the Society to have compassion upon

your weak brethren who by marrying young, and too precipitantly have cast themselves at the feet of the wiser & more happy part of men; and that tho' you are not a father, or husband, you have tender regards for every state of humanity thats honorable the poor and necessitous.

It adds to my calamity that I have 4 negros to maintain, the gift of the parish to successive ministers, two of which are in a manner useless. My successors may gain by them; but I lose, they being unfaithful as well as unhappy wretches: two diseased and two thievish. I cannot be as cruel as some here to slaves, from whose wounds they extract their estates. I might tire the patience of any but a good Christian by this long but true representation of my hard circumstances. Believe me, Sir, I now have nothing to feed on, nor for eleven persons but Indian corn in the house and a little American wheat-flower, and butter, for being 40 miles from Charlestown the only good market and having no ready money (having mortgaged the most part of this years income here to pay Mr. Smith) I almost want bread. If you can serve me by putting my necessities into a just light to the Society, I shall be truly thankful and pray to God to recompense you in the great day of retribution.[77]

A year later, in 1728, he returned to England, embittered and disillusioned, his last dismal report showing that St. John's Parish contained 1,500 Negro slaves and "none of them baptized or instructed in Christianity."[78]

The ownership of slaves by the missionaries created an unique situation. The majority of the Society's workers kept Negroes, and often asked their parishioners to furnish them with slaves. They were to be careful, however, by the Society's order, to instruct them conscientiously in order that they could become examples to the rest of the parish, and the custom seems to have been less a reflection of the Society's attitude toward the institution of slavery, than a positive ap-

[77] Brian Hunt to David Humphreys, St. John's Parish, South Carolina, February 9, 1726-1727 in *S.P.G. MSS.* (L.C. Trans.), B 4, No. 196. The striking change in Mr. Hunt's attitude toward his Negroes seems a reflection of his own poverty and poor health. In contrast may be quoted the statement of Z. Kingsley, a planter, whose slaves, when his own fortune was depleted, "became poor, ragged, hungry and disconsolate. To steal from me was only to do justice—to take what belonged to them, because I kept them in unjust bondage." Cited in U. B. Phillips, *American Negro Slavery,* p. 295.

[78] Brian Hunt to David Humphreys, St. John's Parish, South Carolina, May 6, 1728, in *S.P.G. MSS.* (L.C. Trans.), A 21, p. 102. C. F. Pascoe gives the dates of the Rev. Mr. Hunt as 1723-1726; see his *Two Hundred Years of the S.P.G.,* II, p. 849.

proach to the immediate problem of Negro education. Albert Ponderous, for instance, when appointed catechist for St. James Santee
in 1721, wrote that he was much concerned about the education of
the children, especially that of the young slaves in his mission, because they were entirely neglected;[79] and shortly thereafter he was
"obliged to buy me two slaves for my service."[80] Bishop Gibson's
Pastoral Letters of 1727 to all the missionaries in the English Plantations, advised on this point:

As to those Ministers who have Negroes of their own; I cannot but
esteem it their indispensable Duty to use their best Endeavours to
instruct them . . . both because such Negroes are their proper and
immediate Care, and because it is in vain to hope that other Masters
and Mistresses will exert themselves in this Work, if they see it
wholly neglected, or but coldly pursued, in the Families of the
Clergy . . .
I would also hope, that the Schoolmasters in the several Parishes
. . . might contribute . . . towards the carrying on this work; by being
ready to bestow upon it some of their Leisure Time. . . .[81]

The ownership of slaves by a missionary was not forbidden by the
Society but their careful instruction was an imperative obligation. The
Rev. Thomas Morritt, for instance, when sent to Winyaw in 1731, im-
mediately acquired some Negroes and wrote to London:

. . . I endeavor [to make] myself agreeable to the Honorable Society's
instructions to instruct my negros. I have 4 children which I purpose,
God willing, to teach . . . as soon as my family is settled, and I have
three men and two women more that give some proof of a steady
application . . . which gives me hopes will prove to good effect.[82]

[79] Albert Ponderous to the Society, St. James Parish, Santee, [South] Carolina,
January 20, 1723, in S.P.G. MSS. (L.C. Trans.), B 4, No. 135. Ponderous received a salary of ten pounds per year for two years as catechist from the Society, and was also appointed a missionary to St. James Santee, in order to increase the slight allowance from the inhabitants. This Parish consisted chiefly
of French refugees conforming to the Church of England, there being about 100
French families to 60 English, besides free Indians and Negro slaves.
[80] Albert Ponderous to the Society, St. James Santee, South Carolina, February
20, 1725, in S.P.G. MSS. (L.C. Trans.), A 19, p. 91.
[81] "Pastoral Letter" to the Missionaries in the English Plantations, May 19,
1727, by Dr. Edmund Gibson, quoted in Frederick Dalcho, An Historical Account
of the Protestant Episcopal Church in South Carolina, pp. 112-114.
[82] Thomas Morritt to David Humphreys, May 3, 1731, Winyaw, South Carolina, in S.P.G. MSS. (L.C. Trans.) B 4, No. 244. Of conditions 114 years later,
U. B. Phillips in American Negro Slavery (p. 319) writes, "N. W. Middle-
ton, an Episcopalian of St. Andrew's parish, wrote that he and his wife and sons
were the only religious teachers of his slaves, aside from the rector of the
parish. . . . On the other hand, R. F. W. Allston, a fellow Episcopalian of Prince

Certainly both precept and example were part of the S.P.G. technique, and those of the planters who encouraged the work among their Negroes, were held up as important object lessons for the rest of the parish, by the missionaries.

George, Winyaw, had on his plantation a place of worship open to all denominations. . . . An Episcopalian clergyman in the same parish with Allston . . . held fortnightly services among the negroes of ten plantations, and enlisted some of the literate slaves as lay readers."

CHAPTER III

THE ROLE OF THE VETERANS

IT was inevitable, in such an enterprise as that of the S.P.G. in South Carolina, that men of varying abilities and temperaments would find their way into the field. Thomas and Le Jau, in the early period, had left an indelible stamp on the Society's program in the colony, and upon the attitudes of the colonials themselves. Equally outstanding, in the years after the overthrow of the Proprietary government, were three men whose vigorous constitutions, and purposeful adjustment to conditions, enabled them to complete long terms of successful service. Francis Varnod, William Guy, and Lewis Jones, gaining perspective with each year of service, were important not only for the work in their own parishes, but as advisers and trailmakers for the young missionaries new to the field.

The Rev. Francis Varnod began his term of service at St. George's in 1723, when the parish was re-established following the Yamassee uprising and its accompanying difficulties. His letter of April 1, 1724, sets a confident note:

. . . And it is observed I had a greater number of Communicants at Christmas day than ever had been seen here before, for above 40 people received the Communion, 17 whereof being negroes—40 or 50 people attend commonly the Divine Service besides 29 or 30 negroes . . .[1]

In this same letter Varnod evaluated his work and analyzed the colonial population, composed of various racial and social groups. Like Dr. Le Jau, he was interested in ethnological observations of the surviving tribal customs of both Negroes and Indians. This letter is more than an account of his work: it is an essay on primitive life as he found it, and is worth quoting at length:

[1] Francis Varnod to David Humphreys [St. George's], South Carolina, April 1, 1724, in *S.P.G. MSS.* (L.C. Trans.), B 4, No. 173. These Negroes belonged to Alexander Skene and his sister, Mrs. Hague, previously noted, and Varnod recognized the sustained efforts of this family by commenting further: "I christened Sunday last, . . . three negro children, a boy and 2 girls, two of them belonging to the Honorable Alexander Skeen Esq. and the other to Mrs. Hague, his sister; christened moreover, since 4 white children one boy and three girls, and 5 negro children, 3 boys and 2 girls, 4 of them belonging to Mr. Skeen and one to Mrs. Hague, both taking great pains to have their negros instructed in the Christian religion. . . ."

. . . I wish I could entertain any tolerable hope of converting our negros. But their masters are entirely against it. The most prevailing reason they pretend to have being that thereby their slaves would have an opportunity of gathering together on the Lord's Day to make insurrections. So that except the Civil power permits the ministers and other approved persons to resort to the negro houses when they think it proper, without any molestation, as it is practiced at Martinico, Little or no good can be done that way. I find that some of our negro-pagans have a notion of God and of a Devil, and dismal apprehensions of apparitions. Of a God that disposes absolutely to all things. For asking one day a negro-pagan woman how she happened to be made a slave, replied that God would have it so and she could not help it. I heard another saying the same thing on the account of the death of her husband. And a Devil whereby who leads them to do mischief, and betrays them, whereby they are found out by their masters and punished. They are also sensible that as we are Christians, we do not act accordingly, upon which account a negro boy about 14 who has never been instructed, being blamed by his mistress (as she was going to church) for some things he had done amiss, was heard to say, My mistress can curse and go to church. . . .

But there is a thing that seems to me more practicable, and that is the conversion of our Indians. If some of our nobility and gentry would in imitation of the true Apostolic zeal of the Honorable Society be at the charge of sending a discreet young man in Deacons orders to go with our traders to some of our most considerable Indian Nations, and to settle amongst them, it would be no difficult matter to convert them, or at least their children. I find by experience that these poor Pagans are endued with very good natural parts, of a temper very sedate and easy, and quite opposite to that hot and violent spirit of the negros. They are not altogether as destitute of natural religion as is commonly thought. They entertain a notion of a Supreme Being, to whom the *Charrokees* offer their first ears of Indian corn. They observe several festivals, *as those of the moon.* They believe that there was formerly an universal flood, and that our wild pigeon went out to see for land. And I am credibly informed that some of the Indians near the French territories practise circumcision. Here is a form of prayer used by one of the Indian kings before taking his Cassina in the morning, which deserved to be printed in gold letters.

Thou chief King of all things let this thy day be a prosperous one to me, and favour me with the Continuance of my being, for I thank thee who regardest me.

I find further that all Indians have a notion of a further state; those between us and North Carolina believe the wicked go in a cold country being very lean and naked, feeding only on mens excrements, and that the good go in a very pleasant warm country where nothing is wanting to make them happy. Their notion of a future state further appears by the following relation of an Indian burial which I saw Sunday last, for I spied on them in the woods. A Winiaw Indian (which Nation has about 100 men) perceiving to be very melancholy I asked him the reason for it. He replyed that he had pawned his gun for 2 gallons of rum and having drunk too plentifully of that liquor, had a fever; and that one of his best friends had shot him-self that day, not being able to support the pains of a violent fever which he had got by drinking also too much, saying O fie upon! I went with him to see the dead man in the woods where I staid till 9 o'clock at night, when 4 of his comrades, having been hunting, came. Asking one of them why they went hunting that day, answered, we pray and hunt. Then I prevailed with them to have the dead man buried, which was done in this manner: the dead Indian being six foot tall, they digged a grave hardly 4 foot long, and six deep, laid few boards at the bottom of it, then the deceased was carried upon a deer skin, being covered with another, and having his knees pressed as close as could be to his body, was in that posture put in the grave, having few planks put over him, was buried, the head turned toward the East, according as they told me, to the custom of their country. At the head of the grave he whom they called their Captain, fixed a small fir tree, having bitan of about it the bark in 3 places, and threw hard by an hand full of shot, because they said the man had killed himself: adding the deceased relations were absent and therefore could perform no more ceremonies. I asked them if they thought their dead friend would be happy hereafter. They said no, because he had killed himself.

The Indians in general allow fornication but condemn adultery; some punishing their women guilty of that crime, with death, others by cutting off their hairs as a mark of infamy. Drinking and stealing, but particularly the former vice are two only things the Christians have taught the Indians. . . .

And as the Cherokee Nation is one of the most populous, it is to be wished that attempts were made to plant Christianity there first. They are divided into ten tribes. Their language is very gutteral, some words bordering upon the Hebrew, . . .

Since the writing of my former letter about this matter, I have been informed that the Creeks are at least as great a Nation as the Cherokees, and that their language is understood further upon the mainland than any other. Both Nations laying beyond the settlement of my Parish, and where the Parish lines are not fixed . . .[2]

[2] Francis Varnod to David Humphreys [St. George's], South Carolina, April 1, 1724, in *S.P.G. MSS.* (L.C. Trans.), B 4, No. 173. For emphasis certain parts of the letters of some of the missionaries were underscored. Since this practice adds but little value to the reader, the underscoring has been omitted. See also Herbert E. Bolton, *Arredondo's Historical Proof of Spain's Title to Georgia* (Berkeley, 1925), Introduction, "The Debatable Land, A Sketch of the Anglo-Spanish Contest for the Georgia Country" 100-110; and Verner W. Crane, "The Southern Frontier in Queen Anne's War," in *American Historical Review*, XXIV (April, 1919), pp. 379-395, and *The Southern Frontier 1670-1732* (Durham, 1928). Another valuable book is Denys W. T. Shropshire, *The Church and Primitive Peoples* (London, 1938). For an excellent summary of the strange

Throughout the eighteenth century missionary opinion fluctuated as to the main emphasis the Society should make in its choice of objectives in the New World. Indians, Negroes, and white colonists were all three objects of attention. The practical advantages of activity among the Indians was that it would make of them allies of the Crown in the fight for the continent. Some missionaries, as did Varnod, believed with Sir William Johnson that the Christianization of the Indians was a feasible program. The Negro Christianization was not so much a problem of remoteness on a far-flung frontier as a question in the mind of the owner of the possible loss of slave capital through his religious training and the consequent acquisition of religious rights, a wedge toward civil rights.

The fact that Varnod, whose term of service at St. George's extended from 1723 to 1736, did not abate his efforts in behalf of the Negroes, in spite of the difficulties so ably outlined, is evidenced by his regular reports, showing that every year he had at least twenty to fifty Negro communicants.[3] From time to time he sent the Society a list of the inhabitants of St. George's parish, and that of 1726[4] may be placed here as illustrative of his careful accounts:

| | White people | | | Slaves | | |
	Men	Women	Children	Men	Women	Children
Alex Skeene, Esq.	3	2	1	27	18	32
Peter Cattle	1	1	5	14	13	7

and unexpected ideas of the Indian which seemed incomprehensible to the white man, see Clark Wissler, *Indians of the United States, Four Centuries of their History and Culture.* Ch. XXI, pp. 270-280, "The Mystery of the Indian Mind."

[3] On December 25, 1724, 17 Negroes were communicants, and 3 were baptized [Francis Varnod to David Humphreys, Dorchester, South Carolina, March 21, 1725, in *S.P.G. MSS.* (L.C. Trans.), A 19, p. 60]; from Christmas 1725 to June, 1726, a Negro man "belonging to Mr. Wragg, merchant"; was baptized, and during Whitsuntide of 1726, 24 Negroes were communicants. [Same to same in same. June 14, 1726. B 4, No. 203] On Easter, 1727, 19 Negroes came to the Communion Table. [Same to same in same. May 4, 1727, A 20, p. 81] By Whitsunday, 1728, 3 Negro children had been baptized and of the slaves belonging to Mr. Skene and Mrs. Haigue 19 regular communicants were reported. [Same to same in same. August 26, 1728, A 21, p. 124] Similar accounts were sent to London in 1729 and 1730, the number of Negro communicants increasing to 26 on Whitsunday, 1730. [Same to same in same. July 2, 1730, A 23, p. 215] On Christmas of 1730 there were 24. [Same to same in same, February 13, 1730-1731, A 23, p. 230, also *ibid.,* August 9, 1731, B 4, No. 249] On Easter 1734 Varnod had 19 black communicants and 25 white [same to same in same, April 14, 1734, A 25, p. 85], and by the next Easter he could report 23 Negro communicants, while 7 black children were baptized on Whitsunday of the same year. [Same to same in same, July 15, 1735, A 26, p. 137]

[4] Names and number of the inhabitants of St. George's parish, South Carolina, inclosed in Francis Varnod to David Humphreys, January 21, 1725 [1726], in *S.P.G. MSS.* (L.C. Trans.), A 19, pp. 104-108. (Dissenters are distinguished from Church people by the letter D.)

Name		White people			Slaves		
		Men	Women	Children	Men	Women	Children
John Williams		1	1	1	48	24	22
Thos. Smith—Dissenter		1	1	5	—	—	—
Samuel Smith		1	1	2	—	—	—
Jerem Burros		2	1	0	—	—	—
Debor Stiles		0	1	5	—	—	—
Sam Wraggs Plant[ation]		1	–	–	35	12	10
Nath Wickams Pl:		–	–	–	4	1	1
John Canty		3	4	5	7	11	7
Joseph Child		1	–	2	10	14	14
Jane Canty		1	1	2	3	6	10
Eliz. Diston	D.	2	1	2	19	18	24
Mary Elms		–	1	2	2	2	—
Wm. Wells		2	–	1	1	0	—
Wm. Burckley	D.	2	1	3	—	—	—
Fr. Frewin	D.	1	–	–	—	—	—
Tho. Cater	D.	1	–	–	12	6	10
Nath Bradwel	D.	2	1	3	1	2	1
Mary Brandford		1	1	4	1	2	3
Lilia Hague		1	1	2	15	6	10
Sus: Baker	D.	3	3	5	26	17	18
Angle Coone		1	1	3	—	—	—
Jos. Griffin	D.	1	3	3	1	1	—
Thos: Elms		–	2	3	10	—	—
Dd. Gallandy		1	1	1	—	—	—
Th. Wally		1	1	1	—	—	—
John Baker		3	1	5	6	13	11
Walter Izard		2	1	4	29	23	39
Geo. Burnet	D.	1	1	1	4	5	9
Gilson Clapp		2	1	2	3	3	8
John Postel Sen.		1	1	4	6	8	17
Sam Way	D.	1	1	4	—	—	—
Uriah Edward	D.	1	1	2	1	—	—
Sam Snow	D.	1	1	3	—	—	—
Jos: Osgood	D.	1	1	2	3	1	2
Tho: Baker	D.	1	1	6	2	1	—
Saml. & Jonah Clarke	D.	2	1	4	2	—	—
Jam: Baker	D.	1	1	3	—	1	—
John Hill		1	1	1	—	—	—
Peter Goudling		1	1	2	4	3	4
Geo. Flood		2	2	2	2	2	3
Richard Baker	D.	3	1	6	5	2	7
Wm. Elliot		1	1	1	4	5	5
Richard Warring		1	1	2	4	5	5
Josh. & Joseph Warring		2	–	–	6	3	7
Th. Cutfield		1	–	–	4	—	—
Th. Warring		1	1	5	18	8	15
Wm. Shingleton	D.	1	1	4	1	—	—
Rd. Beadon	D.	3	2	4	7	6	6
Rd. Winn	D.	1	2	2	1	1	2
Rebecca Simons	D.	–	1	6	4	3	3
John Hill		1	1	1	1	—	—
Sam Stiles	D.	1	1	2	—	—	—
Jos. Smith	D.	1	1	–	2	2	4
Ebenezer Way	D.	1	1	2	—	—	—
Joseph Sumner	D.	1	1	7	3	2	4
Wm. Way	D.	3	1	7	3	1	1
Mos. Way	D.	1	1	3	4	2	—
Th. Redd	D.	1	1	4	—	—	—

		White people			Slaves	
---	---	Men	Women	Children	Men	Women	Children
Job Chamberlain		2	1	3	4	5	2
James Rawlins		1	2	1	3	5	4
Benj. Perriman		8	2	9	1	—	1
James Sanders		1	1	4	3	1	—
James Dorton		1	1	1	2	2	—
Elias Thomas		1	1	4	—	—	—
Cha: Diston		1	1	2	1	—	2
Robt. Millerson	D.	1	1	1	5	1	7
John Shute		1	1	3	2	1	—
Robt. Miller, Jun.	D.	1	–	–	3	—	—
Jos: Brunson	D.	3	3	6	2	2	1
John Citchin	D.	1	–	–	1	1	2
Isaac Brunson	D.	2	1	7	2	1	—
Mala Glaze	D.	1	–	–	2	4	6
Wm. Wallace		2	1	4	10	9	11
Aaron Way	D.	2	1	2	—	1	2
John Caswell	D.	1	1	1	1	2	—
Wm. White	D.	1	1	–	—	—	—
John Jones		1	1	1	1	—	—
Th. Way	D.	3	1	1	—	1	1
Th. Satur		3	–	1	3	4	1
Dan Steward		1	1	1	—	—	1
John Gorton	D.	1	1	4	1	—	—
Th. Osgood	D.	1	2	1	—	1	—
Wm. Fishburn	D.	1	1	2	1	1	1
Th. Osgood, Jun.	D.	1	1	3	1	1	1
Step. Dowse	D.	1	1	4	—	—	—
Hugh Fisher	D.	1	1	–	2	1	1
John Tudder		1	1	6	—	—	—
Eliz. Hawks	D.	3	2	–	—	—	—
Abig. Stew	D.	–	2	1	4	4	6
Johan Hosier		–	1	2	—	—	—
John Cousins		1	1	2	—	—	1
John Hawks	D.	1	–	–	1	5	2
Nathan: White	D.	1	1	1	—	—	1
Nathan: Sumner	D.	1	1	4	—	1	—
Th. Bacon	D.	2	–	5	—	1	—
Thom. Boone		1	–	–	16	19	12
Jos: Blake		1	1	3	16	17	20
Franc. Varnod		1	–	–	1	1	1
Wm. Sanders		1	5	–	10	13	13
Laurence Sanders		1	–	–	5	2	3
Widow Izard		–	1	2	2	1	2
James Postel		1	1	2	4	4	6
James Postel, Jun		1	1	2	4	5	4
Benj. Sumner	D.	3	4	2	—	—	3
Roger Sumner	D.	5	2	3	2	1	—
Moses Norman		3	2	3	3	5	1

Free negroes and Indians

		White people			Slaves	
---	---	Men	Women	Children	Men	Women	Children
Robin Johnson, Negro		1	1	4	3	3	3
Guy, a negro		1	–	–	—	—	—
Nero, an Indian		1	–	–	—	—	—
Sam Pickins, Indian		1	1	4	—	—	—
Sarah		1	–	–	—	—	—

This painstaking and revealing list and the other meticulous reports of Mr. Varnod were particularly valuable in enabling the Society to visualize the colonial scene. In 1736, at the end of thirteen years' service in his parish, he could report material as well as spiritual progress in his charge. The Society's abstract of his letter dated June 29, 1736, gives a glimpse of Varnod's success in the work of building up his parish:

. . . the Building the new Church there hath been carried on but slowly hitherto, because it was hard to get in the Subscription for that work; however, they had now got in most of the Money, and had done the Doors and Windows, and should be able to finish the Flooring of the Building. He [Varnod] says, Religion is in as flourishing a Condition in his Parish, as in any Part of the Province, the fashionable Principles of Libertinism and Infidelity having not yet infected any of his present Parishioners: which good Success, next to God, he says, is owing chiefly to the Bishop of *London's* Pastoral Letters.[5]

The notice of Varnod's death was sent by the Churchwardens and vestry of St. George's Parish, South Carolina, to the Rt. Hon. Rev. Edmund Gibson, Bishop of London, three months later, on September 27, 1736: "We cannot easily express the Concern we are under for the loss of the Reverend Mr. Varnod, late minister of the Parish, who after a Short Illness of three days, died on ye 24th Instant." In appreciation of his remarkable record, and at the suggestion of the vestry of St. George's, the Society in 1739 awarded his widow a gratuity.[6]

The career of the Rev. William Guy,[7] who served at St. Andrew's for twenty-two years, beginning in 1719, is revealing not alone for

[5] *An Abstract of the Proceedings of the S.P.G.* Printed with Claggett Sermon (London: 1737), p. 52. (Huntington Library)
[6] *An Abstract of the Proceedings of the S.P.G.* Printed with Butler Sermon (London: 1739), pp. 67-68. (Huntington Library) The entry reads: ". . . The Gentlemen of the Vestry . . . beg leave to recommend to the Society's Compassion the Widow of Mr. *Varnod,* whose narrow Circumstances did not enable him to make a Provision for her, though he was of a good Life and Conversation, and duly performed the Duties of his holy Functions. The Reverend Mr. *Garden,* the Lord Bishop of *London's* Commissary in *South Carolina,* bears witness likewise to Mr. Varnod's having been a good and useful Missionary, and recommends his Widow to the Charity of the Society. The Society hath ordered Mr. Varnod's Salary to be paid up to the End of the Quarter, in which he died, and given his Widow a Gratuity of 25 *l.*"
[7] Guy's term of service was the longest of any missionary sent to South Carolina, extending as it did from 1712 through 1751. Ordained as a priest by the Bishop of London in 1713, he went to Charleston where he served one year with Commissary Johnston. In 1714 he went to St. Helen's, but was forced to leave this parish in 1715 by the Indian uprisings. His service at St. Andrew's, from 1719-1751 completed approximately 40 years in the Carolina field. See C. F. Pascoe, *Two Hundred Years of the S.P.G.,* II, p. 849.

his sound achievements, but as an example of the care with which
the Society proceeded. Over his long period of service Guy reported
an average of about one Negro baptism a year.[8] He confirmed the
view that lack of education among the Negroes was due chiefly to
lack of opportunity, but was content to proceed carefully, if per-
sistently, in this work. His account of January, 1728, gave a good
picture of the state of his parish, and placed it geographically as well:

As to the number of negro slaves in this parish—There are about
1800, and as to what care is taken for instructing them, very little.
The number that have been instructed and baptized in this parish
have been two adults belonging to Mr. John Godfrey, deceased, and
one negro child belonging to ffr; [Francis?] Young, Esquire.
In a word, the parish of St. Andrew is chiefly on the South side
of Ashley River, is bounded to the Southwest by St. Pauls, to the
Northwest by St. George's, to the Northeast part by St. James, Goose
Creek, and partly by St. Philips, Charlestown, and is about 21 miles
in length and 7 in breadth, the lower part of which (viz. James's
Island which is one half of it) is opposite to Charlestown and extends
to the barr.[9]

Further reports of Guy give an excellent picture of the many-sided
phases of the duties of the missionary in the field. In an account of a
missionary journey undertaken by him in 1731 to the adjacent Bahama Islands, the Society summarized from his letters:

. . . last Year he did extend his Labour into another Country, into
Providence, one of the *Bahama* Islands . . . That the Occasion of
his going there was thus. Governor *Rogers,* arriving at *Carolina* from
Providence informed the Reverend Mr. *Garden,* Commissary of the
Bishop of *London* there and Mr. *Guy,* of the extream Want there
was of a Minister in that Government, which had been without one
for some Years, and pressed Mr. *Guy* to go over with him, and officiate there some Months. Mr. *Guy,* upon considering the great Usefulness, and almost Necessity of the Thing, determined to go with
Governor *Rogers.* Accordingly he embarked on this charitable Under-

[8] Guy reported the baptism of a free Negro in the first six months of 1720: see
William Guy to David Humphreys, St. Andrew's, South Carolina, October 17,
1720, in *S.P.G. MSS.* (L.C. Trans.), A 14, p. 78. Three years later he baptized an
adult Negro man and a woman. [Same to same in same, May 23, 1723, B 4, No.
156.] In 1732 he recorded the baptism of one Negro man and a child. [Letter of
January 5, 1732, in *Journal of S.P.G.* (L.C. Trans.), Vol. VI, April 20, 1733.]
and baptisms of two free Negro men and their wives and one slave were reported
in 1738. [Same to same, January 10, 1738-1739, in *S.P.G. MSS.* (L.C. Trans.),
B 7, Part I, p. 221.] One Negro man was baptized by the Rev. Mr. Guy in 1740.
[Same to same in same, March 26, 1740, B 7, Part II, p. 240.]
[9] William Guy to David Humphreys, St. Andrew's Parish, South Carolina,
January 22, 1727-1728 in *S.P.G. MSS.* (L.C. Trans.), A 20, p. 114. This letter is
an historical account of the Church and Parish of St. Andrew's in answer to a
request made by the Society: the request dated June 16, 1727.

taking the 3d of *April* 1731, and arrived at Providence, the 12*th* of the same Month. . . . He began with reading Prayers every *Wednesday* and *Friday,* in a little neat Church built of Wood, which was lately finished, and preached every Sunday in the Forenoon, and read Prayers, and baptized the Children every Sunday in the Afternoon: He was sensible his Stay must be but short among them, he resolved to lose no Time, and therefore visited forthwith as Opportunity gave leave, all the Parts of this Island, notwithstanding the great Fatigue of travelling, on account of the Rocks they are obliged to go over, and the heat of the Day, which is always very great, he baptized in all 89 Children, and 3 Adults. After this he went down to *Harbour Island* and *Islathera,* and two other inhabited Islands in this Government, about 20 Leagues distant from *Providence;* at the former of these he baptized 23 Children, and at the latter 13. Thus during his short Stay in this Government, which was only 2 Months, besides performing the other Offices of reading Divine Service, Marrying, Visiting the Sick &c. He baptized in all 125 Children, and 3 Adults, for each of which, he had the proper Sureties the Church requires. He likewise Administered the Blessed Sacrament twice, but had no more than 10 Communicants at each Time. He writes farther, the People of this Government are in general very poor, it would therefore be a great Charity to send a Missionary to them. He distributed among the People a Number of the Bishop of *London's* first and second Pastoral Letters, which the People very thankfully received. He is now returned to his Parish in *Carolina,* and proceeding in his Duty there.[10]

Such expeditions, frequently mentioned by other missionaries, tacitly established their role as one of the "agents of empire"—a humanizing agent tempering the rougher inroads of trade and government. Also implicit in the account is the intimate connection at this time, by ties of trade and empire, between South Carolina and the West Indies; a relationship that caused the Thirteen Colonies to anticipate island revolts during the American Revolution. In addition to his regular parochial duties, the education and instruction of the Negroes in his parish, the distribution of literature, and such surveys of adjacent fields as the above, the S.P.G. missionary was expected to show gains in the permanent establishment of the Church in the Colony. Guy's letter of May 14, 1733, concerning the building of the Church at St. Andrew's is summarized by the Society in 1734. The church is

. . . now neatly finished in the Inside, the Charge whereof amounts

---

[10] *An Abstract of the Proceedings of the S.P.G.* Printed with Berkeley Sermon (London: 1732), pp. 54-55 and 48-49 which run consecutively due to mistake in paging. (Huntington Library)

to three thousand five Hundred Pounds, that Currency. The Outside is also to be plaistered, and a Steeple built, and a small Gallery for the Use of such as have no Pews. He acquaints further, that the Chapel in James's Island, which was blown down about three years ago by a Hurricane, is now rebuilt, and filled up, so that he can perform Divine Service in it. He hath about 30 constant Communicants and since the 5th of *January* last, hath baptized 13 children and one Adult. That his Parishioners are so zealous in promoting any good Work, that notwithstanding the charge they have been at in enlarging the Church, they have lately subscribed above five hundred Pounds that Currency, towards carrying on the Settlement of the New Colony of Georgia. . . .[11]

The fine fruits of twenty years of successful service are reflected in Guy's letter from St. Andrew's in 1740. This buoyant account of the work in hand and waiting to be done is in vivid contrast to the fears and forebodings sometimes expressed by the young missionary, new to his parish. Busy and confident, in spite of an "ill state of Health," Guy writes enthusiastically to London:

I thought it my Duty . . . to acquaint the Hon[ble] Society with the pres[t] State of my Parish, which is as follows—namely that the Parishioners who profess themselves members of the Church of England are a might[y] well behav'd People constant in their attendance on the Publick Worship of God & very kind & affectionate to me their minister: & that, tho' it has been my misfortune to loose several of the old Inhabitants who were constant Communicants, yet it is matter of great Comfort to me to observe that at X[t]mass last I had three N. Comunicants & hope to see the N[o] of them increase in a Short time.

I have bap[d] since the date of my last twelve Children, one Adult white woman, & an Adult negro man; & continue as usual to read Prayers, & Catchise the Children every Friday in Lent, to which I am encourag'd by the readiness of the Parents in sending them to me.

As the N. Parish of S[t] John's Colleton County remains still vacant, so I visit that Parish at the Recomendat[n] of M[r] Comissary Garden, every eight Sunday; as I do the Chappel on James's Island in my own Parish; & have always a pretty large & well behav'd Congregation. The Inhabitants there are very desirous to have a Minister reside among them, & accordingly did apply to the Hon[ble] Society the last Year for a Supply of that Cure: but as they have not as yet been favour'd wth an Answer, they have desir'd me to repeat their Requests to them for One. And in order to induce a Minister to come over, they have purchas'd a Glebe of ab[t] 300 acres of Land contiguous to the Church, & are now preparing materials

---

[11] *An Abstract of the Proceedings of the S.P.G.* Printed with Maddox Sermon (London: 1734), p. 41. (Huntington Library)

for the building of a House, which is to be of Wood, upon it. The Church is of Brick, but not finish'd in the inside, & is the largest of the Country Churches, except my own. There is the same allowance from the Publick to the Minister of this Parish, as to the other Ministers & the Person who has the happiness to be appointed there, will, (I am well Satisfied) meet wth all suitable Encouragem^t from the Parishioners who are indeed a good sett of People. There is this further necessity of their having a Minister to live among them, as there is of late two dissenting Meeting Houses set up in that Parish, which in time may endanger some of the People, particularly the younger Sort, being seduc'd from the Church; & this is the Occasion of my going there to prevent as much as I can their going astray; tho' it be very inconvenient for me on account of the distance I am from thence, & the ill state of Health which I frequently labour under.

This is all I have at pres^t to lay before the Honble Society. . . .[12]

Typical of the "news flashes" often contained in the missionaries' letters is Guy's reference to the devastating Charleston fire, which destroyed many of the early frame buildings, most of which were rebuilt in the enduring brick which gives Charleston the charm which it retains today. Guy reported capably:

. . . [I] shall finish this Letter wth giving you a short account of the dreadfull Fire which has consumed the most valuable part of Charles town.

It broke out the 18th of Novr about 2 o'clock in the afternoon. The N° of Houses burnt, are computed to be above 300, besides Storehouses, Stables, etc: & the Damage only in merchandize above 200,000 p^{ds} Sterl. Among the Unhappy Suffers I had the misfortunate to be one myself, having lately finish'd a house at a considerable Expence; which join'd to the Loss of some Slaves of late years, makes the misfortunate the greater to me, who have a pretty numerous Family to maintain.[13]

But the affairs of the parish progressed steadily regardless of such setbacks, and by 1742 St. Andrew's contained 180 families, consisting of about 600 whites and 2500 blacks of which 117 families were of the Church of England, and 63 were dissenters.[14] In September of that year Guy related that he had distributed 12 copies of the essay of the Bishop of Sodor and Man, on ". . . Christianity made easy . . ."[15] and continued:

[12] William Guy to Dr. Bearcroft, St. Andrew's Parish, South Carolina, March 26, 1740 (Read October 17, 1740), in *S.P.G. MSS.* (L.C. Trans.), B 7, Part II, pp. 239-240.
[13] William Guy to [Philip Bearcroft], St. Andrew's Parish, South Carolina, February 16, 1740-1741 in *S.P.G. MSS.* (L.C. Trans.), B 9, No. 132.
[14] William Guy to Secretary, St. Andrew's Parish, March 26, 1741-1742, in *Journal of S.P.G.* (L.C. Trans.), IX, July 16, 1742.
[15] This was a reference to the tract on "The Knowledge and Practice of

I have bap^d 15 white children, & one Negro woman & 7 Children, belonging to a Gentleman in my Parish; which Woman & four of her Children who are Adults, having been instructed by the Care of their Master in the Principles of our Holy Religion, were capable of rendering a pretty good Account of their Faith, wch they did before the publick Congregation in my Church: & the other three will be taught, as soon as they shall be able to learn, to say the Creed, the Lord's Prayer, & the Ten Commandments & be further instructed in the Church Catechism.[16]

Guy's death on December 9, 1749, was reported to the Society by the Vestry and Churchwardens of the Parish of St. Andrew's, who wrote with appreciation of his splendid service, and asked that he be immediately replaced.[17]

Meanwhile, in the frontier parish of St. Helen's,[18] the Rev. Lewis Jones wrote often of the slow but actual progress towards the education of Negroes. In 1726 he said, "It is more to be wished than expected that the planters zeal would excite them to encourage schoolmasters for the education of their slaves . . ."[19] and two years later he noted there were 170 Negro slaves in his parish but no care was taken for instructing them.[20]

A missionary on horseback, in a very extensive and sparsely settled charge which included the whole nation of the Yamassee Indians, Jones was a staunch representative of the Society's program in a

---

Christianity made Easy; or, an Essay towards an Instruction for the Indians," composed and published by Bishop Wilson of Sodor and Man in 1741, "on purpose to promote the good Designs of the Society." The Huntington Library copy, page 1 of the Essay, has a decorated border showing savages with wings clustered around a Bible, and surrounded by birds, doves, scrolls, fleur de lys and pots of fruit. Of remarkable interest are the dialogues supposedly carried on between a missionary and an Indian. These Dialogues are in the style of Pilgrim's Progress, Defoe, and the Voyageurs. They have a naïve charm, and convey a real sense of such an encounter, almost unconsciously giving the Indian the better of the argument at times.

[16] William Guy to [Philip Bearcroft], St. Andrew's Parish, South Carolina, September 30, 1742, in *S.P.G. MSS.* (L.C. Trans.), B 10, No. 143.

[17] Vestry of St. Andrew's Parish to Philip Bearcroft, South Carolina, June 20, 1750, in *S.P.G. MSS.* (L.C. Trans.), B 18, No. 192.

[18] On the extreme southern end of the settlement, St. Helen's was farthest from the center of population. Situated just below Port Royal, and cut in two by the Savannah River, its area would have comfortably included the combined areas of St. Paul's, St. George's, St. James's, St. Thomas', St. Andrew's, St. Philip's, and Christ Church. See "A Map of the Province of Carolina, Divided into its PARISHES &c, According to the latest Accounts, 1730," in David Humphreys, *An Historical Account of the Incorporated Society for the Gospel in Foreign Parts,* pp. 80-81.

[19] Lewis Jones to David Humphreys, Port Royal, South Carolina, July 19, 1726, in *S.P.G. MSS.* (L.C. Trans.), A 19, p. 325.

[20] Lewis Jones to David Humphreys, St. Helen's, South Carolina, January 26, 1727-1728, in *S.P.G. MSS.* (L.C. Trans.), A 20, pp. 117-118.

parish which presented some unique problems. He told of the frequent alarms occasioned by the Spaniards and Indians which caused the planters to remove their slaves farther within the colony. Although in January, 1734, Jones reported that one considerable planter in his parish intended to have all his little Negroes taught to read,[21] he explained that the general lack of schools made catechizing a difficult task. Six months later he acquainted the Society of the baptism of one Mulatto woman and 12 children. At the same time, in adapting himself to the needs of his parish, which "chiefly consists of Islands; [and] it is almost impracticable for the remote Inhabitants to attend divine Service duly every Lord's day,"[22] he had obtained the consent of his Vestry to visit them once in five or six weeks.

These frontier parishes, designed to serve as "buffer states" against the Indians, the French, and the Spanish, were becoming increasingly important as sources of wealth, tied as they were to the port of Charleston.[23] Of the continued efforts of Jones and the expansion of St. Helen's Parish, the Society recorded in 1736:

. . . that the remote parts of it begin to settle apace, and that the new Settlers propose to build a Chapel of Ease about 14 Miles distant from *St. Helen's* wherein he [Jones] promised to officiate as often as he can. He hath baptized 11 Children and one Negro Child in his own Family; the Number of Communicants the same as before. . . .[24]

[21] Lewis Jones to Secretary, St. Helen's, South Carolina, January 8, 1734, *Journal of S.P.G.* (L.C. Trans.), Vol. VI, September 19, 1735.

[22] *An Abstract of the Proceedings of the S.P.G.* Printed with Hare Sermon (London: 1735), p. 52. (Huntington Library)

[23] A vivid description of social conditions in the expanding frontier is given in B. R. Carroll, *Historical Collections of South Carolina,* I, pp. 377-378. He writes: "Nor is there the smallest reason to expect that manufactures will be encouraged in Carolina, while landed property can be obtained on such easy terms. The cooper, the carpenter, the brick layer, the ship builder, and every other artificer and tradesman, after having laboured for a few years at their respective employments, and purchased a few negroes, commonly retreat to the country, and settle tracts of uncultivated land. While they labour at their trades, they find themselves dependent on their employers; this is one reason for their wishing at least to be their own masters; and though the wages allowed them are high, yet the means of subsistence in towns are also dear, and therefore they long to be in the same situation with their neighbors, who derive an easy subsistence from a plantation, which they cultivate at pleasure, and are answerable to no master for their conduct. Even the merchant becomes weary of attending the store, and risking his stock on the stormy seas, or in the hands of men where it is often exposed to equal hazards, and therefore collects it as soon as possible, and settles a plantation. Upon this plantation he sets himself down, and being both landlord and farmer, immediately finds himself an independent man. Having his capital in lands and negroes around him, and his affairs collected within a narrow circle, he can manage and improve them as he thinks fit."

[24] *An Abstract of the Proceedings of the S.P.G.* Printed with Lynch Sermon (London: 1736), p. 50. (Huntington Library)

A year later the abstract of Jones' letter of June 4, 1737, published by the Society, related:

... That since his last of the 3d of *June,* 1736, he had baptized thirty-nine Children, one of whom was a *Mulatto,* and another a *Negroe,* but his Number of Communicants doth not exceed twenty; and once in five Weeks he preaches at one place, and once in six Weeks at another place in his extensive Parish very remote from the Church; that the pious Zeal of the venerable Society, and of his worthy Diocesan for promoting Christian Knowledge among the *Negroes* meets with but a cold Reception from them, but he had himself a *Negroe* Girl of seven Years of Age, that reads very prettily in the New Testament, and a *Negroe* Boy of five Years of Age, that spells well, and is apt to learn.[25]

In 1739 Jones discovered a humanitarian in his parish; and this information took precedence over his brief report of Stono's rebellion:

. . . one Considerable Planter, a Man of a Good Solid, Christian Disposition, Expresses an Inclination of Instructing the Young Ones Born in his family, had he an opportunity of a School in yᵉ Neighbourhood he Lives in.

The Desertion of 23 Negroes from this Neighbourhood to St. Augustine, a Spanish Garrison, on a Proclamation Publish'd there of freedom to all Slaves that Sh[all] Desert to them from Any of the English Plantations, will Considerably Encrease the Prejudice of Planters agst the Negroes, and Occasion a Strict hand, to be kept over them by their Several Owners, those that Deserted having been Much Indulg'd.[26]

[25] *An Abstract of the Proceedings of the S.P.G.* Printed with Butler Sermon (London: 1739), p. 69. (Huntington Library)
[26] Lewis Jones to [David Humphreys], St. Helen's, South Carolina, May 1, 1739, in *S.P.G. MSS.* (L.C. Trans.), B 7, p. 233 [Part I]. See also U. B. Phillips, *American Negro Slavery,* pp. 473 and 477-479. Phillips stated, p. 473, in ". . . 1739 . . . on a September Sunday a score of Angola blacks with one Jonny as their leader broke open a store, supplied themselves with arms, and laid their course at once for Florida where they had been told by Spanish emissaries welcome and liberty awaited them." A further account of this uprising is given in B. R. Carroll, *Historical Collections of South Carolina,* I, 332-333: "A number of negroes having assembled together at Stono, first surprised and killed two young men in a ware house, and then plundered it of guns and ammunition. Being thus provided with arms, they elected one of their number captain . . . marching towards the south-west with colours flying and drums beating. . . . In their way they plundered and burnt every house. . . . Governor Bull returning to Charlestown from the southward, met them, and observing them armed, quickly rode out of their way. . . . By a law of the province all planters were obliged to carry their arms to church. . . . The women were left in church trembling with fear, while the militia, under the command of Captain Bee, marched, in quest of the negroes, who, by this time . . . had marched above twelve miles. Having found rum in some houses and drunk freely of it, they halted in an open field and began to sing and dance, by way of triumph . . . the militia discovered them,

Unfortunately, Jones was right in his estimate of the reaction to this rebellion. The South Carolina Slave Code, adopted in the following year, contained a clause which spoke for the planters:

And whereas the having of slaves taught to write, or suffering them to be employed in writing, may be attended with great inconveniences; *Be it enacted,* That all and every person and persons whatsoever, who shall hereafter teach, or cause any slave or slaves to be taught to write, or shall use or employ any slave as a scribe in any manner of writing whatsoever, hereafter taught to write; every such person and persons shall, for every such offence, forfeit the sum of one hundred pounds current money.[27]

A bitter blow to the Society's program for Negro advancement, the remarkable thing about the entire affair is that it did not seem to

---

and stationed themselves . . . to prevent them from making their escape. . . . One party advanced into the open field and attacked them, and, having killed some negroes, the remainder took to the woods, and were dispersed. Many ran back to their plantations in hopes of escaping suspicion from the absence of their masters; but the greater part were taken and tried. Such as had been compelled to join them contrary to their inclination were pardoned, but all the chosen leaders and first insurgents suffered death." For the conspiracy of Denmark Vesey and his followers in 1822, see Phillips, *op. cit.,* pp. 477-479. See also H. T. Catterall, *Judicial Cases Concerning American Slavery and the Negro,* II, pp. 340-341, for the legal account of a conspiracy in July, 1829.

[27] Joseph Brevard, *An Alphabetical Digest of the Public Statute Law of South Carolina* (Charleston: 1814), II, p. 243, Title 157. A discussion of the legal rights of slaves is contained in Roy Smith, *South Carolina as a Royal Province, 1719-1776* (New York: 1903), pp. 143-145. "Special courts for the trial of negro slaves were provided for by an act of 1690. Any justice of the peace, on complaint being made to him, was authorized to issue a warrant for the arrest of the offending slave. He was then to call in another justice of the same county, and the two of them summoned three freeholders to complete the court, and appointed a day for the trial. Trial was without jury and the decision was final. The punishment meted out consisted in whipping, branding, cutting off the ears, or the infliction of the death penalty, according to the severity and frequency of the offense.

"With some changes in detail this method of trial continued in South Carolina as long as slavery existed. By an act of June 7, 1712, the value of all slaves executed according to law was to be fixed by a disinterested board of appraisers and compensation made to the owners out of the public treasury. This proved too heavy a burden on the public; so a law was passed in 1717 providing for a special tax upon the slaveholders of a parish when-ever a negro was executed within its limits. Such a localization of expense probably induced the courts to be too lenient in their treatment of slave criminals. At all events, the old plan of compensation from the public treasury was restored after the Stono insurrection of 1739. The presence of the entire court was required in capital cases, though the vote of one justice and two freeholders or of one freeholder and two justices was sufficient to convict. For minor offenses one justice and two freeholders were sufficient, and the concurrence of the justice and one freeholder enough to convict.

"The slave code adopted in 1740 remained substantially unchanged until the Civil War. It provided that the court for the trial of capital offenses should consist of two justices and not more than five nor less than three freeholders. The most important innovation was the bringing of free negroes under the jurisdiction of the court."

decrease the efforts of its missionaries to assist and instruct the
Negroes. Records of the years following 1740 show the same determination, the same unceasing efforts, and almost equal results. Indeed, the Charleston Negro School, to be discussed later in this volume, was started almost at the exact time of the passage of this
Slave code which, to less courageous men, would have meant the end
of a program. Moreover, the fact that many masters, encouraged
by the missionaries, continued to send their slaves for instruction,
speaks for the healthy state of race relations in some quarters at
least. Miscegenation, and the growing group of free Negroes, doubtless had something to do with this state of affairs. But the fact
remains that, in spite of a prohibitory law, the Negro, both slave and
free, continued to receive, from the S.P.G. missionaries, the opportunity for instruction.

Meanwhile, from St. Helen's, came another echo of these stirring
times. The famous George Whitefield, whose visit to Georgia and
South Carolina had at first excited the interest and then the opposition of the clergy,[28] had been read out of the church by Commissary
Alexander Garden in 1740. Significant again of the remoteness of
St. Helen's is the incident in the same year when Jones permitted
Whitefield to preach in his church, and therefore fell under some
ecclesiastical inquiry. Mr. Jones wrote the following letter explaining
his actions to Commissary Alexander Garden:

I rec^d Both y^r Letters; And in Compliance with yr request Am
to inform you that the Report is here wch you have had of Mr Whitefield's having Preach'd here at his Coming from Georgia, And at
his Return thither: But with^t my knowledge of his being under Any
sentence of an Ecclesiastical Court. Therefore as there was no prohibi-
tion (wch I knew of) of his Preaching and Executing other parts of
his Ministerial office, I Look'd upon it to be a matter of Discretion,
And thought myself at Liberty to Comply with what I found to be
the general Desire of my Congregation, to permit him to preach
in the Church. Other reasons that prevail'd were these, that M^r
Whitefield has upon all occasions declar'd himself a Member of the
Church of England, preach'd Strictly to the Articles, Had the Univer-

---

[28] A contemporary account of Whitefield's visit is contained in B. R. Carroll,
Historical Collection of South Carolina, I, pp. 405-411. Referring to Whitefield's visits to Charleston, this account says (p. 406), "Alexander Garden . . .
who was the Episcopal clergyman of that place, . . . to keep his flock from
straying after this strange pastor, expatiated on the words of Scripture, 'Those
that have turned the world upside down are come hither also;' Whitfield,
with all the force of comic humour and wit for which he was so much distinguished, by way of reply, enlarged on those words, 'Alexander, the copper-
smith hath done me much evil, the Lord reward him according to his works.'"

sal Character of being of an unblemish'd Life, And Conversation, & having had an uncommon Success that attended his Ministry: these, Sir, (notwithstanding my dislike of Some other things) induc'd me to think That I Sh^d have done Greater disservice by opposing than by complying with my Parishoners herein. These are, as I remember, the Reasons wch prevail'd with me, And have done nothing out of Contempt to Authority.[29]

Under the Church of England there had been practical religious freedom in South Carolina for the Puritan, Jew, Quaker, Huguenot, Scotch Covenanter and others. John Wesley, Charles Wesley and George Whitefield regarded themselves as Anglicans but their enthusiasm violated the prevailing Anglican tradition of the time. Whitefield, unlike Wesley, was not an opponent of the slave system.[30]

In another letter to the Secretary of the Society in 1740 Jones wrote:

You have herein Inclos'd a coppy of my Letter to the Revd Mr Garden our Commissary, in Answer to his Letter requiring my reasons for permitting Mr Whitefield to preach in this Church. . . .

I beg Leave to Answ[r] The Honble Society that what I did was not out of Contempt of Authority, And that the reasons mention'd to the Commiss^{ry} were the Genuine Reasons wch induc'd me to Let him preach; neither do I find any ill Consequence from it: whereas if I had oppos'd it, I Sh^d have incurr'd the displeasure of most of my Parishoners, And had put it out of my power of being any further useful here. I have been now 15 years the Honble Society's Missionary in this Parish; And if necessity Sh^d require it, can have a full Testimony from the Inhabitants of this place of having behav'd among them as becomes my office.[31]

Mr. Jones continued by saying that "There are two or three families in this Parish who have been Lately prevailed upon to have their Negroes Instructed in the principles of the Christian faith by the Earnest Persuasions of Mr. Whitefield."[32]

[29] Lewis Jones to Commissary Garden, St. Helen's South Carolina, August 15, 1740, in *S.P.G. MSS.* (L.C. Trans.), B 7, Part II, p. 253 (Copy).
[30] See Edgar L. Pennington, "John Wesley's Georgia Ministry," in *Church History*, VIII, No. 3 (September, 1939), pp. 231-254. See also Elizabeth K. Nottingham, *The Making of an Evangelist* (New York, 1938), pp. 117-174, for an account of John Wesley's career in Georgia which, like Whitefield's furnished ample 18th century evidence of the influence of the new world societies on the old world through repatriation. Wesley was aroused, during his American stay on the frontier, into an adaptation of his amazing abilities to the needs of all of the people of Great Britain.
[31] Lewis Jones to [Secretary], St. Helen's, August 15, 1740, in *S.P.G. MSS.* (L.C. Trans.), B 7, Part II, p. 251; also in *Journal of S.P.G.* (L.C. Trans.), VIII, December 19, 1740.
[32] *Ibid.* It may be noted here that the early Episcopal Churches as the later large nineteenth century churches of Charleston were built with the wide

This statement seems to have explained satisfactorily the use of the Church by Whitefield, for in his letter of the following year, Jones limited his discussion to Negro instruction. He expressed his great satisfaction with the Society's efforts on behalf of the educational program for the Negroes, and pointed to the special advantages to be gained by placing greater emphasis on the training of the young Negroes of the parish. He recognized, if he did not approve, the fact that the economic interest of the planters was the greatest stumbling block in the way of having the grown slaves instructed, and offered to his parishioners the counter-proposition that the young Negroes, who had not yet assumed any economic importance in the plantation regime, become the particular objects of their care.

With a strategist's skill, Jones had assessed the opposition, and offered an almost unanswerable alternative to the masters who had found it impossible to arrange time for the instruction of their working slaves, especially during the busy season of the year. In such a parish as St. Helen's, where the settlements were so distant and remote from each other that the missionary was at a disadvantage, it was particularly necessary to have a workable plan.

Moreover, Jones was quite specific as to the methods of instruction, and offered to his parishioners the example of his own Negroes who were "taught to read, & instructed in the principles of the Xtian faith, as Soon as they are capable of receiving Instruction; two w^{re} of Can read well . . . , and two More Learn to Spell."[33]

---

galleries provided for Negro members attracted in large numbers by emotional oratory. See U. B. Phillips, *American Negro Slavery*, p. 318. "As a rule the greater the proportion of negroes in a district or a church connection, the greater the segregation in worship. If the whites were many, and the negroes few, the latter would be given the gallery or some other group of pews; but if the whites were few and the negroes many, the two elements would probably worship in separate buildings."

[33] Lewis Jones to Philip Bearcroft, St. Helen's, South Carolina, September 25, 1741, in *S.P.G. MSS.* (L.C. Trans.), B 9, No. 137. In this letter Jones also refers to the project of Commissary Garden in Charleston for negro education, discussed later in this volume. He "was with great Pleasure informed of the pious Design of the Society to instruct their little Negroes in the Christian Faith, according to the Scheme of the Reverend Commissary, by purchasing Negroes and fitting them for the Office of Schoolmasters to the young Negroes in their several Parishes; and that, he is in great hopes (as it doth not interfere with the People's Temporal Interest, the great Obstacle to Instruction of grown Slaves) the Generality of them will gladly accept of this Proposal: That he hath always instructed his young Negroes, and had them taught to read; and he hath two at this Time, who can read well in the New Testament; and two more are learning to spell: And he will not be wanting

Jones continued his efforts in behalf of the Negroes in his parish[34] until his death on December 24, 1744, after a "lingring Illness . . . his sound Doctrine, and exemplary Life and Conversation, during his Ministration of near 19 Years . . . gained him the Esteem of every one that knew him."[35]

Varnod, Guy, and Jones represented, each in his own way, the S.P.G. missionary at his best and most effective over a long period of service. Men of vigor, courage, and imagination, they entered their fields almost simultaneously during that difficult period of rebuilding after the Yamassee wars. Resourceful in adjusting to the swiftly-changing scene of the frontier colony, they re-established their missions during a period of unrest and monetary inflation following the overthrow of the Proprietary government in 1720, and participated in the gradual stabilization of colonial affairs which culminated in 1729 when, by act of Parliament, all rights of the Lord Proprietors in the colony were purchased by the Crown.[36] When subsequent action by the English government opened up free lands and encouraged settlement, they saw an influx of immigrants, largely from central Europe,[37] which automatically decreased the proportion of Church of England people by adding to the numbers of the other sects.

---

from Time to Time in helping forward the good Work, and in promoting, as it is his great Duty, the Enlargement of the Kingdom of Jesus Christ . . ." In *An Abstract of the Proceedings of the S.P.G.* Printed with Stebbing Sermon (London: 1741-1742), pp. 55-56. (Huntington Library)

[34] In 1743 Jones was still dissatisfied with his progress in the instruction of Negroes and reiterated his determination to continue in that work. See Lewis Jones to Philip Bearcroft, St. Helen's South Carolina, December 27, 1743, in *Journal of S.P.G.* (L.C. Trans.), Vol. IX, June 15, 1744.

[35] *An Abstract of the Proceedings of the S.P.G.* Printed with Hutton Sermon (London: 1745), p. 53. (Huntington Library)

[36] The details of this purchase are given in B. R. Carroll, *Historical Collections of South Carolina*, I, p. 274. "The purchase was made for seventeen thousand five hundred pounds sterling, to be paid before the end of September, 1729, free of all deductions; after which payment, the province was to be vested in the crown of Great Britain. At the same time seven-eighth parts of the arrears of quitrents, due from the colonists to the proprietors, amounting to somewhat more than nine thousand pounds sterling, were also purchased for the crown for five thousand; so that seven-eighth parts of this vast territory cost no more than twenty-two thousand five hundred pounds."

[37] This type of immigration was encouraged by the Crown, due as much to the lack of skilled craftsmen in the colony as to the desire to add to the population. The town of Purrysburg, established by the Swiss on a grant from the king, was furnished by the Assembly with "400 *l. Sterling* and Provisions sufficient for the Maintenance of 300 Persons for one Year, provided they be all Persons of good Repute, and *Swiss* Protestants, and that they come to *Carolina* within the space of two years." See *ibid.*, II, p. 126. The need for taylors, shoemakers, smiths, potters, vintners, and skillful carpenters "not ashamed to demand 30s. per Day beside his Diet," is elaborated in *ibid.*, II, 130-131.

Meanwhile the wealth of the province was rapidly increasing,[38] and, as the value of their slaves increased, the planters showed a tendency towards becoming more unwilling to release them for instruction[39] both because of the time thus consumed, and because of the current belief, enacted into law by the Slave Code of 1740, that encouragement in the field of education was a contributing factor to the slave insurrections which occasionally broke out. A shift of emphasis on the part of the missionaries is indicated in their reports, which show a growing preponderance of baptisms among the women and children of the slave quarters. Varnod, Guy, and Jones, thoroughly familiar with the tempers and prejudices of the planters, apparently decided to focus attention on women and children, who were neither in as great demand for labor, nor as serious an insurrectionary danger.

Sturdily unperturbed by setbacks, intolerance, hurricanes and fires, the reports of these veterans in the field form an important background for comparison with the bewildered and sometimes despair-

[38] A vivid description of the growing prosperity of the colony in 1731 is given in B. R. Carroll, *Historical Collections of South Carolina*, II, pp. 128-130, 132 (misprinted 123)-140. Signed by John Peter Purry, this account points out the variety of crops which can be raised in addition to those already in production, and points out that "The Trade of *Carolina* is now so considerable, that of late years there has sail'd from thence Annually above 200 Ships, laden with merchandizes of the Growth of the Country, besides 3 Ships of War which they commonly have for the Security of the Commerce, and last Winter they had constantly 5, the least of which had 100 Men on Board. It appears by the Customhouse Entries from *March,* 1730, to *March* 1731, that there sailed within that time from *Charles-Town* 207 Ships most of them for *England,* which carried among other Goods 41957 Barrels of Rice about 500 Pound Weight per Barrel, 10754 Barrels of Pitch, 2063 of Tar, and 1159 of Turpentine; of Deer Skins 300 Casks, containing 8 or 900 each; besides a vast Quantity of *Indian* Corn, Pease, Beans, &c. Beef, Pork, and other salted Flesh; Beams, Planks, and Timber for Building, most part of Cedar, Cypress, Sassafras, Oak, Walnut, and Pine." (pp. 128-129) For reports through 1748 see "A Description of South Carolina containing Many Curious and Interesting Particulars relating to the Civil, Natural and Commercial History of that Colony," (London: 1761) reprinted in *ibid.,* II, pp. 223-241. Wealth had increased "partly owing to the great increase in the Value of ... Exports; and partly to a considerable decrease in ... Imports from the Colonies of New-York, Pensilvania, &c. For those two Colonies used to drain us of all the little Money and bills we could gain upon our trade with other places, in Payment for the great Quantities of Flour, Bread, and Beer, Hams, Bacon and other Commodities of their Produce wherewith they then supplied us, all which, excepting Beer, our new townships, inhabited by Germans, begin to supply us with." (223-224)

[39] The temper of the times is described in *ibid.,* I, p. 299, as follows: "... Each planter, eager in the pursuit of large possessions of land, which were formerly neglected because of little value, strenuously vied with his neighbour for a superiority of fortune, and seemed impatient of every restraint that hindered or cramped him in his favorite pursuit."

ing letters of the younger missionaries transferred suddenly from the halls of Oxford or Cambridge to a frontier which was subject not only to the forays of Spaniards, Indians, and the slaves themselves, but also laced with malarial swamps and boasting a semitropical climate whose quick changes wrought havoc on weak constitutions.

CHAPTER IV

A SURVEY OF OTHER PARISHES

A BRIEF roll call of a number of other parishes throws an interesting sidelight on the expanding social order of South Carolina, during the period from 1730 to 1765.[1] If the first thirty years
of the century laid the foundation and set the framework, then the
period following was to see the structure to the point of completion.
For the missionary, too, it was still a period of construction. He was
beset with the difficulties of illness, indifference, insurrection, and
opposition; but accomplished much. Parish after parish was so thoroughly established as to warrant the withdrawal of the S.P.C. support.
Interestingly enough, the turn of each decade seemed to mark a
milestone in the Society's program: the expansion of the frontier
began in 1730, following purchase of lands by the Crown; in 1740
the enactment of the Slave code; in 1750 the outbreak of Indian
hostilities; and in 1760, following grants by the colonial legislature
of £100 for each of their clergymen, the beginning of the withdrawal of the Society.

Amidst their parochial notations, the missionaries at their several
posts record the events of the frontier. Illustrative of first impressions was a letter of the Rev. John Fulton of Christ Church parish,[2]
who said, in 1730, shortly after his arrival, that he had many Negro
slaves ". . . who make insurrections sometimes [so] that the people
are forced to come to Church with guns loaded."[3] Several of the

---

[1] In general, as throughout this paper, each parish has been completed chron-
ologically, before proceeding to the next. Of special value, in assessing this
period, are the Society's *Abstracts of Proceedings* which draw, in masterly rep-
ortorial style, a brief but graphic picture of the period.
[2] Frederick Dalcho, in *Historical Account of the Protestant Episcopal Church
in South Carolina*, p. 275, describes Fulton's charge: "This parish was established by Act of the Assembly, Nov. 30, 1706; and its boundaries defined by another Act, Dec. 18, 1708, as follows: 'to the North-East by a large Creek, or
River, commonly called Awindaw Creek, or Seawee River, being the bounds
of Craven country, to the South-East by the Sea, to the West by the Wando
River, and to the North-West partly by the said River, and partly by a line
drawn from the Cowpen of Capt. Robert Daniel, or the Swamp of the head
of Wando River exclusive, to the Cowpen of Joseph Wigfal, on the head
of the said Awindaw Creek or Seawee River inclusive."
[3] John Fulton to David Humphreys, Christ Church, South Carolina, December 4, 1730, in *S.P.G. MSS.* (L.C. Trans.), A 23, p. 222.

missionaries, he concluded, had found Negro conversion impracticable because of the incorrigible lives of those who had been baptized.

An excellent example of the steady growth of a parish toward self-sufficiency, is St. John's, where the Rev. Daniel Dwight began his work in 1729. A graduate of Yale college, and one of the few missionaries educated in the colonies, Dwight's busy life is outlined in the Society's report of his work, given in 1732:

. . . he hath been last Year much afflicted with a Fever; but upon Recovery . . . took a Journey into some remote Parts of the Province to visit some poor People, quite destitute of a Minister. They are settled 50 and 70 Miles distant from his Parish. At one Place, 40 People met him at performing Divine Service; at another 30. Among these poor People he distributed many of the small Tracts which he had of the Society, and which the People received very gladly. He recommends those People as very proper Objects of the Society's Charity; and desires he may have 2 or 3 Dozen of cheap Common Prayer-Books, which he will distribute among them. In his own Parish he hath baptized 9 Children, and one *Negroe* Woman, who had been a long while very desirous of it, and had taken much Pains to prepare, and have herself instructed by himself.[4]

A vignette of the progress of affairs and Church and School at St. John's is the report eight years later concerning Dwight:

. . . his Church hath lately been repaired, and is now decent and in tolerable good Order. That by several kind Benefactions, but chiefly by the Benefaction of Mr. *James Child* deceas'd, they have built a Brick House for a Schoolmaster, 40 Feet by 30; and that there is 500 *l.* sterling now at Interest at 10 per Cent for a Salary, but they have not yet been able to get a Person duly qualified for the Office of a Schoolmaster. Mr. *Dwight* adds, that he has been very much assisted in promoting the Affairs of the Church and School by Mr. *Le Jeau,* a Gentleman of a publick Spirit, and a plentiful Fortune, the Son of the late worthy Dr. *Le Jeau,* who died a Missionary of the Society in that Province in 1717.[5]

In the spring of 1741, on a missionary tour, Dwight reported the baptism of "16, all infants 7 of which were Mulattoes,"[6] and two years later his *Notitia Parochialis* showed the number of white inhabitants in St. John's Parish as 500, his communicants numbering

---

[4] *An Abstract of the Proceedings of the S.P.G.* Printed with Berkeley Sermon (London: 1732), p. 54. (Huntington Library)
[5] *An Abstract of the Proceedings of the S.P.G.* Printed with Benson Sermon (London: 1740), pp. 57-58. (Huntington Library)
[6] Daniel Dwight to Philip Bearcroft, St. John's, April 10, 1741 in *S.P.G. MSS.* (L.C. Trans.), B 9, No. 142.

43, with 2600 Negroes.[7] By March 25, 1745-1746 the number of slaves, Indian and Negro, in his parish had reached about 3000.[8]

The reports of the missionaries give striking testimony of the development of the plantation in South Carolina. Again and again the large Negro population stands out against the white minority. This preponderance of the Negro could have been only the result of a slave trade importation.[9] The addition of these new Negroes, no doubt, produced a slave population prone to occasional insurrection and led to uneasiness on the part of the planters. The amazing success of the S.P.G. under these circumstances calls for repeated notice.

The Rev. Levi Durand, formerly of Christ Church, followed Dwight at St. John's, serving from 1750 to 1765. On November 18, 1757, he wrote the Society that his Parishioners had subscribed three thousand Pounds of Carolina money towards building a new Church.[10] From November, 1763, to October 1, 1764, he baptized "16 infants, one of whom was a negro born of Christian parents,"[11] and by 1765 the Society made the following encouraging report of the work accomplished at St. John's; where the

. . . Congregation consists of about 24 Families who are constant in their Attendance on publick Worship. Instead of the old Brick Church, burnt in the Year 1755, a large new one is begun, and 3000 l. Currency subscribed towards it, and 1000 l. more granted them by

[7] Daniel Dwight to [Secretary], St. John's S.C. March 25, 1743, in *Journal of S.P.G.* (L.C. Trans.), Vol. IX, August 19, 1743.
[8] Daniel Dwight to [Secretary], St. John's South Carolina, March 25, 1745-1746, in *Journal of S.P.G.* (L.C. Trans.), Vol. X, July 18, 1746.
[9] For a complete, well documented, story of the Slave Trade in South Carolina see Elizabeth Donnan, *Documents Illustrative of the History of the Slave Trade to America,* IV (Washington: 1935), pp. 235-587. Based on court records, minutes of the Royal African Company, news items, especially from the Charleston *Gazette,* and the valuable letters of Henry Laurens, as well as a wealth of manuscript material of this nature, this work also includes tables estimating the number of slaves entering South Carolina during the eighteenth century. For example, the total number brought in from 1706-1724 is given as 5081 slaves (p. 255); from 1721-1726, 3632 slaves (p. 267); from 1733-1738, no numbers are given, but 56 slave ships entered Charleston harbor (pp. 278-280); from 1739-1751, due to the war with the French, only 24 ships are recorded (pp. 296, 301). Beginning in 1752, when the records of Sales, Vessels, Captains, Sources, Number, and Firm, were recorded in the *Gazette,* the records are more complete. From 1752-1754, 35 ships brought approximately 3,600 slaves (pp. 310-311); in 1755, 16 ships brought approximately 1,000 slaves (pp. 314). From 1756-1764 yearly importations average about 1500 (see pp. 338, 365, 372, 375, 378, 380, 381, 386) and beginning in 1765 the number increased greatly, showing in that year approximately 4700 slaves brought on 48 ships (pp. 411-413). In 1769 about 4200 slaves arrived on 27 ships (p. 428).
[10] *An Abstract of the Proceedings of the S.P.G.* Printed with Ellis Sermon (London: 1759), p. 69. (Huntington Library)
[11] Levi Durand to [Secretary], St. John's, South Carolina, October 1, 1764, in *Journal of S.P.G.* (L.C. Trans.), Vol. XVI, Dec. 21, 1764.

this Government. Till the Church is finished, he officiates in a small wooden Building erected in the Church Yard, at the Expence of Mr. *Cordes,* one of his Parishioners. He has also a very decent Brick Chapel, 9 Miles distant from the Church, where he officiates once a Month to a very regular Congregation. His Parish is 60 Miles long and 10 wide. The poor Settlers, about 25 Miles distant from the Parsonage, have raised a Logg House, 20 Feet by 30, for a Place of Worship; and allow their Schoolmaster a small Salary to read to them on Sundays the Liturgy and Sermons. Once in two Months Mr. *Durand* officiates here, and baptizes their Children, and has many more Hearers than the Building will contain. At the other End of the Parish there is a very neat well finished Chapel, established by Law, where he is obliged to serve every fourth Sunday to a regular and devout Congregation. . . .[12]

The parish of St. John's had progressed so successfully that on Mr. Durand's death in 1765 the Society withdrew its allowance from the parish, "the Provision of 100 *l.* Sterling, made by the Laws of the Province for that and every other Parish, with other Emoluments, being judged a sufficient Support."[13]

At St. Paul's, by way of contrast, the difficulties of the frontier, and the preponderance of dissenters in the parish, made it a difficult post for the Rev. Andrew Leslie, who landed there in 1730. Two years after his arrival the Society reported:

. . . he hath been much afflicted with Sickness since he entred upon his Mission, and hath been for a long time unable to perform the Duties of his Office in Publick. . . . The first Inconvenience he met with, was, that the Church where they met for Divine Worship was not near finished. He immediately set on foot a Subscription for raising Money to finish it: The People at first were backward to contribute, by reason of some Mismanagement in a former Subscription. However, some worthy Gentlemen pursued this Design with Success at last, and at length raised 1800 *l.* of that Country Money, which is thought a sufficient Sum to finish the Church. Mr. Mackuen, a Gentleman of that Parish, is very zealous to carry on this Work, so that now he hopes the Church will be finished in a Month. The Parsonage house is not fit to live in, nor can he guess when it will be repaired, the Parish having been at great Expences in building a Church and purchasing a Glebe. The first time he administered the Holy Sacrament he had but 7 Communicants, at *Christmas* following 15, at Easter 20, and at Whitsunday 26. That when he gave Notice afterwards of the Sacrament being to be administered, he fell, in the meantime, into such Weakness, that he could not attend

[12] *An Abstract of the Proceedings of the S.P.G.* Printed with Yonge Sermon (London: 1765), pp. 88-89. (Huntington Library)
[13] *An Abstract of the Proceedings of the S.P.G.* Printed with Warburton Sermon (London: 1766), p. 39. (Huntington Library)

himself. He says farther, that since his first Entrance upon his Mission, he hath baptized 35 Children, and 5 Adult Persons.[14]

Adjusting to conditions as he found them, and planning for the future, Leslie informed the Society four years later, by letter of December 29, 1736, that, since most of his parishioners were at too great distance to "attend Divine Services every Lord's Day . . . they have petitioned the General Assembly for leave to bring in a Bill, to empower them to build a Chapel of Ease in the Center of the Parish, which will in all probability be the Parish Church in a few Years."[15] In the meantime, services were being held at a planter's house called Beach Hill. Early in the following year he reported that £1100 Carolina money had been raised towards erecting a Chapel of Ease which would be finished by May of 1738.[16]

His account of the Stono rebellion, written in January, 1739, is a brief but graphic bit of reporting.

An Insurrection of ye Negroes happened in my Parish, Sept[r] 16, who murdered 22 of my Parishoners in a most barbarous Manner: our Militia came up wth y[m] next day about 4 in ye Afternoon, &, after a Short Engagem't put y[m] to ye Rout: & in a Second Engagement ye Saturday following, ye Rebels So entirely defeated & dispersed y[t] there never were Seen above 6 or 7 together Since. However, Several of my principal Parishioners, being apprehensive of Danger from ye Rebels Still outstanding, having carried their Families to Town for Safety, & if ye Humour of moving continues a little longer, I shall have but have a Small Congregation at Church. . . .[17]

The planter not only removed his household to town upon such alarms, but slaves, because of epidemics, were at times removed to lodges in the wilderness. This mobility was characteristic of the exposed householders on frontier settlements throughout these dangerous decades.

The Rev. William Orr, who took over Leslie's duties at St. Paul's in 1741 when the latter "was obliged thro' ill Health to return home," took a great interest in the Negroes in his parish, and wrote frequently of his work among them. His *Notitia Parochialis* for 1742

[14] *An Abstract of the Proceedings of the S.P.G.* Printed with Berkeley Sermon (London: 1732), pp. 51 and 44, numbered consecutively due to printer's error. (Huntington Library)
[15] *An Abstract of the Proceedings of the S.P.G.* Printed with Herring Sermon (London: 1738), pp. 46-47. (Huntington Library)
[16] *An Abstract of the Proceedings of the S.P.G.* Printed with Butler Sermon (London: 1739), pp. 68-69. (Huntington Library)
[17] Andrew Leslie to Philip Bearcroft, St. Paul's Parish, South Carolina, January 7, 1739, in *S.P.G. MSS.* (L.C. Trans.), B 7, Part II, p. 243. Also in *Journal of S.P.G.* (L.C. Trans), Vol. VIII, April 18, 1740.

listed the "heathens and infidels" in the parish at 3829 in number, as compared with 456 professors of the Church of England, of whom only 8 were actual communicants.[18] Six months later he wrote:

I am instructing and preparing a negroe woman (who is both very sensible and sober) for the Sacrament of Baptism; and she is very desirous to have her Child Baptised also at the same Time. And I hope, to prevail on others also for the same Purpose.[19]

And on March 30, 1744, he reported of her:

I have after previous Instruction, Baptized a Negroe Woman (who is very sensible, and of a Christian Disposition) who at her Baptism in the Parish Church behaved well, and answered to the satisfaction of every one present. I have also Baptized eleven white Children, and I intend in a short time to Baptise several negroe children, when sufficient Sureties can be proved for them.[20]

However, affairs at St. Paul's were not progressing as Mr. Orr had hoped and in this same letter he remarked upon the poor house in which he lived, which had neither window panes nor plaster, and, when it rained, "I am obliged to put all my books &c into Chests and Trunks to save them from being ruined by Wet; and how very inconvenient that must be to a Person fixed upon his studies one may easily judge."[21]

Two years later he informed the Society that he had been preparing some adult Negroes for baptism ". . . a work of no small labour and difficulty, considering the aversion which many of their owners have to any such thing."[22] But by September 30, 1748, he addressed the Society's Secretary:

Reverend Sir

Since my Last I have Baptised two free nigroe Women after proper Instruction, both of them very sensible and sober; and each of them answered to full Satisfaction, when examined concerning their Belief, and expressed their sincere Desire to be admitted into the Christian Church by the holy Sacrament of Baptised (sic). . . .[23]

The Society removed Orr from St. Paul's in 1744 to St. Helen's,

[18] William Orr to [Secretary], letter of September 30, 1742, in *Journal of S.P.G.* (L.C. Trans.), Vol. IX, Aug. 19, 1743.
[19] William Orr to [Philip Bearcroft], St. Paul's Parish, South Carolina, March 30, 1743, in *S.P.G. MSS.* (L.C. Trans.), B 11, No. 219.
[20] William Orr to [Philip Bearcroft], St. Paul's Parish, South Carolina, March 30, 1744, in *S.P.G. MSS.* (L.C. Trans.), B 12, No. 94.
[21] *Ibid.*
[22] William Orr to [Philip Bearcroft], St. Paul's Parish, Sept. 29, 1746, in *S.P.G. MSS.* (L.C. Trans.), B 16, fo. 182.
[23] William Orr to [Philip Bearcroft], St. Paul's Parish, South Carolina, Sept. 30, 1748, in *S.P.G. MSS.* (L.C. Trans), B 16, No. 142.

the "Vestry of St. *Paul's* having neither settled the Glebe, nor built the Parsonage House, nor elected Mr. *Orr* their Rector, as the Laws of the Province direct. . . ."[24] In this, as in other instances, the Society followed the policy of aiding in the establishment of a parish. As soon as possible the complete support of a parish was to be taken over by the parishioners themselves.

To continue with the roll call, St. Bartholomew's, a frontier parish, had been vacant since it was devastated at the outbreak of the Indian wars in 1715, when the Rev. Thomas Thompson entered upon his duties there in 1734. Faced with the responsibility of rebuilding, Thompson first surveyed his charge. The Society's account of his letter of May 1, 1736, embodied a good picture of the parish as he found it, and his plans for expansion of the work:

. . . there are . . . 120 Families of White People, and 1200 Negroes; that for want of a fix'd Minister among them for some Years past, there are only nine Communicants; that he hath baptized upwards of 100 Children since he first came there, and 16 since he enter'd in the Society's Mission; that the Parish being of large Extent, he offici- ates once a month at *Chikaw,* the remotest part of it, where a convenient Building hath been lately erected for that Purpose; that he hath lately visited *Upper Savannah-Town,* where there is a Garrison kept for the safety of the *Indian* Traders, several of whom constantly reside there; that he performed Divine Service on the *Lord's-Day* within the *Fort,* and baptized ten Children, five of whom were *Indians,* on the Mother's-side.[25]

Two years later he had "the good Fortune to continue in the Favour and Esteem of his Parishioners, a very considerable Step towards being useful among them,"[26] but by September 29, 1739, he consulted the Society concerning his weakened health and asked leave to spend the next summer in England to regain his strength. The Society agreed that he might have leave to come to England.[27]

Thompson returned to St. Bartholomew's, his health improved, and on October 14, 1740, reported 26 communicants in his church.[28] In

[24] *An Abstract of the Proceedings of the S.P.G.* Printed with Hutton Sermon (London: 1745), p. 53. (Huntington Library)
[25] *An Abstract of the Proceedings of the S.P.G.* Printed with Clagget Sermon (London: 1737), pp. 53-54. (Huntington Library)
[26] *An Abstract of the Proceedings of the S.P.G.* Printed with Butler Sermon (London: 1739), pp. 70-71. (Huntington Library)
[27] Thomas Thompson to [Secretary], St. Bartholomew's, South Carolina, September 29, 1739, in *Journal of S.P.G.* (L.C. Trans.), Vol. VIII, April 18, 1740.
[28] Thomas Thompson to [Secretary], St. Bartholomew's South Carolina, Oc- tober 14, 1740, in *Journal of S.P.G.* (L.C. Trans.), Vol. VIII, January 16, 1740- 1741.

1743 Thompson's place at St. Bartholomew's was taken by the Rev. Charles Boschi,[29] who began his service in 1745.

In a letter of October 30, 1745, Boschi told "of his arrival at his parish on April 12, and on the following Sunday, being Easter day [he], first officiated and has since baptized 26 children, one white adult, and one negroe girl, after proper instruction."[30] In the same letter he spoke of the "dearness of living there" and asked for an increase in salary of £10 a year in order that he might get out of debt. The Society granted him the gratuity, but specified that it was not to constitute a yearly increase.[31] Six months later he was concerned over the fact that his parishioners seemed rather inclined to keep their Negroes from the knowledge of Christianity and blamed him for continuing his efforts on behalf of the Negro girl mentioned in his former letter. However, he was determined not to be discouraged[32] and the next June he was able to report her baptism, and spoke cheerfully of his congregation:

. . . from y[e] 9 of Septemb[r] in 1746: to the 25 of March in 1747: I baptized 12 Infants, & one Adult Negroe Girl. This is the same person that I mention'd in several of my former Letters that I did expect with the assistance of divine power to have her baptiz'd as soon as I would have found her sufficiently instructed for the holy sacrament of Baptism. I brought her at last with a great deal of pains & trouble to the knowledge according to her Age fit for that holy sacrament . . . several Presbiterians, as well as Negroes continues to appear at our divine worship.

The above mention'd Negro Girl she is belong to the worthy Col. Hym, one of my parishioners.[33]

On August 22, 1747, Boschi informed the Society that, having been appointed "Chaplain to the Garrison lately established in the Island of *Ruatan* in the Neighbourhood of the *Moskito Shore,* he was preparing to remove thither; . . ."[34] and offered his services on

[29] Boschi was "formerly a *Franciscan* Fryer, but approved to be a worthy Proselite to our Church, by his diligent and laborious Service in it for seven Years last past. . . ." See *An Abstract of the Proceedings of the S.P.G.* Printed with Bearcroft Sermon (London: 1744), p. 53. (Huntington Library)
[30] Charles Boschi to [Secretary], St. Bartholomew's South Carolina, October 30, 1745, in *Journal of S.P.G.* (L.C. Trans.), Vol. X, Sept. 19, 1746.
[31] *Ibid.*
[32] Charles Boschi to [Secretary], St. Bartholomew's, South Carolina, April 7, 1746, in *Journal of S.P.G.* (L. C. Trans.), Vol. X, July 18, 1746.
[33] Charles Boschi to [Philip Bearcroft], St. Bartholomew's, South Carolina, June 20, 1747, in *S.P.G. MSS.* (L.C. Trans.), B 16, fol. 176.
[34] *An Abstract of the Proceedings of the S.P.G.* Printed with Thomas Sermon (London: 1747), p. 64. (Huntington Library) The S.P.G. activities on the Mosquito Shore are discussed by the Author in "The Efforts of the S.P.G. to Christianize the Mosquito Indian, 1742-1785," in *The Historical Magazine of the Protestant Episcopal Church,* Vol. IX, December, 1940, pp. 305-321.

behalf of the Indians there. Boschi's offer was accepted by the Society, but in August, 1749, he received notice that the Crown had ordered the reduction of the garrison at *Ruatan,* and therefore asked to be continued in his mission at St. Bartholomew's,[35] where he died within the year.[36]

The Rev. Robert Baron succeeded Boschi at St. Bartholomew's and, according to the *Abstract of Proceedings,* he

. . . landed at *Charles Town* on the 1st Day of *June* 1753 and went thence to St. *Bartholomew's* Parish, and officiated for the first Time in his Church on Whitsunday, but was afterwards taken ill, and had a pretty severe Seasoning; that he had not seen the half of his Parish, it being settled for near thirty [miles] and extending to an hundred Miles, but he finds his Neighbours a regular well-behaved People, many of them intermarried with Presbyterians who are numerous, but they live in good Friendship, and come to Church when there is no Preaching at their Meeting house.[37]

By the next year the number of his communicants had doubled, and one additional Chapel was "near finished, and Workmen agreed with for another."[38] This remarkable growth continued, and, in 1761 the Society commended the

. . . two very handsome Brick Chapels, which were so far finished as to be fit for public Service two Years ago, but some Ornaments within are yet wanting, together with Bibles and Common Prayer Books for the Reading-Desk, which he desires may be sent him, and be deducted out of his Salary: . . . in Approbation of his good Intention in relation to the Bibles and Common Prayer Books, the Society hath ordered them, to be sent him upon their own Account.[39]

Baron died in April, 1764,[40] leaving his parish so well-established that he was not replaced by the Society.

At the extreme northern end of the colony a newly-created parish, Prince Frederick's,[41] was flourishing under the Rev. John Fordyce

---

[35] Charles Boschi to [Secretary], St. Bartholomew's, South Carolina, August 3, 1749, in *Journal of S.P.G.* (L.C. Trans.), Vol XI, November 17, 1749.
[36] C. F. Pascoe, *Two Hundred Years of the S.P.G.,* II, p. 849.
[37] *An Abstract of the Proceedings of the S.P.G.* Printed with Drummond Sermon (London: 1754), pp. 62-63. (Huntington Library)
[38] *An Abstract of the Proceedings of the S.P.G.* Printed with Hayter Sermon (London: 1755), p. 57. (Huntington Library)
[39] *An Abstract of the Proceedings of the S.P.G.* Printed with Newcome Sermon (London: 1761), p. 61. (Huntington Library)
[40] C. F. Pascoe, *Two Hundred Years of the S.P.G.* II, p. 849.
[41] Prince Frederick's parish was "taken off from Prince George, Winyaw, by Act of Assembly, April 9, 1734; and March 29, 1735. Its bounds were directed to 'begin at the South-Westmost part of the plantation of John Du Bosc, on Santee River, from thence on a line to the head of John Green's Creek, and

who served successfully from 1736 to 1751. To the Society Fordyce wrote a letter, on July 25, 1737, summarized thus:

... That the State of his Parish from *Sept.* 29, 1736 to that time was, as follows: The Number of Inhabitants about one thousand seven hundred, of whom about two hundred and thirty were Members of the Church of *England,* and he had baptized twenty-five white Children, and one *Negroe* Woman, and six of her Children *Mulattoes;* she herself and her three elder Children could read well, and repeat the Church-Catechism; and two of the remaining three could repeat the Creed and the Lord's-Prayer; he catechizeth constantly on *Sundays* in *Lent,* and preacheth and reads Lectures on the Catechism on the other *Sundays,* (except in the excessive Heats) throughout the Year, and through God's Assistance will do his Endeavours to discharge his Duty to the Edification of his People, and to the Satisfaction of the Society.[42]

By February, 1738-1739, his parish contained 1200 Christians of whom 400 were of his congregation, and 35 of them communicants, while 800 were dissenters of various sorts, with 1400 "heathens and infidels." He had, moreover, baptized "one black woman who gave an account of her faith and read several portions of Scripture."[43]

In 1742 Fordyce's letter to London contained the information that

I have Baptised within this Parish 39 white Children, 5 Black, 2 Mullato's & 3 adults. . . . The 13th of June I preach'd at Williamsburgh, about 30 miles west from hence, where I had a large congregation of Church people, & several of the Irish Dissenters, & Baptis'd 10 Children & 5 Negro D° with the proper God-Fathers &c. . . .[44]

Regularly each year his reports came in: in 1743 he baptized "42 white and 2 negro children";[45] in 1744, "35 children, 4 Negro Children, and Two Adult Negro Women";[46] and in 1745 "4 Mulattoes—

down the said Creek to Black River, thence over Black River to the plantation of John Bogg, and from the said plantation of John Bogg to be included in the town Parish, in a due north line to Peedee River, and that part of the said Parish wherein the Parish church now is, shall and hereby is declared to be a distinct Parish. . . .'" Dalcho, *Historical Account,* p. 319.

[42] *An Abstract of the Proceedings of the S.P.G.* Printed with Butler Sermon (London: 1739), p. 71. (Huntington Library) See also the Rev. Mr. Fordyce to [Secretary], Frederic Parish, Wynyaw, South Carolina, July 25, 1737, in *Journal of S.P.G.* (L.C. Trans.), Vol. VII, August 18, 1738.

[43] John Fordyce to [Secretary], Prince Frederick's, South Carolina, Feb. 1, 1738-1739, in *Journal of S.P.G.* (L.C. Trans.), Vol. VIII, May 18, 1739.

[44] John Fordyce to [Philip Bearcroft], Prince Frederick's Parish, South Carolina, December 1, 1742, in *S.P.G. MSS.* (L.C. Trans.), B 10, No. 149. Also in *Journal of S.P.G.* (L.C. Trans.), Vol. IX, April 15, 1743.

[45] John Fordyce to [Secretary], Prince Frederick's South Carolina, October 24, 1743, in *Journal of S.P.G.* (L.C. Trans.), Vol. IX, Feb. 17, 1743-1744.

[46] John Fordyce to [Philip Bearcroft], Prince Frederick's Parish, South Carolina, Oct. 3, 1744, in *S.P.G. MSS.* (L.C. Trans.), B 12, No. 90.

children and 1 Mulatto Man, 30 years old."[47] Three years later he mentioned that a number of dissenters attended his church when there was no preaching at their own, and added that in the preceding half year he had baptized 6 white children and a Negro child.[48] The preponderance of dissenters on the frontier is revealed by Fordyce's account of a missionary journey to the Pedee River, during which he met many Anabaptists, and wrote the Society that "there are such ignorant Enthusiastick Preachers among them, that one scarce can beat a Bush, but comes a Preacher . . ."[49] These bare items recorded the introduction, of course, of the whole S.P.G. program. The masters had been approached, supplied with the Pastoral Letters, copies of famous Sermons, small tracts and appeals, and induced to send the Negro children for regular instruction. The existence in the community of an educated and scholarly man as a representative of a humanitarian view towards slavery was at least an entering wedge in the formation of opinion. On October 23, 1751, the Churchwardens of Prince Frederick's reported that "our late worthy Rector the Rev. Mr. Fordyce (to our great grief and loss) died the 24th of June last."[50]

To progress to another parish, the charge at St. George's was assigned on Varnod's death in 1736 to the Rev. Stephen Roe, who had thirteen Negro communicants at Easter in 1738, and twelve during Whitsuntide. With the impatience of a young man new to his parish he wrote indignantly:

That it gives me much concern to find how little success I have yet had in my endeav[rs] to bring more persons of discretion to a constant communion . . . by public as well as private exhortations . . . That my concern is increased w[n] I observe y[e] gross neglect, not to say y[e] unchristian Aversion of too many to instruct their Negroes in Christian Principles & bring them to Baptism; to their own great disadvantage & the reproach of Protestants & the Christian Name. . . .[51]

Roe told in 1741 of a trip he took in May and June through the

[47] John Fordyce to [Philip Bearcroft], Prince Frederick's Parish, South Carolina, Nov. 4, 1745, in S.P.G. MSS. (L.C. Trans.), B 12, No. 92.
[48] John Fordyce to [Secretary], Prince Frederick's Parish, South Carolina, April 18, 1748, in Journal of S.P.G. (L.C. Trans.), Vol. XI, Sept. 16, 1748.
[49] John Fordyce to [Secretary], Prince Frederick's, South Carolina, November 4, 1745, in Journal of S.P.G. (L.C. Trans.), Vol. X, April 18, 1746.
[50] Churchwardens to Philip Bearcroft, Prince Frederick's Parish, S.C. October 23, 1751, in S.P.G. MSS. (L.C. Trans.), B 19, No. 147.
[51] Stephen Roe to David Humphreys, St. George's, South Carolina, December, 1738, in S.P.G. MSS. (L.C. Trans.), B 7, pp. 223-224 [Pt. 1], also in Journal of S.P.G. (L.C. Trans.), VIII, June 15, 1739.

newly settled townships of Amelia, Orangeburgh, and Saxe-Gotha, all contiguous to his parish, and spoke of the poverty of the people there. He further reported eleven Negro communicants for Easter, 1740,[52] and the baptism of one Negro slave in the last six months of 1741. A parochial report of December 28, 1741, gave a numerical analysis of his parish.

1. Number of inhabitants — One hundred & thirty nine Families containing about 468 white Persons, & having ab^t three Thous^d three hund. 47 Slaves belonging to y^m, tho some settled at Remote Plant[ati]ons out of ye Parish.

2. No. of the Baptized — Four hundred & Thirty or thereab^{ts} of every Denom of whites, & abt one hundred negroes, &c.

3. No. of Adult Persons Baptized this Half-year — One Negro Slave, Baptized (four more of ye Same being under Instrucon for Baptism)

4. No. of actual Communicants of the Church of England — Forty eight white Persons, & ab^t fifteen Negroes.

5. No. of those who profess themselves of the Church of England — Seventy eight Families containing ab^t 295 white Persons & ab^t 85 Negroes.

6. . . .

7. No. of Heathens and Infidels — Three thous^d two hundred 87 Negro & oth^r Slaves. Few or no wandering Indians.[53]

Three months later, in a leetter of Feb. 20, 1742, he left his parish to be chaplain of the Fort of Boston, to try to improve his health, and his letter of resignation mentioned that he had lately baptized 5 adult Negroes.[54]

The *Notitia Parochialis* made in 1748 by his successor, the Rev. William Cotes,[55] shortly after his arrival is interesting by way of comparison:

[52] Stephen Roe to [Secretary], St. George's Parish, South Carolina, January 6, 1740-1741, in *Journal of S.P.G.* (L.C. Trans.), Vol. VIII, May 15, 1741.
[53] Stephen Roe to [Secretary], St. George's Parish, South Carolina, December 28, 1741, in *S.P.G. MSS.* (L.C. Trans.), B 10, No. 174.
[54] Stephen Roe to [Secretary], St. George's Parish, South Carolina, Feb. 20, 1741-1742, in *Journal of S.P.G.* (L.C. Trans.), Vol. IX, June 18, 1742.
[55] In 1747 the Society reported that Commissary Garden "commends the Reverend Mr. *Cotes* that had been lately ordain'd by the Lord Bishop of *London,* and had brought thither very good Testimonials . . . and the Churchwardens and Vestry of St. *George's* Parish, after Tryal of Mr. *Cotes's* Abilities and Behaviour having made the . . . Request, the Society have appointed Mr. Cotes to that Mission." See *An Abstract of the Proceedings of the S.P.G.* Printed with Thomas Sermon (London: 1747), pp. 63-64. (Huntington Library)

1. Number of Inhabitants about   Whites Settled.
                                        410 viz. 91 families besides others
                                        which are generally transient, being
                                        hired from year to year.

2. N° of the Baptized from July 1748   27 White & one Negro—Child
   to Christmas 1748

3. N° of Adult persons baptized from   one white man & one negroe woman.
   ditto &c.
    . . .[56]

Of special interest today is the notation regarding families "Which
are generally hired from year to year." Presumably these were tenants
or sharecroppers, suggesting that already on the fringe of the plantation society the social group was arising which has assumed such
large proportions in the present scene in the South. Unlike Ludlam,
who had sensed the implications of the plantation structure, Cotes
recognized in these people only a missionary problem. Commenting
only on the larger number of "Heathen" in his parish, he continued
with a word regarding the Negroes, showing that the slave, in company with his white master, was taking his part in the expansion of
the settlement.

. . . I comprehend most of the Negroes, for I believe there is but few
of them baptized and the few Negroe Communicants that I have
heard off [sic] in my Predecessors time, upon Enquiry, I find they
were sold and dispersed into various parishes.
    The Reason why I can give no account of the baptized among
them, is, 1st they are not liable to be registered by our Law (which
has provided a Register distinct from the Minister) So that there is
no easy way of knowing who were baptized in Church or meeting.
    2dly if any of my Predecessors keept a private Register, of those
that were baptised by them, they have neglected to leave it behind
them. But I shall endeavour to keep a list of the Negroes baptized,
in my time; and if I should Chance any way to find out the Number
of the Negroes baptized, before my time, I shall not fail to transmitt
it.[57]

By letter of April 17, 1751, he described his long illness, during
which his church was "but poorly provided for," but in spite of
handicaps, he had 30 communicants, and since September, 1749-1750
he had baptized 8 whites and 6 Negro children.[58]

[56] William Cotes to Philip Bearcroft, St. George's Parish, Dorchester,
South Carolina, Jan. 4, 1748-1749, in *S.P.G. M.S.S.* (L.C. Trans.), B 16, No. 147.
    [57] *Ibid.*
    [58] William Cotes to Philip Bearcroft, St. George's Parish, Dorchester, South
Carolina, April 17, 1751, in *S.P.G. MSS.* (L.C. Trans.), B 19, No. 140. Also in
Journal of S.P.G. (L.C. Trans.), Vol. XII, Nov. 15, 1751.

Seven months later Cotes commented regarding the attitude among the planters:

As for the Case of Negro baptisms which I was in hopes of seeing go forward, it is now and will be at a stand. A horrid practice of poisoning their Masters, or those set over them, having lately prevailed among them. For this practice, 5 or 6 in our Parish have been condemned to die, altho 40 or 50 more were privy to it. One of Col. Blake's, who had been baptized, told me, that notwithstanding what was alleged against her, she still hoped to be saved, because she believed in Christ (a vague phrase much in use among our sectaries). I endeavoured to show her the true import and meaning thereof, and at last she made some kind of confession, and desired to be remembered in our prayers.

How it happens I don't know, but my observation and information we find the most, of those that were poisoned, were noted for their leni[ent]cy and indulgence, and from this many have taken occasion to exclaim against the perverseness of negroes and are discouraged to bring them to the Christian Ordinance of baptism; all which, for a time, I must in a great measure endure, and wait till their passions are abated, before I can have any reasonable hopes of convincing them to the contrary.[59]

Mr. Cotes died suddenly on Sunday, July 19, 1752, "after having that day performed divine services."[60]

Meanwhile at St. Andrew's the Rev. Charles Martyn was appointed by the Society to succeed the venerable Guy who died in 1751. Martyn wrote on June 25, 1752, that there were about 1500 Negroes and 100 Indians in the parish, all of whom he would willingly instruct, but as to the Indians, "their shyness and strong aversion to instruction is a bar . . . and as to the negroes, their masters seem rather averse to their instruction because, as they say, from experience they find they become lazy and proud."[61] But in December of the same year, he reported the baptism of "one adult negro man who gave a very rational account of the principles of the Christian religion."[62]

Particularly revealing as an account of community life is the Society's abstract of Martyn's letter of July 7, 1757:

. . . his Ministry is attended with some Success, tho' not so great as

[59] William Cotes to Philip Bearcroft, St. George's, Dorchester, South Carolina, December 2, 1751, in *S.P.G. MSS.* (L.C. Trans.), B 19, No. 141.
[60] Churchwardens of St. George's, South Carolina, to [Secretary], August 24, 1752, in *S.P.G. MSS.* (L.C. Trans.), B 20, No. 139.
[61] Charles Martyn to [Secretary], St. Andrew's, South Carolina, June 25, 1752, in *Journal of S.P.G.* (L.C. Trans.), Vol. XII, Nov. 17, 1752.
[62] Charles Martyn to [Secretary], St. Andrew's, South Carolina, December 28, 1752, in *Journal of S.P.G.* (L.C. Trans.), Vol. XII, May 18, 1753.

he could wish, being obstructed by a scandalous Practice lately introduced of carrying on the usual Labour of the Week, even on *Sundays,*
during the Season of making Indico; but Mr. *Marten* hath done his
Duty in endeavouring to convince his people of the Crime of their
profaning the Lord's Day; ... he preaches every fourth *Sunday* at a
Chapel in the furthest Part of the Parish, where, among others, a considerable number of Persons, educated in the Presbyterian Way
attend, and several of them produce Common Prayer Books, and
make the Responses; and, he hopes, will in Time become steady Members of the Church. Mr. Marten had, within the twelve Months preceding, baptized 36 Children, and two adult *Negroes* . . . and there
have been five worthy Persons within the same Time added to his
Communicants.[63]

The reference to "the Season of making Indico" suggests the
growing importance of this comparatively new crop in the plantation
scheme. Indigo, which was not introduced into the colony until about
1743, had for its sponsor "one of America's greatest women, Eliza
Lucas, afterward the wife of Charles Pinckney (chief justice of the
province) and the mother of the two patriot statesmen, Thomas and
Charles Cotesworth Pinckney."[64] Rice remained, as it had been, the
staple plantation crop, but the cultivation of indigo, which could be
raised in conjunction with rice,[65] was expanding each year, increasing

---

[63] *An Abstract of the Proceedings of the S.P.G.* Printed with Johnson
Sermon (London: 1758), pp. 50-51. (Huntington Library)

[64] U. B. Phillips, in *American Negro Slavery,* pp. 91-92. Phillips continued
regarding this amazing young woman: "Her father, the governor of the British
island of Antigua, had been prompted by his wife's ill health to settle his family
in South Carolina, where the three plantations he acquired near Charleston
were for several years under his daughter's management. The girl while attending her father's business, found time to keep up her music and her social
activities, to teach a class of young negroes to read, and to carry on various
undertakings in economic botany. In 1741 her experiments with cotton,
guinea-corn and ginger were defeated by frost, and alfalfa proved unsuited
to her soil; but in spite of two preliminary failures that year she raised
some indigo plants with success. Next year her father sent a West Indian
expert named Cromwell to manage her indigo crop and prepare its commercial
product. But Cromwell, in fear of injuring the prosperity of his own community, purposely mishandled the manufacturing. With the aid of a neighbor,
nevertheless, Eliza not only detected Cromwell's treachery but in the next
year worked out the true process. She and her father now distributed indigo
seed to a number of planters; and from 1744 the crop began to reach the rank
of a staple."

[65] A discussion of these two crops written about 1755, is reprinted in B. R. Carroll, *Historical Collections of South Carolina,* II, 202-204: ". . . each good working hand employed in a Rice Plantation makes Four barrels and a half of Rice,
each Barrel weighing Five Hundred Pounds neat; Besides a sufficient Quantity of Provisions of all Kinds for the Slaves, Horses, Cattle, and Poultry of
the Plantation for the ensuing Year . . . An Acre of good Land may produce
about Eighty Pounds Weight of good Indigo; and one Slave may manage Two
Acres and upwards . . . But I cannot leave this subject without observing

the wealth of the planters,[66] while it added to the working hours of the slaves.

It was the missionaries' responsibility to divert some of this growing wealth into channels indicated by the Society's program, and a terse report concerning Martyn at St. Andrew's, read: "his Parishioners . . . have actually purchased an Organ, and paled in the Church-yard; and he hopes to see soon a Charity school for the Education of their poor Children, established."[67] Thus to both practical and humanitarian ends Martyn was building. So well did he build that by 1761

. . . his Affairs calling him to England, [Martyn] attended the General Meeting of the Society in *September* 1761, resigned the Missionary's Salary, thinking the Ministers of St. *Andrew's* sufficiently provided for without the Society's Allowance; and received their [the Society's] thanks for his past good Conduct, as well as his generous Behaviour on this Occasion.[68]

In conclusion, the parish of St. James, Goose Creek, so ably served by the pioneers, Le Jau and Ludlam, offers in its reports an excellent summary of this period, and an evaluation of the work accomplished. Under the Rev. Timothy Millechamp, who arrived there in 1732,[69]

---

how conveniently and profitable, as to the charge of Labour, both Indigo and Rice may be managed by the same Persons, for the Labour attending Indigo being over in the Summer Months, those who were employed in it may afterwards manufacture Rice in the ensuing Part of the Year, when it becomes most laborious; and after doing all this, they will have some Time to spare for sawing Lumber and making Hogsheads, and other Staves, to supply the Sugar Colonies."

[66] Harriette Kershaw Leiding, in *Historic Houses of South Carolina* (Philadelphia: 1921), pp. 112-113, describes the Winyaw Indigo Society, formed about 1740. "The old Oak Tavern, which stood in Bay Street was the scene of these monthly reunions. On the first Friday of May, each year, the anniversary meeting took place . . . Fees and contributions were paid in the staple crop of the section—indigo—and by the year 1753 the club was a rich association. A proposal was made that the surplus funds be devoted to the establishment of an independent charity school for the poor. The meeting rose to its feet. 'Every glass was turned down without staining the table cloth,' and the school of the Winyah Indigo Society was established and has continued its good work to this day."

[67] *An Abstract of the Proceedings of the S.P.G.* Printed with Hayter Sermon (London: 1755), p. 56. (Huntington Library)

[68] *An Abstract of the Proceedings of the S.P.G.* Printed with Hume Sermon (London: 1762), p. 63. (Huntington Library)

[69] The influx of immigration into Goose Creek, as a result of the opening of free lands by the Crown in 1731, is described in Harriette Kershaw Leiding, *Historic Houses of South Carolina*, p. 22: "In 1732 . . . an advertisement appeared in the *Gazette* designed 'To encourage Tradesmen to settle contiguously in the Parish of St. James's on Goose Creek, John Lloyd, Esq., will grant building leases of 64 acres of land, viz., 8 Lotts consisting of 8 acres each Lott, all fronting the Broad Path, from the Brow of the Hill Mr. Rich Walker

affairs had settled down to routine management. The church was now an old and established one,[70] and the work went on in spite of the frequent illnesses of Millechamp, which, on two occasions, necessitated his return to England.[71] The instruction of the Negroes in the parish seems to have suffered as a result, for Millechamp complained that in the entire year of 1734 he had baptized only one Negro man, and that in addition several books had disappeared from his library, evidently stolen.[72]

In 1736 the Society reported of Goose Creek as follows:

... many of that Parish were removed to *Cape-Fear;* that his Congregation is now very much reduced; that he sometimes administers the Sacrament at the Chapel at *Wassamsaw,* where the People are at too great a distance to come to Church. He says he is just recover'd from a dangerous Fit of Sickness, and desires to leave to return home next Spring, or whenever else the want of Health should oblige him.[73]

This report, in common with many similar S.P.G. records, gives valuable information on frontier conditions relating to the rapid migration of people from place to place, the illness of the missionary and other persons and the long distances in a plantation economy. Hardship was universal and death came early.

Millechamp's *Notitia Parochialis* reported on October 15, 1741, that there were 2160 unbaptized Negroes and 20 Indians in his parish;

---

now lives on, to the Fence joining Mr. Hume's Land, on the North West side of the Broad Path. The Land is all cleared, and very proper for either Pasture, Corn or Rice, within 20 miles of Charlestown, and four of Goose Creek Bridge; and the Trades thought most proper to settle on it are, a Smith, Carpenter, Wheel-right, Bricklayer, Butcher, Taylor, Shoemaker and a Tanner."

[70] The church at Goose Creek is pictured in *ibid* (opposite page 22) and the author notes that: "Goose Creek, sometimes spelled 'Goose Crick,' is one of the oldest settlements in the state outside of Charleston. The church still standing there was begun in 1714 and completed in 1719. Tradition has it that it was spared during the Revolution because of the fact that above its chancel there are the Royal Arms of England."

[71] The Society's *Abstract of Proceedings* for 1739 (p. 70) report that Millechamp, then in England, "acquainted the Society on the 15th of *September* 1738, That he purposed through God's Blessing to return forthwith to his Mission, with which, the Society being well pleased, they gave him 10 *l.* towards the Expences of his return to his Parish." Again in 1746 the *Abstracts* (p. 57) report that Millechamp "is returned to England with their Leave, for the Recovery of his Health, with recommendatory Letters from the Churchwardens and Vestry of his Church; and purposes, God willing, to return in a short time thither again."

[72] Timothy Millechamp to David Humphreys, Goose Creek, South Carolina, May 28, 1735, in *S.P.G. MSS.* (L.C. Trans.), A 28, p. 134; also in *Journal of S.P.G.* (L.C. Trans.), Vol. VI, September 19, 1735. On Whitsunday, 1734, the entire number of communicants (black and white) numbered only 15.

[73] *An Abstract of the Proceedings of the S.P.G.* Printed with Clagget Sermon (London: 1737) pp. 52-53. (Huntington Library)

and that of the 91 white families only 10 were dissenters,[74] while by 1742 there were 98 families and 2752 slaves in the parish.[75] On Christmas day of that year there were 20 white and 2 Negro communicants, and on Easter 21 whites and 2 Negroes: nine families and 202 slaves having removed from the parish.[76]

When the Rev. Robert Stone succeeded Millechamp at Goose Creek in 1748 he commented on the unhealthy state of South Carolina and said he had buried 8 people in the first nine weeks he took over his Parish. Forty-five was the age looked upon as the average life span of man.[77] In the same letter Mr. Stone advised that he had baptized one adult black and "should have baptised another, but his master sent me word that he desired to speak to me first."[78] His cheerful report two years later was testimony of a growing confidence in himself and in the value of his work.

. . . The beginning of Lent last year I set apart the afternoons on Sunday for the instruction of negroes, and continued so to do until I was [taken ill]. Such numbers crowded the church before, that they were very off[ensive] to the whites. To show how acceptable it was to them, they sent six of the old men with a present of poultry to thank

[74] Timothy Millechamp to [Secretary], St. James', Goose Creek, South Carolina, October 15, 1741, in *Journal of S.P.G.* (L.C. Trans.), Vol. IX, February 19, 1741-1742.
[75] Timothy Millechamp to [Secretary], St. James, Goose Creek, South Carolina, November 3, 1742, in *Journal of S.P.G.* (L.C. Trans.), Vol. IX, May 20, 1743.
[76] Timothy Millechamp to [Secretary], St. James, Goose Creek, South Carolina, April 12, 1743, in *Journal of S.P.G.* (L.C. Trans.), Vol. IX, Aug. 19, 1743.
[77] Robert Stone to Philip Bearcroft, Goose Creek [South Carolina], March 6, 1749-1750, in *S.P.G. MSS.* (L.C. Trans.), B 7, No. 182. A description of the hazards to health presented by the colony is given in B. R. Carroll, *Historical Collections of South Carolina,* I, p. 383, as follows: "As this climate differs so much from that of Britain, Ireland, and Germany, and every where has great influence on the human constitution, no wonder that many of these settlers should sicken and die by the change, during the first state of colonization. In the hot season the human body is relaxed by perpetual perspiration, and becomes feeble and sickly, especially during the dog-days, when the air is one while suffocating and sultry, and another moist and foggy. Exhausted of fluids, it is perhaps not at all, or very improperly, supplied. Hence intermittent, nervous, putrid and bilious fevers, are common in the country, and prove fatal to many of its inhabitants. Young children are very subject to the worm-fever, which cuts off multitudes of them. The dry belly-ache, which is a dreadful disorder, is no stranger to the climate. An irruption, commonly called the prickly heat, often breaks out during the summer, which is attended with troublesome itching and stinging pains; but this disease being common, and not dangerous, is little regarded; and if proper caution be used to prevent it from striking suddenly inward, is thought to be attended even with salutary effects. In the spring and winter pleurises and peripneumonies are common, often obstinate, and frequently fatal diseases."
[78] Robert Stone to Philip Bearcroft, Goose Creek [South Carolina], March 6, 1749-1750 in *S.P.G. MSS.* (L.C. Trans.), B 17, No. 182.

me. I returned their present and told them I should be well satisfied for my pains, if they would make good use of it. I have received thanks from several of their masters and mistresses who thought that they behaved much better since they frequented the church. As soon as I was recovered they came and desired me to do like again. Which I shall always comply with whilst health will permit. I have baptized since my last only two grown blacks and seven white children . . .[79]

The Rev. James Harrison, who took over the parish of Goose Creek in 1752, after Stone's death, also found that an "obstinate aversion" to having their slaves baptized, prevailed among the masters, chiefly founded on their belief that the Negroes became less governable.[80] The temper of the times, and the additional perils of the frontier during this difficult decade, are capably described in a paragraph, by Commissary Alexander Garden of Charleston:

. . . Tho in the midst of the almost general Commotions & Confusions of War in N. America, we in this Province have enjoyed a profound Peace, yet we are now likely to be engaged in a dangerous Indian war with the Cherokee Nation. One half of the Inhabitants from the Age 16 to 60 years are drawn but to march at an hours Warning, & our Governor is set out with a Body of Men for that Country, upon whoes Success depends our Safety; whilst the other half of the Militia is employed in Guarding agst. the Insurrections of our numerous Negro Slaves; So that I am affraid Religion will make but little Progress amidst these Confusions.[81]

Ulrich B. Phillips, in his *American Negro Slavery*, suggested that such plots and similar disturbances were more notable for the frenzy of the public than for the formidableness of the menace. The rebellion at Stono, in 1739, had been real enough but early accounts attribute its cause to a Spanish plot rather than to educated Negroes. Certainly a white population so heavily outnumbered by the slaves whom they held in subjection, was apprehensive, and quick to imagine an incipient insurrection.[82] Only two genuine uprisings (in 1720 and

[79] Robert Stone to [Philip Bearcroft], St. James, Goose Creek, South Carolina, March 22, 1750-1751 in *S.P.G. MSS.* (L.C. Trans.), B 18, No. 186. Also in *Journal of S.P.G.* (L.C. Trans.), Vol. XII, June 21, 1751.

[80] James Harrison to [Secretary], St. James', Goose Creek, South Carolina, January [13?] 1756, in *Journal of S.P.G.* (L.C. Trans.), Vol. XIII, May 21, 1756.

[81] Alexander Garden to David Humphreys, Charlestown, South Carolina, October 31, 1759, in *S.P.G. MSS.* (L.C. Trans.), B 4, No. 284; *Journal of S.P.G.* (L.C. Trans.), Vol. XIV, April 18, 1760. For Negro disturbances in 1712 and 1741 at New York see U. B. Phillips, *American Negro Slavery*, pp. 469-471; for the South Carolina uprisings see p. 473.

[82] Helen T. Catterall, in *Judicial Cases Concerning American Slavery and the Negro*, II, p. 362, cites the case *State v. Green*, in 1836, when "the husband

1739) seem to have taken place during the period studied. But a
consciousness of the murderous potentialities of the situation ac-
centuated by the increase of the slave trade from 1730 on,[83] is reflected
in legislative action,[84] and formed a real obstacle to the S.P.G. mis
sionary, anxious to educate and assist "the poor Negroes . . . [whose
condition] is yet nearly as hard as possible, their servitude most
laborious, their Punishments most severe."[85]

Harrison, at Goose Creek, was an excellent example of the results
to be gained by staunch but diplomatic efforts in this direction. Woven
through all of his reports, which reflect the excessive difficulties of
the period during which he served, is a sturdy confidence; and particularly to be noted is the striking success he could report in his
work with the Negroes who formed a large proportion of his congregation. In 1758 the Society commented:

of the prisoner, [Mrs. Green], was shot by some unknown person, she instantly
cried out, 'Henry is killed—the negroes have risen—we shall all be killed' . . .
there did not appear to have been any apprehensions of a rising among the
negroes . . . it was, she said, Tommy Ray's negro man, Edom, who killed him."
Edom was tried and acquitted and Mrs. Green was found guilty of being an
accessory before the fact.
   [83] See Elizabeth Donnan, "The Slave Trade in South Carolina Before the
Revolution," in the *American Historical Review*, XXXIII (July, 1928), pp.
804-828. A table of importations appears on p. 807. Rice formed the basis of
exchange until about 1733, after which "factors" in Charleston were required
to "make good all bad Debts, to remit 2 thirds of the Value in 12 Months,
the other one third in 2 Years after the Day of Sale." (p. 812) By 1763 the
value of slaves had so increased that "a cargo averaged between £33 and £34,
the best men yielding £320 per head, and small Boys £260 to £280." (p. 822)
   [84] A discussion of legislative efforts to reduce the proportion of Negroes to
whites by import duties may be found in W. E. B. Du Bois, *The Suppression
of the African Slave Trade* (New York: 1896), 9-11. "South Carolina had the
largest and most widely developed slave-trade of any of the continental colonies," says Du Bois. "This was owing to the character of her settlers, her near-
ness to the West Indian slave marts, and the early development of certain
staple crops, such as rice, which were adapted to slave labor." Due to increased demand, and in spite of imports, South Carolina, in 1760, totally prohibited the slave-trade, an action promptly disallowed by the Privy Council,
but "the colony declared that 'an importation of negroes, equal in number to
what have been imported of late years, may prove of the most dangerous consequence in many respects to this Province, and the best way to obviate such
danger will be by imposing such an additional duty upon them as may totally
prevent the evils.' (Cooper, *Statutes*, IV, 187). A prohibitive duty of £100
was accordingly imposed in 1764."
   [85] *Annual Sermon of the S.P.G.* . . . on Friday, February 20, 1740-41, by
Thomas Secker, Lord Bishop of Oxford (London: 1741) p. 8. (Huntington
Library) Secker makes a bold attack on the attitude of the planters who "are
habituated to consider [their slaves] as they do their Cattle, merely with a View
to the Profit arising from them . . . Others, by obliging them to work on Sundays to provide them the Necessaries, leave them neither Time to learn Religion in it, nor any Prospect of being able to subsist, if once the Duty of
resting on that Day become Part of their Belief. And some, it may be feared,
have been averse to their becoming Christians, because, after that, no Pretence
will remain for not treating them like Men."

... it is impossible to ascertain the exact Number of white Inhabitants of that Parish, as it is unbounden to the North West; and those unfortunate People, whom the Terrors and Calamities of War drive from the more Northern Provinces, are continually changing their Places of Residence. Mr. *Harrison* is informed by some, who have brought their Children from 80 to 200 Miles Distance to be baptized, that there are about 30 Families scattered about here and there among them. The Number of Communicants within the more settled Part of the Parish, is 30 Whites, (10 of them added within the last Year) and 17 Negroes; and he had baptized 13 White and 3 Negroe Children, and 7 adult Negroes in that Year. Mr. *Harrison* adds, that Mr. *Peter Taylor* a good and worthy Parishioner hath made a Present of a Negroe Girl for the Use of the Minister of that Parish, as a small Encouragement to him for his endeavouring to propagate the Gospel among the Slaves of the Parish; (to use the Words of the Entry of this Donation in the Vestry-book) and Mr. *Harrison* promises, that his sincere Endeavours in this good Work, as far as is consistent with other Duties incumbent on him, shall speak his Gratitude for this Benefaction.[86]

A year later, concerning his report of May 28, 1758, the Society announced:

... his Congregation is considerably increased, and he hath twenty-six white and twenty regular negroe Communicants, and he had baptized eighteen white Children and five Adult negroes after proper instruction, in the preceeding half year.[87]

Harrison's letter of May 12, 1759, contained a *Notitia Parochialis,* which the Society summarized with the remarkable skill found in all its *Abstracts of Proceedings:*

... there are about two hundred Families resident in a Tract of Land one hundred and eighty Miles in Length, and from ten to fourteen Miles in Breadth; and his Congregation generally consists of about one hundred and fifty Whites, and from fifty to sixty Negroes; and that about sixteen Miles from the Church, at ... *Wassamsaw,* are eight Families settled in a Neighbourhood of a Chapel, where he officiateth five or six times in a Year. According to Mr. *Harrison's Notitia Parochialis* he had baptized fourteen Children, and nine Adults in the preceding Year; and his Communicants consist of thirty-one white, and twenty-six Negro Persons.[88]

[86] *An Abstract of the Proceedings of the S.P.G.* Printed with Johnson Sermon (London: 1758), pp. 51-52. (Huntington Library)
[87] *An Abstract of the Proceedings of the S.P.G.* Printed with Ellis Sermon (London: 1759), p. 70. (Huntington Library)
[88] *An Abstract of the Proceedings of the S.P.G.* Printed with Ashburnham Sermon (London: 1760), pp. 61-62. (Huntington Library) Also in *Journal of S.P.G.* (L.C. Trans.), Vol. XIV, Dec. 21, 1759.

Regularly each year the Society recorded his progress. By April 14, 1760, in spite of the war with the Cherokees:

. . . he had baptized, since the Date of his preceeding Letter, nineteen Children and five Negro Adults, and he had thirty-two White and twenty-eight Black Communicants; but that the War in which they were unhappily engaged with the *Cherokees,* made it impossible for him to inform the Society . . . of the Number of Inhabitants in that Parish; he can only say in general, that they are greatly increased, many of the Frontier People having, for the greater Security, come and settled among them.[89]

The situation was no better in January 26, 1761, when:

. . . by the Calamities of the War with the *Cherokee Indians,* the Number of Inhabitants in his Parish is considerably lessened, many of the unfortunate People, who were driven from their Settlements, having retired to the Northern Provinces, to procure that Protection and Maintenance, which they saw but little Likelihood of in *South Carolina.* He has 31 White, and 26 Black Communicants; has baptized since his last 15 Children, and 2 Adult Negroes.[90]

A year later Harrison had "38 white Communicants & 18 Negroes who communicate";[91] and he mentioned that peace has been concluded with the Cherokee Indians. By January 20, 1764, there were "26 white Persons who communicate constantly, and 16 Negroes:[92] and two years later, of the 1300 Negroes in his parish, 150 or more were Christians, and 30 communicants.[93] These South Carolina records throughout illustrate Dr. Carter G. Woodson's thesis that there is no separate Negro History in the United States. In American History the Negro has his part, but it is interlaced with that of the white man.

So faithful were the Negroes, as contrasted with the white members of his parish, that by October 18, 1768, they far outnumbered

[89] *An Abstract of the Proceedings of the S.P.G.* Printed with Newcome Sermon (London: 1761), pp. 60-61. (Huntington Library) Also recorded in *Journal of S.P.G.* (L.C. Trans.), Vol. XIV, July 18, 1760; and in *S.P.G. MSS.* (L.C. Trans.), B 5, No. 230.

[90] *An Abstract of the Proceedings of the S.P.G.* Printed with Hume Sermon (London: 1762), pp. 62-63. (Huntington Library) Also recorded in *Journal of S.P.G.* (L.C. Trans.), Vol. XV, Sept. 18, 1761; and in *S.P.G. MSS.* (L.C. Trans.), B 5, No. 231.

[91] James Harrison to Philip Bearcroft, Goose Creek, So. Carolina, July 16, 1762, in *S.P.G. MSS.* (L.C. Trans.), B 5, No. 232. Also recorded in *Journal of S.P.G.* (L.C. Trans.), Vol. XV, January 21, 1763.

[92] James Harrison to Daniel Burton, Goose Creek, South Carolina, January 20, 1764, in *S.P.G. MSS.* (L.C. Trans.), B 5, No. 233. Also recorded in *Journal of S.P.G.* (L.C. Trans.), Vol. XVI, April 13, 1764.

[93] James Harrison to [Daniel Burton], Goosecreek, S.C., August 8, 1766, in *S.P.G. MSS.* (L.C. Trans.), B 5, No. 234. Also recorded in *Journal of S.P.G.* (L.C. Trans.), Vol. XVII, Dec. 19, 1766.

their masters in attendance. Marking the indifference of his white
congregation Harrison told that for about 2 months in the spring
the Church was pretty well filled, but during the rest of the year
there were seldom more than 30 or 40 white people as compared with
about 100 Negroes who attended. He had 16 constant white communicants, 16 who communicated occasionally, and 35 faithful Negro
communicants. Since his last he had baptized 56 white children (but
not all of his parish), 3 adults, and 7 Negro children.[94] By this time
he was practically alone in the field, the Society having followed its
policy of withdrawing missionaries as each parish found itself able
to carry on the work independently.

Twelve years earlier, in 1757, the Annual Report had noted that
the Assembly of South Carolina "hath been pleased to augment the
Stipend of their officiating Ministers to 100 *l.* Sterling per Annum,"[95]
and in 1759 the Society voted not to provide missionaries for the
vacant posts of those to be empty henceforth.[96]

[94] James Harrison to [Secretary], St. James, Goose Creek, S.C. October
18, 1768, in *Journal of S.P.G.* (L.C. Trans.), Vol. XVIII, January 20, 1769.
[95] *An Abstract of the Proceedings of the S.P.G.* Printed with Keene Sermon
(London: 1757), p. 57. (Huntington Library)
[96] C. F. Pascoe, *Two Hundred Years of the S.P.G.*, I, pp. 18-19. Pascoe comments "By the example of the Society and its Missionaries, the Colonists were
led to take a real interest in spiritual things, and they showed their gratitude
by building and endowing Churches and Schools, and making such provision
that in 1759 the Society voted not to fill up the existing Missions in the Province
as they became vacant." In 1765 a request for a missionary reached the
Society. See Petition of Louis De St. Pierre, Esq. in behalf of himself, and
other Inhabitants of the Township of Hillsborough, or New Bourdeaux in
Granville County, South Carolina, to the Respectable Society for the Propagation
of the Gospel in Foreign Parts, dated South Carolina [1765] in *S.P.G. MSS.*
(L.C. Trans.), B 5, No. 256, which reads: "That, your Petitioner is a Justice
of Peace and Captain of a Company of Militia composed of French Protestants,
who quitted their native Country in order to settle in his Majesty's American
Dominions; And that your Petitioner, being come to England to lay before
Government, the probable Success of two valuable Branches of Commerce in
those Parts, if properly encouraged (viz.) The Culture of the Vine and of raw-
Silk; he thinks it equally his Duty, as a faithfull Subject and a Christian, to
acquaint this respectable Society with the deplorable State he and his Brethren
of the said Colony are in, with regard to Religion; and earnestly to sollicit
your charitable Advice and Assistance thereupon.
That, the Inhabitants of Hillsborough, or New Bordeaux Township (amounting in number to 300 Souls) have had no Pastor among them but the late
Rev[d] M[r] Boutiton, who came with them thither from France, and died shortly
after their entering upon their present Settlement in 1763; and that ever since
that time, they have been deprived of the use of the Sacraments, and every
other means of Public Instruction and Edification.
That, besides the French Colony of Hillsborough or New Bourdeaux there
are many English and Irish Settlers in their Neighbourhood, who would gladly
and thankfully partake with them in the Blessings of a regular and pious
Ministry, were the Colony provided with a proper Person, in Episcopal Orders, and capable of preaching both in English and French.
That, there is actually such a one, as yet unprovided for, in South Carolina;

An account of the Society's refusal to supply a vacancy at St. George's in 1759 gives a careful statement as to the reasons for their action:

... the Society, upon mature Consideration are of opinion, that as by an Act of the Assembly of *South Carolina* 100 *l.* Sterling *per Annum* is allowed by the Province to the officiating Ministers in every Parish, in which no Mission is settled, it will best answer the good Purposes of the Society not to fill up the Missions in this Province as they become vacant, but to proceed to erect new Missions in such Places as through the Poverty of the Inhabitants stand very much in need of their charitable Assistance.

But at the same Time not to neglect *South Carolina* in such religious Matters as really want the Society's Assistance: They have assisted the Rev. Mr. *Immer,* a Swiss Clergyman, that lately arrived in *England,* and hath been ordained Deacon and Priest in the Church of *England,* in order to go and officiate ... to the Church of Purrysberg in this Province composed of *French* and *German* Protestants, the Languages of whom he understands and is to officiate in; the Expences of himself and of his Family from *Switzerland* to *England,* and of his necessary Stay here having so far exhausted his small Stock of Money that without the charitable Aid of the Society he was utterly unable to proceed on his Voyage thither.[97]

By 1763 only four missionaries were supported by the S.P.G.: Garden at St. Thomas', Durand at St. John's, Baron at St. Bartholomew's, and Harrison at Goose Creek.[98] And two years later, in 1765, the Society regarded with satisfaction the condition of South Carolina

---

both able and willing to undertake that Duty (The Rev[d] M[r] Peter Sevrier by Name) to whose sound Doctrine and good Morals many Persons of Worth are ready to bear Testimony: and that your Petitioners are very desirous of retaining him for their Pastor, but unfortunately want the means, their Infant Colony having as yet but the bare Necessaries of Life.

That your Petitioners, confiding in the Society's known Zeal and Charity, presume to lay their pityable case before them, earnestly intreating, that some pecuniary assistance may be issuing out of their Funds, as a Salary to their Pastor, for the Space of two or three years only; after which, they hope, with the Blessings of God upon their labors, to be able to maintain him themselves." Apparently this request was refused.

[97] *An Abstract of the Proceedings of the S.P.G.* Printed with Ashburnham Sermon (London: 1760), pp. 62-63. (Huntington Library) The Society did send in 1769 the Reverend Mr. S. F. Lucius to Coffee Town. The inhabitants had made a special call on behalf of "the Protestant Palatines in South Carolina." Having emigrated from Europe, they were "greatly distressed for want of a minister, ... The Lords Commissioners of Trade and Plantations referred their petition to the Society. ... In six months he baptized 40 children and 30 adults. ... Mr. Lucius continued among them as the Society's missionary until the end of the American Revolution." C. F. Pascoe, *Two Hundred Years of the S.P.G.,* I, p. 19. Mr. Pascoe gives a brief account of the work of the Rev. Mr. Lucius.

[98] *An Abstract of the Proceedings of the S.P.G.* Printed with Egerton Sermon (London: 1763), p. 37. (Huntington Library)

where there were "19 Parishes all filled at present with regular Clergy, besides one or two Itinerants; who have all 100 *l.* Sterling from this Government, except the Missionaries who are allowed but 70 *l.*"[99]

[99] *An Abstract of the Proceedings of the S.P.G.* Printed with Yonge Sermon (London: 1765), p. 89. (Huntington Library)

CHAPTER V

THE CHARLESTON NEGRO SCHOOL

SPECIAL experiments in education were attempted by the Society for the Propagation of the Gospel in every area of its work. Attempts to train native leaders by their removal for education in England were made in several notable cases: from Africa, Philip Quaque with other students,[1] and from South Carolina, the Yamassee Indian Prince.[2] Special schools, such as the one in Philadelphia run by the Bray Associates,[3] and in New York by the S.P.G.,[4] were set up. The Charleston Negro School, begun in 1743 by Commissary Alexander Garden, represented an unique contribution not only to the Society's program for the Christianization of slaves, but also to the wider field of Negro education. Garden was one of the first to see in the Negro himself the potentialities for the enlightenment of the whole race, for the fundamental concept of his school was that it was to be conducted by trained Negro teachers, an important recognition of the abilities of the race. Furthermore, its efficacy depended upon the scholars themselves, who were, in turn, to impart their knowledge to their fellows, unable through lack of opportunity, to

[1] See Frank J. Klingberg, "Philip Quaque: Pioneer Native Missionary on the Gold Coast, 1765-1816," in *The Journal of Negro Education* (October, 1939), VIII, pp. 666-672. An African aristocratic freeman, Philip Quaque was educated by the Society in England, and sent back to the Guinea Coast where he worked for half a century, from 1765 to 1816, in the heyday of the slave trade.
[2] The visit of the Yamassee Indian Prince to England is to be the subject of a separate paper.
[3] The story of the Negro school in Philadelphia, begun in 1758 by the Bray Associates with the active assistance of the S.P.G. is told in Edgar Legare Pennington, *Thomas Bray's Associates and their Work Among the Negroes* (Worcester: 1939) pp. 65-73. See also Richard I. Shelling, "Benjamin Franklin and the Dr. Bray Associates," in *The Pennsylvania Magazine of History and Biography*, LXIII (July, 1939), pp. 282-293. Franklin's interest in the Negro school found practical expression. He met with the Associates, recommended that other such schools be founded in New York City, Williamsburg, Virginia, and Newport, Rhode Island, and corresponded with church leaders requesting their assistance in organizing these schools. When they were established, he "made it a point to visit the schools and sent a report to the Associates. . . . Not only did he keep in constant touch with the three schools in America, but also looked after the needs of various groups which desired books" (pp. 286-287).
[4] See Frank J. Klingberg, *Anglican Humanitarianism in Colonel New York*, (Philadelphia: 1940) pp. 124-139, for the story of the Negro School established by Elias Neau in New York City, beginning in 1705 and continuing to the American Revolution.

attend the school. Granted that the underlying motive was religious training, this school, nevertheless, remains a monument to the Society's belief in the intelligence of the Negro and his equal rights to the benefits of religion and education.

To assess properly this experiment, it must be placed in its social setting. Centered in a plantation economy, where the Negro represented not only the chief unit of labor, but a primary source of capital wealth,[5] it had of necessity to oppose the immediate economic interest which begrudged the slave both the time and the opportunity for bettering himself. Further opposition was found in the forebodings of a white population so heavily outnumbered by a race held in subjection. As has been seen throughout this study, a prevailing fear of any equalitarian efforts formed a continual obstacle to the Society's program, based so fundamentally on humanitarian motives. Garden founded his school in Charleston where, alone in the province, the white and the Negro populations were about evenly divided.[6] Here he might count on at least some white sympathy and could select his scholars to the greatest advantage from many possible candidates.

Charleston itself, the spiritual and cultural center of the colony, had the advantage of a regional location which gave it a natural geographic position of monopoly. It was the only good defensible port between the Spanish settlements to the South and the Virginia settlements to the North, and an all but land enclosed harbor made it safe for shipping. These natural attractions brought in a steady stream of settlers not only from the West Indies, but from the home land, together with French Huguenots, Germans, and even Yankees from New England. Acadians, being Roman Catholics, did not receive a welcome into this cosmopolitan society. French and Spanish and Indian threats kept colonial South Carolina in a state of alarm and the Acadians might conceivably identify themselves with their fellow religionists to the South and West.

[5] For a table showing the proportion of the value of slaves to total personal property, see Arthur Henry Hirsch, *The Huguenots of Colonial South Carolina* (Durham: 1928) pp. 176-178. He comments, "it is safe to say that more than one-half of the personal property owned by the Huguenots of the tidewater consisted of slaves. . . . So numerous had slaves become in Carolina by 1735 that planters in stocking new plantations were no longer forced to depend on slave brokers for a supply. They could be secured from the numerous auction sales and by private transfer." Among the slave owners listed by Hirsch is Francis Le Jau, probably the son of the early missionary who "died penniless." The value of Le Jau's personal property is listed at £16,456-06-9, three-fourths of which (£11,831-00-0) is in the assessed value of his seventy slaves.
[6] See B. R. Carroll, *Historical Collections of South Carolina*, II, p. 484 for a statement, written in the year 1763, that in Charleston "The white inhabitants are about four thousand, and the Negro servants near the same number."

To the eighteenth century observer, the future of Charleston was as promising as that of New York, Philadelphia, or Boston. Today, the historic, beautiful city is a monument of its past. Victim of the Civil War and of the earthquake of 1886, it has nevertheless survived as a relatively small eighteenth century community, its growth not having overwhelmed its early character and charm.

Commissary Alexander Garden was himself an intimate part of the Charleston scene. Arriving in the city in 1719 during the death throes of the Proprietary government, he was first appointed rector of St. Philip's parish in Charleston, and in 1726 became commissary for North and South Carolina and the Bahama Islands, by order of Dr. Edmund Gibson, Bishop of London.[7] A native of Scotland,[8] Alexander Garden was not only one of the community's "few literary men,"[9] but proved himself a vigorous and sometimes vitriolic exponent of all that he found good and just. His controversy with Whitefield[10] received notice on both sides of the Atlantic, due as much, perhaps, to his form and forthright style as to the implications of

[7] Frederick Dalcho, *An Historical Account of the Protestant Episcopal Church in South Carolina*, pp. 98, 103.

[8] *The Dictionary of National Biography*, XX, pp. 406-407, is authority for the statement that Alexander Garden was born in Scotland in 1685, going to Carolina in 1719. He is not to be confused either with his nephew, the Rev. Alexander Garden, who was a missionary for the S.P.G. at St. Thomas' from 1744-1765, nor with his son, or his grandson, both of whom bore his name. It is his son, Alexander Garden (1730?-1791) who is listed in the *Dictionary of National Biography* as a botanist of note, educated in medicine at the University of Edinburgh, who returned to America in 1752, taught in King's College [Columbia University], New York, and later returned to Charleston to practice medicine, and pursue his studies in natural life in the colony, which were augmented by correspondence with Bartram, Peter Collinson, John Ellis and Linnaeus. He sent many new plants to Europe, among them the magnolias. The Cape Jessamine Ellis named in his honor, the "Gardenia." Siding with the Crown in The Revolution, he returned to England where he served as vice-president of the Royal Society. In turn, his son, Alexander Garden (1757-1829) although educated at Westminster and Glasgow, was a Patriot during the Revolution, joined the continental army and, at the end of the war, received his father's estates, which had been confiscated by the Patriots.

[9] Carl Bridenbaugh, *Cities in the Wilderness* (New York: 1938), p. 463.

[10] Some echo of the violence of this controversy has been preserved in the pamphlets published by both Whitefield and Garden. The degree of Garden's indignation may be judged from the following written by him in 1742: "Had I been engaged with any *other* than *that* Gentleman, my Pen might have run in a little smoother Stile; But as it happened to be with him, the most virulent, flaming, foul-mouthed *Persecutor* of the Church of God, that ever appeared in any *Age* or *Country,* no wonder if such Company proved *infectuous,* and somewhat embittered my Pen." From Alexander Garden, M.A., *The Doctrine of Justification According to the Scriptures, and the Articles and Homilies of the Church of ENGLAND, explained and vindicated in a LETTER to Mr. A. Croswell of Groton in New England. Being a reply to the said Mr. Croswell's Answer to Mr. Garden's three first Letters to Mr. Whitefield* (Charleston; MDCCXLII). (Huntington Library)

the controversy itself. Typical of Garden is his statement in 1743 that "As to the State of Religion in this Province, it is bad enough,— Rome and the Devil have contriv'd to crucify her between two Thieves, Infedelity and Enthusiasm."[11] A further commentary on Garden may be quoted as an analysis of his character:

Mr. Garden, in the discharge of the duties of this high office [Commissary of the Bishop of London], was strict and impartial. Improper conduct on the part of Clergymen was immediately noticed, the delinquents brought to trial, and the Canons of the Church were enforced against them. . . . He was attentive to the religious education of his Children and Servants. . . . In all cases he was a strict observer of rules and forms, and would not lightly depart from them. . . . His charity was in like manner measured by rule. The exact tenth of his whole income was yearly given to the poor. In every thing he was methodical. He carefully digested his plans, and steadily adhered to them. Strict himself, according to the forms of his religion, he required strictness from others. Under his Pastoral Care, a profession of religion was no slight matter. It imposed a necessity of circumspect conduct regulated in all respects by the prescribed forms of the Church.[12]

These distinguishing traits are amply portrayed in the correspondence between the Commissary and the S.P.G. These records also present the inception and progress of the Charleston Negro School in revealing detail.

In a long letter, written in May, 1740, Commissary Garden outlined his School plans in a challenging prospectus which took cognizance of a wide range of unfavorable factors, inherent in a slave economy.

Touching the most effectual Method, for Instructing the Negro & Indian Slaves, in the principles of our holy Religion, as it has been a Matter of my long and Serious Attention, I shall now humbly offer my final sentiments upon it, to the Hon[able] Society, in these few following Conclusions.

1st This good Work must not be attempted in the Gross, or inclusive of the whole Body of Slaves, of so many various Ages, Nations, Languages &c. For in this View it allways has, & ever will appear insuperable. But

2dly It must commence, & be carried on among such of them only, as are Home-Born, and under the Age of Ten years.

3dly Neither will the work thus limited ever turn out to any toler-

[11] Quoted from the New York *Journal*, May 30, 1743, in Carl Bridenbaugh, *Cities in the Wilderness*, p. 423.
[12] See Frederick Dalcho, *An Historical Account of the Protestant Episcopal Church in South Carolina*, pp. 176-8, wherein the above quotation is quoted from Ramsay's, *South Carolina*, II, p. 466.

able Effect, in the Hands of the Masters and Mistresses of Slaves; much less in the hands of any White School^mrs or Mistresses that may be sent from England, or any otherwise employed in it, And therefore

4. My 4th Conclusion is, that the above effectual Method of Proceeding in the Work as above limited, must be by *Negro* Schoolmasters, Home-born, & equally Property as other Slaves, but educated for this Service, & employed in it during their Lives, as the others are in any other Services whatsoever.

Pursuant to this last Conclusion I long since Proposed, that every owner of Eighty or a Hundred Slaves, ('mong whom there are seldom fewer than Ten or Twelve Children from Ten years old and under) should be at the charge of sending to School One or other of the Males, as should appear most capable and best disposed, 'till he be Taught to read the *Bible,* to say the *Church Catechism* by heart, and to use the *Common Prayer;* and who from thenceforth should be employ'd by the Said Owner, as a Schoolmaster, and in that Service only during his life, to instruct in the same manner all the Slave children not only of that Plantation, but of the smaller Plantations, that may be in the Neighbourhood. But alas! this Proposal how practicable soever allowed to be, yet it contains in it the loss of the Annual Profit from the labour of One Slave, no Body would be prevailed with to put it in Practice. I then consulted the Members of our Assembly here whether the Proposal might not be Enforced by a Law, or Act of Assem[bly] passed for the purpose; but was answer'd, that as it would touch on [not clear] Properties, they could pass no such Law (or rather would not do it, being most of them Parties concerned) I farther also had some thoughts [not clear] whether the Honble Society might not obtain his Majesty's Recommendation for the Passing such a Law in the respective Colonies; But observing how frequently such Recommendations, or even Instructions are either postponed or otherwise evaded, when there is no Mind to comply, I have likewise laid aside all such thoughts, and finally concluded—

5. In the last Place, to rest the Matter wholly on the Bottom of Charity; and in no hands so proper or promising of Success, as those of the Honble Society. . . .[13]

Granted that all ameliorative institutions must accept at least part of the social order, for footage in order to institute change, this agent of the S.P.G. on the ground offered an intelligent survey in order to discover what could be done, and by what exact methods. Commissary Garden, in this comprehensive plan, showed the most careful weighing of conditions in that he proceeded by rejection of a number of plausible plans which, by experience, he anticipated would fail. He then laid down his five-point program, with the convincing clearness of an expert observer. He had seen the variety of

[13] Alexander Garden to [Philip Bearcroft], South Carolina, May 6, 1740, in *S.P.G. MSS.* (L.C. Trans.), B 7, Pt. II, p. 235 ff.

skilled craftsmen among the Negroes[14] to which he wished to add
the trained schoolmaster, carefully selected and educated for his life-
long job. This slave, "home born, and equally property as other
Slaves," Mr. Garden was convinced, would no more upset the regime
than other skilled slaves "in any other Services whatsoever." He continued:

... And therefore I humbly Propose
That the Hon[ble] Society in order to proceed the most effectually in
this good Work, do appoint Three or Four or more of the Clergy of
this Province, for Instance (meaning the same method as the rest)
their Attorneys, with Directions to purchase for them (the said Society) and their Successors, in their Name, for their use, and at there
(sic) Charge [bound in, maybe charges] Three Four or Five (more
or fewer, as present Circumstances may allow, and to be added to
from Time to Time as Occasion may require, and future Circumstances enable) Home Born Male Slaves, not under the Age of
Twelve, not exceeding that of Sixteen Years, and who shall appear
to be of Sober docile Dispositions; and that the said Slaves be forthwith instructed in the Principles of the X[tn] Religion as contained in
the Church Catechism, to read the Bible, and to make use of the Book
of Common Prayer—And this accomplished (as I conceive it may
be in the Space of two years) then to direct that the said Slaves be
employ'd as Schoolmasters, in Such Places, and under the immediate
Care and Inspection of Such Persons, as shall be deemed most proper
by the said Attornies, for promoting the like Instruction of Slave
Children as per 2[d] Conclusion. This may perhaps appear like doing the
Work by halves, but in Event it is doing the whole, and by the alone
Method, at least the most effectual, (as I conceive) that the whole ever
will, or by ordinary Humain means can be done.
As among us Religious Instruction usually descends from Parents
to Children, so among them it must at first ascend from Children to
Parents, or from young to Old.
They are as 'twere a Nation within a Nation. In all County Settle-
ments, they live in contiguous Houses and often 2, 3 or 4 Famillys
of them in one House, Slightly partitioned into So many Apartments.
They labour together and converse almost wholly among themselves,
so that if once their children could but read the Bible to them, and
other Tracts of Instruction of Evenings & other spare Times, specially

[14] Of interest are the numerous South Carolina cases involving apprenticeship of slaves cited in H. T. Catterall, *Judicial Cases Concerning American
Slavery and the Negro*, II, especially *Collin v. Green*, p. 309; *Rice ads. Spear*,
p. 324; *Rantin v. Robertson*, p. 407; and *Compton v. Martin*, p. 427; and
White v. Arnold, pp. 435-436. Showing slaves apprenticed to bricklayers, tailors,
carpenters, shoemakers, and blacksmiths, these cases hold the master craftsman
responsible not only for proper instruction over a considerable period of years,
but also for "sufficient meat, drink, working clothes, lodging and washing, fitting
for an apprentice, during the said term" (p. 407), placing the Negro apprentice on a par with the white during his term of apprenticeship.

Sundays; this would bring in at least a Dawning of the blessed Light amongst them; and which as a Sett or two of those children grew up to Men and Women, would gradually diffuse and increase into open Day.—Parents and Grand Parents Husbands, Wives, Brothers, Sisters, and other Relatives would be daily Teaching and learning of one another. In a word I verily believe, were this method of Instructing the Young Slaves continued, in this or any other Colony, but for the Space of Twenty Years, the Knowledge of the Gospel 'mong the Slaves of such Colony in general (excepting those newly Imported) would not be much inferior to that of the lower sort of white People, Servants & Day Labourers, (Specially in the Country) either in England or elsewhere. . . .[15]

His intention, not to have foreign white teachers, especially from England, the plan to take advantage of the pliability of the young, to select those with good linguistic ability, and especially to develop leadership within the race, showed a conviction and knowledge that progress would come from the Negro himself. While emphatic in his observation of the Negro as a "Nation within a Nation," he was equally firm in his assumption that the Negro's progress would not be inferior to that of white men under similar conditions of life and labour. Confident of the Negro's future, in a final paragraph, he outlined the part the Society could play in setting the plan in motion:

. . . I shall only add on the Subject at present that I'm in great hopes, if once the World could but see this Work undertaken, and carried on, in one uniform and promising Method by the Society, and as a *distinct Branch* of the general good Work they are engaged in; there would be found many Charitable & well disposed Christians both at Home, and in the respective Colonies concerned, who will contribute with a liberal Hand towards it. And if God continues my Life, I dare promise in behalf of this Colony, that immediate Care shall be taken to provide for the Maintenance & Education of such Slaves as shall be purchased by the Society for this Service in it, And I doubt not but in Time they may be reimbursed also from hence the first Cost and Charges.[16]

Of all the many schemes for Negro education, under the institution of slavery, none was more fundamentally wise, practical, far-seeing, than this comprehensive proposal for a plantation school system, freed in advance from features that would cause it to be still-born, or doomed to early failure.

Garden's letter was referred to a Committee of the Society, and

[15] Garden to Bearcroft, May 6, 1740, *op. cit.*
[16] *Ibid.* This important letter can also be found in the *Journal of the S.P.G.* (L.C. Trans.), Vol. VIII, September 19, 1740.

by October of 1740, the members agreed to use £1500 Old South Sea Annuities appropriated for the instruction of Negroes, for support of Mr. Garden's proposal, and that he, together with the Rev. Thomas Hasell of St. Thomas',[17] and the Rev. William Guy of St. Andrew's be empowered to buy two male Negro children such as they should judge most proper for instruction.[18] Further, the Secretary asked Commissary Garden to inform the Society what immediate care should be taken for the maintenance and education of the pupils, and also to inform it by what methods he proposed to introduce them, when instructed, among other slaves to carry out the scheme.[19]

Garden's reply was clear and confident. His methodical mind and personal interest in the expanding project were reflected in his letter in May, 1741, which elaborated on the original scheme as follows:

I have communicated your Letter to my Brethren *Hasell & Guy* & the hon[ble] Society may depend on our punctual Complyance with their Directions for purchasing two young home born male Negroes for them, as soon as we can find such to be disposed of as we shall judge most promising to answer the proposed End. Their Maintenance & Education shall be my own particular care, without any Charge to the Society.

The Method by w[ch] I propose their Service (when Instructed) for the Instruction of others, I perceive has escaped the observation of the Society, contained in the following Words of my former Letter, viz. "And this (that is, the Instruction of the Society's Slaves) accomplished (as I conceive it may be in the Space of two years) then to direct that the S[d] Slaves be employed as "Schoolmasters, in such Places, & under the immediate Care & Inspection of Such Persons, as shall be deemed most proper by their s[d] Attornies for promoting the like Instruction of Slave-Children as *p* 2[d]/ Conclusion."

More clearly to explain my Meaning When the two Slaves, now ordered to be purchased by the Society, shall be duely instructed, I would propose that one of them be appointed a Schoolmaster for the Instruction of the Negroe or Slave Children of Charlestown, under the Care & Inspection of myself & two more such Persons as should appear most likely to make due conscience of discharging the Trust. A Convenient Schoolhouse, if God spares my Life, shall be provided by the Time, where all such Children may be sent for Instruction, & where I doubt not to see a great Number Sent Out of Land for that great & good End.—The other Slave to be employed in like Manner in one or other of the best Settled Country Parishes under the Care &

[17] At Hasell's death on October 9, 1743 or 1744, the Commissary's nephew, the Rev. Alexander Garden, Jr., was appointed as his successor. See C. F. Pascoe, *Two Hundred Years of S.P.G.*, Vol. II, pp. 849.
[18] Report of Committee on Mr. Garden's proposals, in *Journal of S.P.G.* (L.C. Trans.), Vol. VIII, October 17, 1740.
[19] The Committee also asked the Society to consider if this scheme could be of use in the Society's Plantation in Barbados, *ibid.*

Inspection of the Missionary & two other proper Persons of such Parish who will provide also that a School house be erected in such place, as the greatest number of children for 2 Miles round may attend.* And as the Maintenance of such Schoolm[r] will amount but to a meer Trifle not exceding £5 Ster. per Year, the Missionary must have a very poor Influence or very few good X[nts] in his Parish, if ever the Society be put to a penny of any such charge.
* And so on in this Method, as the Society may encrease their Number of such Schoolmasters till the Several Parishes be all supplied. [Footnote in Garden's letter].[20]

Thoroughly convinced by this further exposition of his purposes, the Society hastened to concur in the plan for the schoolmasters as set forth by the Commissary.[21] The ready support of the Society had the backing of the other missionaries in South Carolina, a fact which is all the more striking when it is remembered that the law of 1740 had prohibited "any person from teaching or causing a slave to be taught, or from employing or using a slave as a scribe in any manner of writing."[22] Hasell and Guy were already working with Garden in the organization of the school, and a letter from the Rev. Lewis Jones, of St. Helen's, spoke vigorously for the whole group:

I have Inform'd the Inhabitants of my Parish of the pious design of the Hon[ble] Society of Instructing their Little Negroes born in their respective families in the Principles of the Christian faith, and of

[20] Alexander Garden to (Philip Bearcroft), Charlestown, South Carolina, May 20, 1741, in *S.P.G. MSS.* (L.C. Trans.), B 9, No. 124; same letter in *Journal of S.P.G.* (L.C. Trans.), Vol. VIII, September 18, 1741. Commissary Garden gave the site for the school building. See Mrs. St. Julien Ravenel, *Charleston, The Place and the People* (New York: 1906), pp. 115-116. The repeated assurances that the Society would be placed at little expense in carrying out the plan are a reflection not only of Garden's resourcefulness, but also of the somewhat depleted condition of the Society's funds in England. In 1742 a grant by Royal Letter of £11,444 assisted in meeting the growing deficit. For a table showing income and expenditure of the Society, 1701-1900, see C. F. Pascoe, *Two Hundred Years of the S.P.G.*, Vol. II, pp. 830-832.
[21] Report of the Committee on Mr. Garden's proposals in *Journal of S.P.G.* (L.C. Trans.), Vol. VIII, October 16, 1741.
[22] Quoted from C. W. Birnie, "Education of the Negro in Charleston, South Carolina, prior to the Civil War," in *Journal of Negro History*, XII (January, 1927) pp. 13-21. Birnie assumes, as have other scholars, that the Charleston school, as a result of this law, was composed largely of free Negroes rather than of slaves. It will be noted that the S.P.G. manuscripts definitely establish that, both in concept and in practice, the emphasis was on the education of slaves as well as of the free Negroes, and this in spite of the law. One explanation of this is given in Henry H. Simms, "A Critical Analysis of Abolition Literature 1830-1840," in *The Journal of Southern History*, Vol. VI, No. 3 (August, 1940). Simms says, (p. 372) "Taken at face value, the slave codes were very severe, more so after the rise of the northern abolitionists than before; but slavery was a 'peculiar institution' and what laws normally indicate in regard to public sentiment might not necessarily hold true in the case of these laws. The slave codes were there for use, if necessary, but were not strictly applied, except in case an insurrection had occurred, or threatened, . . ."

Learning them to read, As God Shall Enable them by the Charitable Contributions of Good & well dispos'd people to Carry on the Same. I have also Exhorted them both in publick & in private to Embrace the kind offer, w^n it is in their power. And in Great hopes that (as the Proposal doth not Interfere with their temporal Interest wch has hitherto been the great Stumbling-block in the way of having Grown Slaves Instructed) the Generality of people, If not all, will thankfully accept of So Gracious & good an offer. I have always had my own Negro-Children taught to read, & instructed in the principles of the X^{tian} faith, as Soon as they are capable of receiving Instruction; two wre-of Can read well in the N. Testam^t, and two More Learn to Spell. Our Settlement here are So distant & remote one from ye other, that it renders the Erecting of Schools very difficult & Inconvenient; and Conseq[uen]tly it will require the Longer time & Greater Expence to render this Laudable design of universal Benefit and Advantage. However we need not doubt but God will bless all Sincere Endeavours of promoting his own Glory in the Enlargement of his kingdom: And the faithful promises of Christ's Universal Empire Sh^d Excite & raise our Zeal & diligence to be Instrumental in Our Several Capacities, in Encreasing the Number of his faithful Subjects, & of making the Heathen their Inheritance, & the utmost parts of the Earth his possession. I shall not be wanting from time to time in promoting So Good a work, & in Executing the other branches of my function. . . .[23]

Encouraged by the interest and support his plan had received, Garden lost no time in carrying out the Society's orders. Within six months after the committee had met, he reported to London the purchase of two carefully-selected Negro boys:

. . . the Business of this is to acquaint the Honble Society, that pursuant to their Order, we have purchased Two Negro Boys. (One of 14, & the other 15 years of Age,) in their Name, and for their Use, and have drawn for the Purchase Money (£59:9:3½) on their Treasurer, as directed.

My Brethren & myself endeavoured all we could to comply with the Society's Order sooner, but could not do it to our liking, before January last. The Boys belonged to the Estate of *Alexander Skene* of this Province lately deceased; were both Baptized in their Infancy, & could Say the Church Catechism, when we purchased them, but knew not a Letter of the Alphabet.

The Original Price at Vendue amounted only to £52:5:9 Sterling. But being obliged to purchase also with them their proportional Share of Corn Provision for 4 Months, and to Pay 2½ Month's Interest on

[23] Lewis Jones to Secretary, St. Helen's, South Carolina, September 25, 1741 (brought to England by Mr. Norris, late missionary at Georgia), in *S.P.G. M.SS.* (L.C. Trans.), B 9, No. 137, also in *Journal of S.P.G.* (L.C. Trans.), Vol. VIII, December 18, 1741.

the whole, before the Executors could adjust the Sale, amounts to the remainder of the Sum for which we have drawn. They have been ever since under my Roof, and sent daily to School, and so shall be continued till qualified for the intended Service, which I doubt not they will be in 18 or 20 Months Time.—

The Society may rely on my punctual & especial Care of their Maintenance and Education, & that during my Life they Shall be at no farther Charge about them.

. . . .

P.S. The Two Boys are named, the one *Harry* and the other *Andrew*. I shall cause the Bill of Sale for them to be Recorded, & shall transmit an attested [copy] to the Society.[24]

This business-like account of the progress of a plan grounded so firmly in humanitarian ideas, marks Garden as no visionary carried away by his own enthusiasm for a program. It is a commentary on the curious combination of practicality, vision and courage, characteristic not only of Garden, but of the entire program of the S.P.G. The Bill of Sale, an essential document in putting the plan into operation, by which the Society became a direct slave owner in South Carolina as it already was at Codrington in Barbados, is given in full:

Know all men by these presents that I William Cattell of South Carolina Esq[r] for and in Consideration of the sum of Three hundred and Sixty pounds Current Money of South Carolina to me in hand paid at and before the Sealing and Delivery of these presents by the Reverend Mr. Alexander-Garden & William Guy Attorneys to the Society for the Propagation of the Gospel in Foreign parts, the Receipt whereof I do hereby acknowledge. Have bargained and sold and by these presents do Bargain, Sell and Deliver unto the said Society for the propagation of the Gospel Two Negro boys Named Andrew and Harry, To have and to hold the said Negros Named Andrew and Harry unto the said Society for the propagation of the Gospel their Successors and Assigns to their only proper use and behoof for ever. And I the said William Cattell my Heirs, Ex[ors] and Administrators, the said bargained Premises unto the said Society Their Successors and assign's from and against all persons shall and will Warrant and forever defend by those Presents In Witness whereof I have hereunto set my hand and seal Dated at CharlesTown the fourth day of April in the fifteenth year of his Majesty's Reign Annoque Domini 1742.
Sealed and Delivered/In the presence of Will. Walter Pr. Cattell
W. Cattell
Seal

[24] Alexander Garden to (Philip Bearcroft), Charlestown, South Carolina, April 9, 1742, in *S.P.G. MSS.* (L.C. Trans.), B 10, No. 138. *Journal of the S.P.G.* (L.C. Trans.), Vol. IX, July 16, 1742.

July the 3rd 1742

This day Personally appeared before me Wm. Walter Esqr and being duly Sworn upon the Holy Evangelist of Almighty God, made Oath he as Witness to the within bill of Sale did see Wm Cattell Senr Esqr&Sign the aforesaid bill of Sale."

Ric^d Walter

South Carolina

Secretarys office 4 Septme^r 1742. This Contains a true copy of the Original Bill of Sale Recorded in this office in Book 22. ffot. 103 Esca, J. Hammerton Sec^{ry}.

So. Carolina

Endorsed 1 S. Carolina
            Copy of a bill of Sale
            Of two Negroe Boys
            April 4th 1742
            Read 13 Dec^e 1742[25]

In the same terms, Philip Bearcroft, secretary of the Society, acknowledged the purchase of the Negro boys, completed the business of the transaction, and expressed the belief that "from your [Garden's] kind care and Inspection over them, . . . they will answer the Pious design of their Instruction."[26]

By September, 1742, Commissary Garden was able to report the rapid progress of the two Negroes. He wrote to the Secretary of the Society,

One of the S^d Boys proves of an excellent Genius, & can now (in the Space of 8 months) read the N. Testament exceeding well. In six months more he will be thrôly qualified for the intended Service; & by that Time, with God's Blessing, I shall have a Schoolhouse ready near my own & every thing necessary prepared for his entering upon it here at Charlestown; . . . As to the other Boy, he is of a somewhat slower Genius, but of a milder and better Temper, & to the best of my Judgement will require less Authority and Inspection over him, when he comes to the intended Service, thô possibly 3 or 4 Months later, than the former.[27]

During the next twelve months, Garden's energies on behalf of his school were divided on three fronts. He continued to supervise the education of the two prospective teachers; he solicited funds and

---

[25] Original in *S.P.G. MSS.* (L.C. Trans.), B 10, No. 140.
[26] Philip Bearcroft to Commissary Alexander Garden (Charterhouse, London), September 14, 1742, in *S.P.G. MSS.* (L.C. Trans.), B 10, No. 199.
[27] Alexander Garden to Philip Bearcroft, Charlestown, South Carolina, September 24, 1742, in *S.P.G. MSS.* (L.C. Trans.), B 10, No. 139; also in *Journal of S.P.G.* (L.C. Trans.), Vol. IX, December 17, 1742.

materials for the actual building of the schoolhouse; and lastly, by "publick notice," as well as "Discourses on the subject from the Pulpit,"[28] he educated the people of the parish itself on the desirability of Negro education and urged them to send the slave children to the school. His success is evidenced by the Society's announcement that "assisted by the voluntary Contributions of some good Christians, . . . the School was actually opened on Monday, the 12th Day of *September* preceding [1743], when several Negroe Children were sent thither for Instruction."[29]

The immediate success of the school reflected not only the thoroughness of Garden's initial plans, but the eagerness of the slaves for such an opportunity. Here was factual refutation of the argument sometimes used that the Negroes were both unwilling and unfit to enter scholastic pursuits. Garden wrote in October of 1743:

The N° is already (a Month's time) increased to 'bout 30, & is daily increasing, so as I soon expect more than one Master can well manage. And therefore as the other Youth, [Andrew] of a slower Genius but willing Disposition, is not yet sufficiently qualified to teach by himself, I shall employ him as an assistant in this School for his Improvement, & 'till some other Parish shall provide proper Accommodation for him.

Thus the Society have charitably opened a Door (& with God's Blessing an effectual One) by wch the Light of the Blessed Gospel will speedily & plentifully pour in among the poor Negroes of Charlestown; & without the least farther Charge to the Society (a few Books only excepted) for many years. After the first two Years, the School will annually turn out 30 or 40 young ones, capable to read the Scriptures, & instruct in the Chief Principles of X^tnty amounting in the Space of 20 years to nigh half the Negroes in this Parish; & who will all along be diffusing the same Light and Knowledge to the others, their Parents, Relations, Countrymen & Fellow-Servants. The Service of a young healthy Slave (as the Society's employ'd in the s^d School is) may reasonably be computed at 30 or 40 years; & I hope that none of my Successors will ever impose on the Society any Charge for his Maintenance; for not only will the Masters & Mistresses of the Children he instructs, readily contribute such a Trifle, but 'een the very Slave Parents themselves wou'd gladly do it, thô they should pinch it off their own Backs, & out of their own Bellies; but no such Charge shall either the one or other be put to during my time.

The only Difficulty at present is the want of the following Books,

[28] Alexander Garden to Philip Bearcroft, Charlestown, South Carolina, October 10, 1743, in *S.P.G. MSS.* (L.C. Trans.), B 11, No. 206; *Journal of S.P.G.* (L.C. Trans.), Vol. IX, February 17, 1743-1744.
[29] *An Abstract of the Proceedings of the S.P.G.* printed with Gilbert Sermon (London: 1743-1744) p. 53. (Huntington Library)

wch I pray the Society would be pleased to send me as soon as possible, viz.

Spelling Books 100
Testaments   50
Bibles   50
Psalters with Common Prayer (printed by *March* for Staners) 50[30]

There is, perhaps, no more vivid appeal in all literature for the right of the Negro to education, than is contained in this letter. Depending as it did on the organizational ability of one man, Garden's school was, nevertheless, grounded strongly in his own confidence in a race which sought education for its children "tho they should pinch it off their own Backs, & out of their own Bellies." Garden's enthusiasm for the Charleston school in action was shared by the Society in London, which is borne out by their reception of Garden's report. Speaking for the Society, its Secretary wrote:

Your Letters of Octr 10th and of Jan: 31st have both been laid before the Society, which rejoices much in the happy Progress of the Negroe School, and to help it forward have sent you with this, 50 Bibles, 50 Common Prayer Books, 50 N: Testaments and 100 Spelling Books, as likewise 100 Copies of Observations on the Conduct of the Methodist, 50 of the last Anniversary Sermon, 20 of the Englishman Instructed in the Choice of His Religion, and 12 of the Rational Communicant to be distributed among all the Missionaries, as you shall think proper.[31]

On its first anniversary the school was flourishing, the number of pupils having doubled. Garden's account of the progress of the scholars was a tribute to the young Negro, Harry, who was presiding in the schoolroom. The Commissary wrote:

The Society's Negro School, under my Care, succeeds even beyond my first Hopes or Expectation. Upwards of Sixty Negro Children are now Daily taught in it, the Principles of our holy Religion, & to read the Scriptures; (15 of which are now capable to read the Testament very well, & 20 more are in Psalters, & the rest in the Alphabet and Spelling Books) and the Number still gradually increasing, so as sufficiently to employ both the Society's Youths to Teach them. And indeed one of the said Youths, named Andrew, tho an exceeding good natur'd & willing Creature, yet proves so weak on understanding, that I'm afraid he will not be soon Qualified to Teach alone; & wish the Society would give a discretionary Power to sell him, & Purchase another of better Genius for Learning in his Room.

[30] Alexander Garden to [Philip Bearcroft], Charlestown, South Carolina, October 10, 1743, in *S.P.G. MSS.* (L.C. Trans.), B 11, No. 206; *Journal of S.P.G.* (L.C. Trans.), Vol. IX, February 17, 1743-1744.
[31] Philip Bearcroft to Commissary Garden (Charterhouse, London), July 7, 1744, in *S.P.G. MSS.* (L.C. Trans.), B 13, p. 52.

. . . The poor Negro School is in Distress for want of Books, and I'm in Pain lest those I wrote for last year, be taken into France or Spain, on their way; for they are not yet come to hand.[32]

Apparently the problem of Andrew's progress, which had been troubling the Commissary for some time, had reached the point of decision. A request, in the previous March, from the Rev. William Guy, and the vestry of St. Andrews, that one of the Negroes purchased by the Society be sent to them, promising to use their best endeavor "to promote so pious and laudable [a] design,"[33] may have forced Garden to the reluctant conclusion that Andrew, the logical choice for this position, would never be able to teach alone. Therefore, he requested from the Society discretionary power to sell the amiable Andrew and purchase a Negro "of better Genius." In place of this expedient, the Society gave Commissary Garden instructions to send Andrew to Mr. Alleyne, the Society's Manager on the Codrington Estates in Barbados. Philip Bearcroft wrote to Garden,

. . . as to the Negroe Youth Andrew, they desire you to send him to M[r] Alleyne the Society's manager to their Plantations at Codrington College in Barbados, by the first opportunity, and that you Purchase another Negroe Youth to be bred Schoolmaster in his stead, and draw upon the Society's Treasurer, Thomas Tryon Esq[r] in Crutched Fryers for the Expence of sending Andrew to Barbados, and for the Purchase of the other in his stead. . . .[34]

Commissary Garden answered this proposal in person, on a visit to England during the summer of 1746.[35] Because Andrew and his parents were natives of South Carolina, he asked that the youth be allowed to remain there instead of being sent to Codrington College.

[32] Alexander Garden to [Philip Bearcroft], South Carolina, October 18, 1744, in *S.P.G. MSS.* (L.C. Trans.), B 12, No. 119; also in *Journal of S.P.G.* (L.C. Trans.), Vol. X, March 15, 1744-1845.
[33] William Guy to Philip Bearcroft, St. Andrew's Parish, South Carolina, March 26, 1743-1744, in *Journal of S.P.G.* (L.C. Trans.), Vol. IX, September 21, 1744. This letter can also be found in the Vestry Minutes of St. Andrew's Church, *S.P.G. MSS.* (L.C. Trans.), B 12, No. 84.
[34] Philip Bearcroft to Commissary Garden, Charterhouse, London, April 27, 1745, in *S.P.G. MSS.* (L.C. Trans.), B 13, p. 349. Andrew was to be employed as a servant in Codrington College, see *Journal of S.P.G.* (L.C. Trans.), Vol. X, March 15, 1744-1745. For an account of the Codrington College and Estates, see F. J. Klingberg, "British Humanitarianism at Codrington" in *Journal of Negro History*, XXIII, No. 4 (October, 1938), pp. 451-486.
[35] Commissary Garden was in ill health, afflicted with palsy of his head, and thought a visit to England would help him. He arrived June 24, 1746, and returned to South Carolina in the fall of that year. John Fordyce, from Prince Frederick's parish had commented on Garden's illness in November, 1745, while mentioning an epidemic of yellow fever in Charleston. See John Fordyce to [Secretary], Prince Frederick's parish, South Carolina, November 4, 1745, in *Journal of S.P.G.* (L.C. Trans.), Vol. X. April 18, 1746.

Garden also asked that the Society give him a power of attorney,[36] in order that he could complete the sale of Andrew and with the money thus obtained, purchase another Negro youth in Andrew's stead. To this the Society agreed.[37]

The highlight of Garden's trip to England was his address before the Society as to the progress of the Charleston Negro School. The Society's abstract of this great defense of the Negro, and his right to learning was as follows:

. . . the Society's Negroe School at *Charles Town* which had then subsisted but two Years and eight Months, had sent out 28 Children, sufficiently instructed according to the Intention of that School; and that it was increased to the Number of 70, *viz* 55 Children taught of Days, and 15 grown Slaves taught of Evenings, when their Days Work is over; That he plainly perceives a very general and earnest Desire

[36] *Journal of S.P.G.* September 19, 1746. (L.C. Trans.), Vol. X, Garden was given the power of attorney in order to sell Andrew. It can be found in *S.P.G. MSS.* (L.C. Trans.), B 1, No. 241, pp. 878a, October 13, 1746.

Know all Men by these presents That the *Society* for the Propagation of the Gospel in Foreign Parts, *have* made, constituted & appointed, & by these presents Do make Constitute & appoint the Reverend Alexander Garden, Clerk, Rector of the parish of St. Philip, in Charles Town, his parish, in the province of South Carolina in America, & Commissary in ye s⁴ province of the Right Rev⁴ Fa[the]ʳ in God Edmund Lord Bishop of London, their lawfull Attorney, the said province, for them the s⁴ Society, & in their Name and behalf, to contact & agree for the Sale & Disposal of & to sell & also to execute & perfect any Bill of Sale or Deed of Conveyance for one Negro youth being the property of the s⁴ Society, & Called or known by the Name of Andrew, to any person who shall be inclined to purchase yᵉ s⁴ Negro, & for the best price that reasonably can be gotten for yᵉ same; And to do acknowledge & perform all manner of things, whatever, wch shall be requisite to make such Sale & Conveyance most absolute & effectual; The s⁴ Society hereby giving their whole power & Auth^ity . . . unto their s⁴ Attorney. And Ratifying & confirming, & promising to hold for good, firm, valid & effectual All that he shall legally do or cause to be done in the p'rmes by virtue of these presents. *In witness* whereof the s⁴ Society have caused to be hereunto affixed their Common seal this day of Octoʳ, in yᵉ 20th year of yᵉ Reign of our Sovereign Lord, Geo, yᵉ 2d, by the Grace of God, of Gr. Br, France, & Irel⁴, K, Def of yᵉ Faith, & so forth, & in yᵉ year of our Lord 1746. By order of the Society

Drt Power of Atty

Endorsed   Society   Oct 1746
              to   dv
              Com^ry Garden   (Delivered)   13. Oct. 1746

[37] Andrew was not sold until 1750, the reason for the delay being because he had received a bruise on his breast, and much care was taken to heal the injury before he was sold. See Alexander Garden to [Philip Bearcroft], Charles Town, September 9, 1750, in *S.P.G. MSS.* (L.C. Trans.), B 18, No. 182. Philip Bearcroft acknowledged receipt of the sale price, 200 pounds currency, or 28£ 11s, 5d, Sterling with a comment on the school as follows: ". . . the Money for the Negro Andrew hath been receiv'd by the Treasʳ of the Society, which return with their Thanks to you on that Accᵗ & for yr good Care and prudent Managemᵗ of the Negroe School, the Success of which they rejoice in. . . ." See Philip Bearcroft to Alexander Garden, Charterhouse, London, August 5, 1751, in *S.P.G. MSS.* (L.C. Trans.), B 19, p. 15.

among Negroe Parents of having their Children instructed, and also an Emulation among many of them that are capable of Instruction; and therefore, as he is now convinced by Experience, that the same Method will answer in other Places, he humbly recommends it to Practice.[38]

Garden's plan was no longer only a theory. It was an actuality whose results had justified its existence, and he had no hesitation in recommending to the Society the expansion of the project into other spheres of its work. Perhaps unconsciously speaking for the whole race were the grown slaves, coming for instruction in the evening, "when their Days Work is over"; and the earnest desire of the Parents to have their children attend the school. In August, 1747, the Society received word that the School was full of children and in the past two years forty scholars had been discharged capable of reading the Bible and well instructed in the Church Catechism. In addition, many grown slaves continued to come in the evenings for instruction.[39] Reports for the next two years showed that about fifteen completed their courses in 1748, and five or six others were nearly finished with their work.[40] Again the next year, Commissary Garden told of his successes:

I have only to add that the Society's negro school at Charles Town continues to go on with all desirable success and last year discharged about 17 scholars duly qualified as proposed. . . .

P.S. I hope to receive a fresh supply of books for the negro school by the first ships, now on their way, hither from London. . . .[41]

Such a request for books, contained in almost every letter, is worthy of consideration both because it points again to the function of such an agency as the S.P.G. in supplying a pioneer colony with reading material, and also because of the type of books requested. Not only ecclesiastical matter, but spelling books, primers, and the like, the tools of reading and writing, were requested for the Charleston school. Dr. Carter G. Woodson has pointed out the difference between instruction for the purpose of religious education, and the ap-

[38] *An Abstract of the Proceedings of the S.P.G.* Printed with Thomas Sermon (London: 1746), pp. 55-56. (Huntington Library)
[39] Alexander Garden to [Philip Bearcroft], Charlestown, South Carolina, August 22, 1747, in *Journal of S.P.G.* (L.C. Trans.), Vol. X, January 15, 1747-1748.
[40] Alexander Garden to Philip Bearcroft, Charlestown, South Carolina, December 22, 1748, in *S.P.G. MSS.* (L.C. Trans.), B 16, No. 146.
[41] Alexander Garden to Philip Bearcroft, Charlestown, South Carolina, September 9, 1750, in *S.P.G. MSS.* (L.C. Trans.), B 18, No. 182; success of school also noted in *An Abstract of the Proceedings of the S.P.G.* Printed with Trevor Sermon (London: 1750).

proach of some sects which depended entirely upon testimony and experience and whose work among the Negroes might be termed "Religion without Letters."[42] In general, the Anglican church encouraged the practice of properly instructing the Negroes before baptism and thus, in addition to the human rights which baptism signified for the Negro, he gained a literacy which marked an important step in his advance as time went on.

At the end of eight years of the school's existence, Garden was able to describe its progress in glowing terms:

... I sincerely wish that the Society were eye witnessess of the success of their negro school in Charlestown and how serviceable it proves for spreading the light of the blessed Gospel among these poor heathens, and how much they rejoice in it. I take leave to repeat my request for a fresh supply of books for them, of the several sorts and numbers as sent formerly, only taking leave to observe that Dyches spelling books are much more proper and useful than those which were last sent.[43]

So firmly was the school established that when, in 1752, a violent tempest[44] blew ". . . the Negro School flat to the Ground and destroyed among other things most of the poor Negroes Books."[45] Garden was able to write stoutly that "About a month after . . . I had another ready prepared for that service; and the said school goes on with the usual success."[46]

Alexander Garden resigned as commissary in 1755, returning to England where he intended to live the rest of his life. But his interest in the missionary work in progress in South Carolina, and in the colony itself, brought him back to Charleston, where he died in 1756.[47]

Garden's successor as Commissary was the Rev. Richard Clarke,

[42] See Carter G. Woodson, *The African Background Outlined* (Washington, D.C.: 1936), p. 339.
[43] Alexander Garden to Philip Bearcroft, Charlestown, February 14, 1750-1751, in *S.P.G. MSS.* (L.C. Trans.), B 18, p. 183.
[44] This hurricane, famous in the annals of Charleston, is described in B. R. Carroll, *Historical Collections of South Carolina,* II, pp. 474-476 with the conclusion that "many people were drowned, and others much hurt by the fall of houses: For about forty miles round Charlestown, there was hardly a plantation that did not loose every out-house upon it, and the roads, for years afterwards, were incumbered with trees blown and broken down."
[45] *An Abstract of the Proceedings of the S.P.G.* printed with Drummond Sermon (London: 1753), pp. 53-54. (Huntington Library)
[46] Alexander Garden to Philip Bearcroft, Charlestown, South Carolina, December 29, 1752, (post script) in *S.P.G. MSS.* (L.C. Trans.), B 20, No. 134.
[47] An interesting account of Garden's farewell sermon at St. Philip's, is given in Frederick Dalcho, *The Protestant Episcopal Church in South Carolina,* pp. 167-171.

rector of St. Philip's Church in Charlestown.[48] His continued interest in the school was shown by the Society's report concerning him in 1755 that he . . .

acknowledges the Receipt of a Box of Books, which he had taken Care to deliver as directed, together with the Letters to the Missionaries of that Province, and promises to tread in the Steps of his very worthy Predecessor Mr. Garden (who, disabled thro' Infirmities, had resigned that Church) in inspecting the Negroe School begun by him, which continued to do much Good, and consists of near 70 Boys and Girls, for whose Use the Society, at Mr. Clarke's Request, hath sent Bibles, Common Prayer Books, Psalters, and other proper pious Books.[49]

The Society agreed to send Clarke £5 worth of books, and a year later the Abstract of Proceedings reports:

The Rev. Mr. Clarke . . . writes, that the Negroe School there is full of children and well attended; but he laments the great negligence of the White People in general in regard to the Blacks, there not being so much as one Civil Establishment in the Colony for the Christian Instruction of fifty thousand Negro Slaves. The Clergy do their duty towards it, but besides many other difficulties and obstructions in their way, it is by no Means in their Power to perform the more immediate Duties of their proper Stations. . . .[50]

Worthy of special note is Clarke's comment on the lack of a "civil Establishment" for the instruction of the slaves. This fragment very possibly points to the Society's ultimate goal, that of state-supported schools for the Negroes. In the same way had the S.P.G., on its entry into the colony, pioneered in the movement for free schools "for the instruction of youth in grammar and other arts and sciences, and also in the principles of the Christian religion." Evidence of this work are the Assembly laws of 1710 and 1712, lending state support for such schools, in view of the fact that "several well-disposed Christians by the last will had given several sums of money for the founding of a free school."[51]

[48] Richard Clarke is listed as a dissenter by John Cooke in *The Preachers Assistant (After the Manner of Mr. Letsome) containing . . . the Texts of Sermons . . . By Divines of the Church of England and by the Dissenting Clergy. . . ,* (Oxford, 1783) I, p. 2, and II, p. 79 (Title of Volume Two—*An Historical Register of all the Authors in the Series alphabetically disposed, with their Titles, Degrees, and Preferments. . . .*)

[49] *An Abstract of the Proceedings of the S.P.G.* printed with Hayter Sermon (London: 1755), p. 57. (Huntington Library)

[50] *An Abstract of the Proceedings of the S.P.G.* Printed with Cornwallis Sermon (London: 1756), p. 50. (Huntington Library)

[51] Quoted from a paper entitled "Colonial Education in South Carolina," by Edward McCrady, Jr., printed in, Colyer Meriwether, *History of Higher Education in South Carolina with a Sketch of the Free School System* (Washington:

The Rev. Mr. Clarke's successful term of supervision lasted until 1759 when the care of the school fell to the Rev. Robert Smith, who was to play so important a role in the re-organization of the church following the Revolution.[52] Smith's first letter to the Society, after taking over his duties, read in part:

Upon ye Resignation of ye Revd Mr Clarke, ye late Rector of St Philips Charl's Town; was by ye Vestry appointed to ye charge of ye Parish. And being informed that Mr Clarke transacted ye Business of ye Society in dispersing ye Pamphlets etc. which ye Society thought proper to send over. As it is ye Duty of every Clergyman to further & promote every Step necessary to ye advancement of Religion, especially in these parts, will I hope apologize for ye Liberty of these Times. As far as my Abilities can be of Service, shall always be ready to obey ye Commands of ye Society. . . . The School for ye education of Negro's, (of which ye Society were founders) falls now under my Care; & as I find Mr Clarke receiv'd Books for ye Children, which are now all disposed of; if Primers, Common prayer Books, & Bibles are sent over, they will be very Acceptable to ye School, which is now in a very flourishing State, there being 50, or 60 Negro Children. . . .[53]

In 1760, Smith disclosed that the school was not in as flourishing a condition as he could wish, due to the ravages of ". . . Small Pox; which was very fatal in March and April: . . .[54] At the same time the Cherokee war, then in progress, added to the insecurity of the colony

---

1889), pp. 211-222. McCrady states (p. 213) that "South Carolina during colonial times was very little, if any, behind even Massachusetts in the matter of public education."

[52] Smith's influence on the established church in South Carolina is described in C. C. Tiffany, *History of the Protestant Episcopal Church* (New York: 1895), pp. 234-5. "Though an Englishman educated at Cambridge University, he was a decided and consistent patriot. At first inclined to sustain the crown, on the appeal to arms he sided with the colonists, stirring up the people to resistance by his preaching, and, at the siege of Charleston, serving in the ranks. To his influence and example is to be largely attributed the fact that, while in the Northern colonies not one in ten of the church clergy opposed Great Britain, in South Carolina, three-fourths of them were patriots. His banishment by the British, when Charleston surrendered to them, only endeared him the more to the people on his return after the war. He at once set to work with characteristic energy to restore the waste places. It was mainly by his advice that the church in South Carolina sent her delegates to the earliest General Convention held at Philadelphia for the organization of the Protestant Episcopal Church; . . . he was elected the first bishop of the diocese of South Carolina in 1795."

[53] Robert Smith to [Secretary], Charl's [sic] Town, South Carolina, July 25, 1759, in *S.P.G. MSS.* (L.C. Trans.), B 5, No. 252. In response to his request for books "the Society have given Directions to be sent to Mr. *Smith* with their Thanks for his very obliging Letter." See *An Abstract of the Proceedings of the S.P.G.* printed with Ashburnham Sermon (London: 1760), p. 62. (Huntington Library)

[54] Robert Smith to Secretary, Charles Town, South Carolina, November 18, 1760, in *S.P.G. MSS.* (L. C. Trans.), B 5, No. 253.

and it was not until April of the following year that the school returned to normal.[55]

The Charleston school was deemed an important and useful institution until 1764. It announced each year a large enrollment and a
number of graduates. At about this time Harry, the teacher, died
and as no other Negroes were found competent to take charge of the
school, it was discontinued.[56] It is not clear why the S.P.G. did not
attempt to continue the school. In some measure it was probably due
to the fact that the Society had discontinued financial assistance in
South Carolina, and transferred its sphere of influence to other
centers. Something of the initial enthusiasm had doubtless died with
Alexander Garden and Harry, the Negro teacher, both pioneers and
creators. The courageous leadership of the founders, in the period
of the Society's activity, evidently did not carry over vigorously into
the period of home rule of the church. Then loss of the Society's
stimulus began to be felt and the experimental school felt the force
of the prohibitory law of 1740, and of the pressure of reaction which,
during the Revolutionary period and thereafter, was to gain strength.
It is, therefore, a fair assumption that the death of the two leaders,
and the withdrawal of the Society from the scene, ended the School.

Certain it is that such laboratories were a powerful means of
examining the arguments against the education of slaves. And more
important still, they were the beginnings of a tradition built so well
that it survived the period of reaction at the opening of the nineteenth
century, and found vivid expression in the words of a planter who,
in May, 1845, at a most critical time in race relations wrote from
the parish of Prince George, Winyaw:

. . . Of my own negroes, and those in my immediate neighborhood, I
may speak with confidence: they are attentive to religious instruction,
and greatly improved in intelligence and morals, in domestic relations,
&c. Those who have grown up under religious training are more intelligent, and generally, though not always, more improved than those

---

[55] Robert Smith to Philip Bearcroft, Charles Town, South Carolina, April 29,
1761, in *S.P.G. MSS.* (L.C. Trans.), B 5, No. 254. In this same letter Mr. Smith
thanks the Society for the books he received from them.

[56] Frederick Dalcho, *An Historical Account of the Protestant Episcopal Church
in South Carolina*, p. 192 ff. See Footnote, p. 149, in which is stated that in 1819
there were colored persons in Charlestown who were taught to read by Harry
and Andrew. Mrs. St. Julien Ravenel, *Charleston, the Place and the People*
(New York, 1906), pp. 115-116, states, "The school . . . went on prosperously for
twenty years. The one 'boy' died and the other took to evil ways. Why none of
their scholars were put in their places is not known, but the plan was discontinued."

who have received instruction as adults. Indeed the intelligence which, as a class, they are acquiring is worthy of deep consideration."

R. F. W. Allston[57]

On the plantation and in subsequent Negro schools, in South Carolina,[58] Garden's convictions regarding the right of the Negro to education, and the example of Harry, who shared his skills with his race, endured, offering a challenge even today to the people of the white race and the black.

[57] See *Proceedings of the Meeting in Charleston, South Carolina, May 13-15, 1845, on the Religious Instruction of the Negroes, together with the Report of the Committee and the Address to the Public.* (Charleston: 1845), p. 35. (Huntington Library)

[58] For an account of other Negro schools begun before 1860, see C. W. Birnie, "Education of the Negro in Charlestown, South Carolina, prior to the Civil War," in *Journal of Negro History,* XII (January, 1927), pp. 13-21. See also Rufus E. Clement, "The Church School as a Factor in Negro Life," in *ibid.,* pp. 5-12 wherein he shows that 70% of the institutions of higher education for Negroes in the South are Church schools, and analyzes their contributions (p. 9) "along four important lines. First, they have taught race pride; second, they have developed Negro leadership; third, they have been instruments working for the adaptation of the Negro to his environment; fourth, they have been centers of independent thought." Herein is well expressed the heritage of the Charleston Negro School.

CHAPTER VI

IN BROAD REVIEW

THE S.P.G., as the original interventionist in South Carolina in the eighteenth century, uncovered all the problems of race relationships between the white men and the Negro that have appeared at any time since. The ideology behind the Society can best be analysed in its Instructions to the Clergy, the early Annual Reports, and the Annual Sermons[1] preached before it by eminent men of the calibre of Berkeley, Butler, and Shipley, the friend of Franklin. The wide scope of S.P.G. experimentation must be kept in mind. It was not the assignment of the missionary on the ground to agitate for emancipation. This policy would have ended his usefulness at once, both in the West Indies and in the South. In general, as the opposition to the slave trade gained momentum, as it did after the third quarter of the century, the pressure of opinion against slavery itself increased. The outburst of Bishop Warburton in his Sermon, February, 1766, may be described as a blistering attack upon the slave trade, the true parent of many evils connected with slavery itself.

In the beginning, the Society based its program on an acceptance of slavery and racial inequality of status. But it became convinced, through its missionary reports, that, though the program would be slow of realization, the Negro in slavery could be Christianized and educated, in order that he could assume his proper role in the social structure.[2] Furthermore, this effort was seen as an inescapable Chris-

[1] For an analysis of the leading ideas of the Sermons, showing the developing and changing mood of the century see F. J. Klingberg, *Anglican Humanitarianism in Colonial New York*, pp. 11-48. Some of the most famous sermons were those by: William Beveridge, Bishop of St. Asaph, 1707; William Fleetwood, Bishop of St. Asaph, 1711; George Berkeley, Dean of Londonderry, 1732; Joseph Butler, Bishop of Bristol, 1739; Martin Benson, Bishop of Gloucester, 1740; Thomas Secker, Bishop of Oxford, 1741; Philip Bearcroft, Secretary of the Society, 1745; William Warburton, Bishop of Gloucester, 1766; Jonathan Shipley, Bishop of St. Asaph, 1773; Beilby Porteus, Bishop of Chester, 1783. An almost complete file of these sermons can be found either in the Huntington Library or the Library of Congress. The Sermon was often printed with the Abstract of Proceedings for the previous year.

[2] For a discussion of the growing movement for "instruction as a prerequisite to emancipation," see Carter G. Woodson, *Education of the Negro Prior to 1861* (Washington, D.C. 1919), pp. 93-121.

tian duty. How, asked Bishop Fleetwood, as early as 1711, could the slave owner hope for salvation himself, while denying it to his Negroes?[3] The force of such an argument in an eighteenth century world, is reflected in the attitudes of some of the planters, as the missionaries often report. In order to attain these ends, the Society tried to modify the plantation discipline, designed for economic productivity, to the extent that some time for its activities could be set aside.

The Negro, as against the Indian and all immigrant groups, had been brought by violence[4] from his lost African world, and was therefore without normal contact with a home base culture of his own. This isolation predisposed him for an adaptation to the white man's civilization.[5] Here in South Carolina, thus separated from his African tribes, he could not, under slavery and in a white community, work out a completely distinct African culture, nor did he, as Philip Alexander Bruce anticipated in 1889, revert to African mores, of which he was losing knowledge. He learned readily, eagerly came to Church in large numbers, and so impressed his ability upon the missionaries that, as early as 1713,[6] they were ready for legislative action towards compulsory education. At the same time they recognized, in the opposition such a plan aroused, the seeds of reaction which might liquidate the entire program and place the Negro more definitely as an isolated group in society, rather than as an integral part of it.

Properly to assess this policy on the part of the S.P.G. missionaries, it must be borne in mind that the environment in which they found themselves was dominated more by rice than by righteousness. From its introduction at the beginning of the century, concurrently with the Society, this cereal was the backbone of an expanding commercial prosperity which, by 1765, made South Carolina "perhaps

[3] See *Sermon* preached before the S.P.G. by William Fleetwood, Lord Bishop of St. Asaph, February 16, 1710-1711 (Huntington Library), reproduced in Frank J. Klingberg, *Anglican Humanitarianism in Colonial New York,* pp. 195-212, especially p. 204.

[4] Broadly speaking, the assumption is here made that kidnapping of the white man in Europe was on a relatively small scale and that even penal transportation does not compare in volume with the African slave trade. Indian slavery, likewise, was not on a large scale.

[5] For the story of this recurring pattern of race relationship in the South from 1815 to the present, see Ch. X and XII in Ralph Henry Gabriel's *The Course of American Democratic Thought;* Ch. X, "The Civil War and the American Democratic Faith"; Ch. XII; "The Re-Creation of the American Union, 1865-1917."

[6] See "Instructions of the Clergy of South Carolina given to Mr. [Gideon] Johnson on his coming away for England . . ." in *S.P.G. MSS.* (L.C. Trans.), A 8, pp. 427-430, printed earlier in this study.

the most prosperous area on the continent."[7] This prosperity, instead
of consolidating British domination, served to heighten the desire
for self-determination, which underlay all South Carolina history,
from the overthrow of the Lords Proprietors in 1720, through the
American Revolution, and which finally culminated in the Civil War.
If the question is raised as to why missionaries of the Church of England did not more vigorously pursue their efforts toward legislative
action in behalf of Negro education, the answer may be found in the
results of such action in the political field in 1776. As representatives
of British humanitarian sentiment, the S.P.G. missionaries were probably more correct in their assessment of the force of an aroused
hostile colonial opinion than were the civil authorities in London.
Adjusting their work to conditions as they found them,[8] they en-
deavored with tact and vigor to forward the advancement of the
Negro in slavery. As has been seen, some of them left legacies toward
the support of schools. And a vital part of the program to help the
Negro develop leaders among his own race was the parallel effort
to interest the white man in cooperation to this end.

Pertinent is the position of the free Negroes in Charleston before
the Civil War. They, as "a respectable, economically independent, and
class-conscious group,"[9] achieved material and cultural gains, while
living in a slave system,[10] which have been largely overlooked by stu-

[7] From Ulrich B. Phillips, *American Negro Slavery*, p. 88. Phillips states
(p. 87) that in 1765 the rice export of South Carolina was 32,000 tons valued
at £225,000 sterling.

[8] The unique position of South Carolina in the colonial scene, is given in *The
Cambridge History of the British Empire*, I, pp. 394-395. The tropical climate
and culture of rice, which demanded black labor in the Charleston district, was
not echoed in neighboring North Carolina. The quoted population figures support
this statement graphically. In 1763 South Carolina had approximately 70,000
blacks to 30,000 whites, while in North Carolina in the same year these figures
were reversed, showing 77,000 whites, and 16,000 blacks in 1760. In North
Carolina, as stated in Charles M. and Evangeline W. Andrews (Editors), *Journal of a Lady of Quality, 1774-1776*, p. 153, there existed "a most disgusting
equality." Over Virginia, where the social structure was more like its own,
South Carolina had the advantage of the colonial center of Charleston.

[9] See E. Horace Fitchett, "Traditions of the Free Negro in Charleston, South
Carolina," in *Journal of Negro History*, XXV, 2 (April, 1940), p. 143. This study
reveals that "in 1819 they [free Negroes] were listed in thirty branches of work.
Among them were 11 carpenters, 10 tailors, 22 seamstresses, 6 shoemakers and
one owner of a hotel. Thirty years later they were listed in fifty different types of
work. In 1859 there were among them 50 carpenters, 43 tailors, 9 shoemakers, and
21 butchers. In these trades some of them became wealthy. In the above mentioned years, 353 persons paid taxes on property and one-hundred-and-ninety were
slave holders. The property on which they paid taxes was assessed at $724,570,
and the amount paid on slaves aggregated $1,170."

[10] Population statistics for this period, as quoted in U. B. Phillips, *American
Negro Slavery*, p. 95, reveal how thoroughly slavery had established itself. To

dents. As the artisans of the community, these people were not only
acquiring economic independence, but with their own organizations,
such as the Brown Fellowship Society (organized in 1790), were cooperating with white men in building institutions of education and
benevolence for the benefit of the entire race.

In the light of the Negro's subsequent emancipation by edict, the
S.P.G. program and policies also raise some questions. Did sudden
emancipation open to the Negroes, in the north as well as the south,
the opportunities for education and self-advancement within the
social system which slavery had often denied him? Or did it tend, in
some cases, to remove such foothold as he had attained by an innate
diplomacy and natural aptitudes, as well as by intervention on his
behalf, and tend temporarily to isolate him from opportunity as a
racial group?[11]

The tenets of the thesis of cooperation rather than segregation,
advocated by the S.P.G. are borne out in many quarters and by
various leaders of the Negro race. After a recent act of the New
York Legislature placing heavy penalties upon union discrimination,
a statement was made by the Negro president of one Union: "The
Negro workers are part and parcel of all workers . . . [but] they
cannot hope to gain equality within trade unions by legislation."[12]

---

quote Phillips: "In the four South Carolina parishes of St. Andrew's, St.
John's Colleton, St. Paul's and St. Stephen's the census-takers of 1790 found
393 slaveholders with an average of 33.7 slaves each, as compared with a total
of 28 non-slaveholding families. In these and seven more parishes, comprising
together the rural portion of the area known politically as the Charleston District, there were among 1643 heads of families, 1318 slaveholders owning 42,949
slaves."

[11] A recent study of Negro educational opportunities is described by Gould
Beech, "Schools for a Minority," in *Survey-Graphic*, Vol. 28 (Oct., 1939), pp.
615-618. He reports that in the Mississippi Delta and South Carolina Tidewater
counties, difference in outlay between Negroes and whites is 15-1 for education.
In the north the difference is in the age and attractiveness of school buildings and
the relative ability of teachers, or in "individual discrimination" in mixed schools.
In 18 states and the District of Columbia, segregaton is mandatory by law, while
in the northern metropolitan centers there is a *de facto* segregation.

[12] See "Equality by Law" in *Time*, February 12, 1940, p. 21. The beginnings of
racial discrimination in a competitive skilled labor market even before emancipation have been pointed out by Carter G. Woodson, and are indicative of attitudes
which emancipation fostered in some cases. Says Woodson, "Before 1860 most
southern mechanics, machinists, local manufacturers, contractors, and railroad
men with the exception of conductors were Negroes. Against this custom of
making colored men such an economic factor the white mechanics frequently
protested. The riots against Negroes occurring in Cincinnati, Philadelphia, New
York, and Washington during the thirties and forties owed their origin mainly
to an ill feeling between the white and colored skilled laborers. The white artisans
prevailed upon the legislatures of Pennsylvania, Maryland, and Georgia to enact
measures hostile to their rivals." See Carter G. Woodson, *Education of the
Negro Prior to 1861*, p. 284. Also see *ibid.*, p. 235, for the statement that "As
late as 1840 there were more intelligent blacks in the South than in the North,"

Even Lincoln, in his plans for the removal to the West Indies and Central America of experimental groups for colonization there, seems to have been surprised that it was impossible to get any considerable number of free Negroes to agree to remove themselves from their homes and their country in America. But the S.P.G. missionaries saw them as permanently of this country, and an integral part of the American world.

Only in recent times, when the animosities bred by the slavery controversy and reconstruction have begun to clear, has this point of view come to be fully understood. Not as a people apart, but as a "nation within a nation," in the words of Alexander Garden, is the Negro receiving full credit for his important role in the building of America; and his participation, in common with the whites, in the triumphs and in the trials of this nation. The effects of Negro migration to the North in recent times, the new movement towards the West, along with that of uprooted early native white stock have not yet been sufficiently assessed. But in the course of the new industrialization of the South, it may be expected that the same problems as with white labor will emerge. Sir John Harris' tour of the South, reported in the Manchester *Guardian*[13] during which he noted many conditions of life as lower than the standards of living in Africa,[14] confirms the convictions that white and black, in the lower economic levels, have suffered together from the same conditions.[15]

Of some special significance, in this connection, is the fact that the missionaries of the S.P.G. received moral support as well as financial assistance from far-away England, and were thus furnished a back-

[13] See Sir John Harris, "In the Cotton Belt," a series of two articles appearing in the Manchester *Guardian*, Vol. 37, Nos. 13 and 14 (September 24, 1937 and October 1, 1937). Harris says (p. 255), "For my part I have never seen such poverty and squalor,—not even in Central Africa." The system "which still holds the South in the grip of slavery," dominated by absentee ownership, landlords and sharecroppers, produced more poverty-stricken whites than Negroes, "the proportion being approximately 5,000,000 whites to 3,000,000 coloured persons." An awareness of the implications of this situation is more acute, he believes, in the South than in the North. He concludes (p. 276), "the South is showing a . . . recognition that the Negro is its job, . . . if only because otherwise the South will sink with him. It is agreed on all hands that pro-Negro sentiment is waning in the North without much good reason, while it is waxing in the South for solid reasons."

[14] For a comprehensive and able report of African living standards today see Lord Hailey, *An African Survey* (London: 1938). Particularly interesting for comparison with conditions in the South are the chapters on "Law and Justice," VII; "The Problems of Labor," XI; "Health," XVII; "Education," XVIII; and "Co-operative Organization," XXI.

[15] See "Visit of the Secretary of the Society to the United States of America" in *Anti-Slavery Reporter and Aborigines' Friend*, V, Vol. 27, No. 4 (January, 1938), pp. 171-172; and Maury Maverick, "Let's Join the United States" in *Virginia Quarterly Review*, XV, No. 1 (Winter, 1939), pp. 64-77.

log against the opposition and indifference which grew from economic roots. Perhaps it is not entirely by chance that the Revolution, which put an abrupt end to the Society's program, in the thirteen colonies, was followed by so reactionary a policy toward Negro education that "by 1835 it was almost impossible for a Negro to attend school below the Mason and Dixon Line except when disguised."[16]

Indeed the dates which marked the eclipse as well as the rise of efforts toward Negro education in the post-Revolutionary period, remarkably parallel those of the dormancy of the Church itself and its rebirth into an active force. Further, the fact that the Charleston district seems to have been less affected by the depressive effects during this period than most other areas, also points to the sound groundwork laid by the S.P.G. there both in the field of race relationships and in ecclesiastical matters. Tried in the crucible of the revolutionary mood, subject to vituperative attacks from anti-British sources, and shorn abruptly of influence and support, the Church, throughout the thirteen colonies, had need to call on all its resources to retain the breath of life. The bitterest attacks came in New England, where the Anglicans had always been in the minority, and most of the clergy remained loyal to the crown.[17] At the same time the established state Church of Virginia, supported by public funds, suffered equally, finding itself staggering and supine when state sup-

[16] See Carter G. Woodson, *The African Background Outlined*, pp. 332-333. Woodson's discussion of this period shows the important part played by the Negro as well as the white man in preserving a degree of educational continuity during this difficult period. He writes, "Fortunately the Negroes, who themselves had become sufficiently interested in the movement to appreciate its worth to themselves, were sometimes in a position to support such efforts on their own resources. Stimulated, too, by the thought of being deprived of a forbidden fruit, they struggled more earnestly to keep alive such institutions. In their poverty-stricken state they could not accomplish all which they had undertaken, but the spirit of the oppressed struggling for liberation, made up to some extent for what they lacked in resources . . . clandestine schools . . . were not merely those of Negroes. . . . A study of these schools clearly shows that the majority of them were conducted by sympathetic whites rather than by the Negroes themselves. They were usually in some secluded spot in a narrow street or a building in a back yard; the adults attending went late at night and the children who frequented them in the day time disguised themselves as bearers of bundles of clothing in which they had their books concealed."
[17] It is nevertheless true that from the handful of northern clergy who sided with the colonies came the vigorous leadership which guided the formation of the Protestant Episcopal Church, and set up the first bishoprics. Accustomed to opposition, they seemed more able in meeting the obstacles presented by a patriotic aversion to the church which was an aftermath of Independence. The career of Bishop William White in Pennsylvania as told in Walter H. Stowe, *The Life and Letters of Bishop William White* (New York, 1937), is an example of such leadership.

port was withdrawn.[18] But in South Carolina, by a policy which closely parallels the conciliatory attitude of the missionaries toward the problem of slavery, the church survived the withdrawal of public funds and was "fortunate in regard to an early episcopate, as she had been in the earlier colonial church settlement."[19] The colorful part played by the clergy of South Carolina in the Revolution, and later in the formation of the Protestant Episcopal Church, was thoroughly in the tradition of peaceful but purposeful progress of these earlier adventurous decades.[20] Equally interesting, as a heritage

[18] The story of the church in Virginia has been ably and briefly outlined by G. MacLaren Brydon, whose address, "Diocesan Beginnings," has been printed in *Addresses delivered at the Centennial Celebration of the Diocesan Missionary Society of the Protestant Episcopal Church in the Diocese of Virginia* (Richmond: 1929), pp. 39-56. "The Church had been a ward of the government," he writes (pp. 43-44), "and in a very real sense had been more hopelessly its victim than ever the Baptists or Presbyterians were. These denominations faced the future well organized with leaders and people trained to govern and support themselves. The Episcopal Church had no training or experience in either, and had . . . no one with the authority even to call a meeting." Discontinuance of salaries in January, 1777, was followed by confiscation of church properties, and finally, in 1786, by the denial of the right of incorporation to the church. Early ministers, maintained on farms, taught school to augment the income of the glebe, and received little or no money salary. The Diocesan convention met only twice between 1799 and 1812. The election of the Rev. Richard Channing Moore as Bishop of the Diocese in 1814 marked the beginning of consolidated effort for re-establishment.

[19] C. C. Tiffany, *A History of the Protestant Episcopal Church in the United States,* p. 391.

[20] Describing the church during this period Frederick Dalcho wrote: "Most of the Episcopal Clergy in Carolina, Joined the Colonies in the Revolutionary contest. Five, only, out of twenty, adhered to Great Britain and left the country. The late Bishop Smith, was banished by the British to Philadelphia, and the Rev. Mr. Lewis, of St. Paul's, to St. Augustine. The Rev. Mr. Purcell, was a Chaplain in the Army, and Deputy Judge Advocate Gen. The Rev. Mr. Warren, of St. James', Santee, being on a visit to England, refused a Living there, with a promise of promotion, and returned to Carolina, in 1778. The Rev. Mr. Percy delivered the first address on the anniversary of our Independence, and on the fall of Charles-Town, was forbid, by Col. Balfour, to officiate, on pain of imprisonment; others, animated their Parishioners, by patriotic discourses, to persevere in the great cause in which they had righteously engaged.

"The successful termination of the Revolution, procured civil liberty for the state, and ecclesiastical independence to the Church. No longer nursed by the hand of government, the Church sought among its worshippers that support, which, before, it had derived from the public treasury. The Salaries allowed by law to the Clergy, and the sums appropriated for the repairs of Churches, ceased with the Royal government. The Vestries of St. Philip's and St. Michael's, met Dec. 7, 1778, and made arrangements for raising the necessary supplies by private subscription. Both Churches were incorporated as one body, by an Act of Assembly, March 24, 1785, by the name of The Vestries and Churchwardens of the Episcopal Churches in the Parishes of St. Philip and St. Michael, Charlestown. This Act authorized the Vestries to assess the Pews, until the rents of Lands, and the interest of monies should be sufficient to defray the expenses of said Churches. Each Church was made a separate Corporation, Dec. 20, 1791. . . ." See Frederick Dalcho, *The Protestant Episcopal Church in South Carolina,* p. 206.

of the S.P.G., was the formation of such a group as "The Protestant Episcopal Society for the Advancement of Christianity,"[21] in 1810, and of other such organizations within the church. Approximately thirty years later, the formation of "The Society for the Promotion of the Instruction of the Negroes in the State,"[22] was a legitimate offspring of the ideas and ideals expressed by the S.P.G. a century and a half before. One of the first organizations of its kind, this Society contributed much to the re-instatement of Negro education after the reactionary period during which it was forbidden.

A glimpse of the continuity of the S.P.G. conceptions and aims is clearly presented in "The Proceedings of the Meeting in Charleston, South Carolina, May 13-15, 1845, on the Religious Instruction of the Negroes, together with the Report of the Committee and the Address to the Public," which sharply reveals a consciousness that religious instruction was a duty towards, and a means of improvement of, race relationship and reciprocal security. All the denominations were at one in this realization and objective. Methodists and Baptists,[23] as the records indicate, were participants on a large scale in this fundamental tradition established by the S.P.G. early in the eighteenth century. The continuing stream of history is well illustrated in these later phases of work.

[21] Formed for the purpose of providing means for building churches in places where they had been destroyed, or where the building was delayed by lack of funds, this Society was organized "for obtaining the means by a fund instituted by the private subscriptions of the pious. . . . Subscriptions are received to *The Church Building Fund,* which are invested in public stock, and by compound interest will continually increase. The Protestant Episcopal Society, being a corporate body, hold this Fund in Trust." See Frederick Dalcho, *The Protestant Episcopal Church in South Carolina,* p. 214, footnote.

[22] Formed in February, 1884, this Society had 1 catechist at St. Marks, Clarendon, a year later. Its purpose was outlined as follows: ". . . Our object is twofold—First: to employ throughout the state *proved and efficient catechists* who shall be members of the Protestant Episcopal Church, and act under the direction and supervision of the ministry . . . and aid them exclusively in the instruction of the negroes. And second: *to send ordained ministers of the P. E. Church as Missionaries among the negroes* to such portions of the state in which they are needed and the planters are willing to receive and to aid them." See report of Thomas W. Hanckel, in *The Proceedings of the Meeting in Charleston, South Carolina, May 13-15, 1845, on the Religious Instruction of the Negroes.* (Charleston: 1845), p. 40.

[23] The role of the Baptists and Methodists, together with other dissenting sects, and the religious climate of South Carolina are well analyzed in William E. Dodd, *The Cotton Kingdom,* Ch. V, "Religion and Education" (pp. 97-117). While "no gentlemen would chose any but the Episcopalian way" (p. 99) ; and "Presbyterians, . . . grew more aristocratic as . . . members became more wealthy and better educated . . . the larger part of the work of saving souls fell to Baptists and Methodists" (p. 102). The chapter also includes a discussion of the split within the churches preceding the Civil War.

Reporting from the Sumter District, J. Dyson, an Episcopal clergy-man, gives an analysis of conditions in his parish which echoes re-markably the letters written by S.P.G. missionaries a century earlier. Dyson wrote:

There are between 2 and 3,000 negroes in the parish of St. Marks . . . from 70 to 100 attend the Episcopal Church: 9 of whom are com-municants. One Episcopal clergyman and one catechist are employed by the vestry & wardens of St. Mark's Church, who are specially engaged in importing religious instruction to our coloured people: likewise several persons of the Methodist denomination—ministers and others—are engaged in this work. Ten plantations are attended by our catechist weekly: 420 adults and 160 children are regularly cate-chised: and every Sunday afternoon the Rector of St. Marks delivers a sermon for the special benefit of the negroes. . . .
. . . The rapid progress of the negroes under my instruction, par-ticularly the children—under the excellent system of our catechist, has surpassed every expectation I had entertained, and realized the fondest hopes. . . . Inducing or compelling slaves to abstain from the use of ardent spirits will be found a powerful auxiliary to religious instruc-tion. In this respect, I have seen but little difficulty, *where the master sets the example. . . .*[24]

And from the parish of Prince George, Winyaw, containing about 13,000 slaves of whom 300 were Episcopalians, 3,200 Methodists, and 1,500 Baptists, a plantation owner, R. F. W. Allston, himself an Episcopalian, discussed his own methods of religious instruction for his slaves:

I have a place of worship for my negroes open to all denominations of Christians. . . . The Methodist missionary preaches to my people every alternate Sabbath, after catechizing the children, about 50. By the rules of my plantation the Methodists and Baptists have prayer meetings at given houses, each twice in the week, besides Sunday, when they meet, and pray and sing together. These meetings are ex-

[24] See *The Proceedings of the Meeting in Charleston, South Carolina, May 13-15, 1845, on the Religious Instruction of the Negroes,* pp. 29-30. (Huntington Library) This report, published as the result of a questionnaire submitted by a committee to clergymen and laymen of all denominations, gives an excellent pic-ture of conditions in regard to Negro education in the period leading to the Civil War. The questions included in the questionnaire are, in themselves, of interest. They inquired (1) as to the number of Negroes in each parish, and their membership in each church; (2) the number of ministers or teachers (black and white) according to denomination, who were working in behalf of educa-tion; (3) the specific plans used for instruction, and the number of Negro chil-dren thus catechized; (4) the comparative results of religious training among children and adults; (5) the degree of benefit to the Negroes of religious in-struction, especially as to morals, marriage, chastity, truthfulness, recognition of property rights, and the observance of the Sabbath; and (6) the influence of religious instruction on the discipline of the plantation.

clusively for the negroes of my own plantation. I have had this custom 15 years and it works well. . . .[25]

Summing up the work as revealed by the printed reports, the Commission concluded regarding the work in the Episcopal diocese of South Carolina:

There is no *Diocese* more engaged—and doing more for the negroes than that of *South Carolina*. There are several clergymen acting as missionaries who are wholly given to this work, and some catechists . . . while almost the entire body of the clergy are . . . engaged in it. The laity also of this Diocese, embracing many of the most distinguished and wealthy citizens, are supporters of the work: contributing not only of their substance, but giving their own personal attention to it. . . .[26]

On the broad front of Negro advancement the comments of the Commission show that the Negro was well along in the process of Americanization on the one hand, and on the road to full-fledged Christianization on the other. The America of many migrant groups included, especially in the South, this large contingent of peoples from Africa, and to a very large extent, even though in slavery, they were participating in the creation of the culture of the New World. They were gaining industrial and agricultural skills, learning the English language, and acquiring an American stamp more definitely than the second generation European who continued links of association with the lands of his national origin. Religion had no small part in cementing him to his new country.

The S.P.G. activities in South Carolina are significant not only in the short view of achievement from year to year, decade to decade, but can be measured in the clearer light of a long-term perspective. The historian, in this case as always, must be an interpreter not only of the minutiae of the immediate scene, but must keep in mind the long-term significance of earlier events. The broad fact is that the Negro of the United States became a Christian and so regards himself today. After three quarters of a century of intense activity by the S.P.G. in South Carolina, the parishes of the colony were firmly established with home rule, and the inhabitants took over their religious management, including work with the Negroes. The possibilities for the Negro's Christianization and education had been carefully studied and a blueprint for future efforts, not alone in South Caro-

[25] See *The Proceedings of the Meeting in Charleston, South Carolina, May 13-15, 1845, on the Religious Instruction of the Negroes,* p. 34.
[26] *Ibid.,* pp. 68-69.

lina, but in all parts of the world, was made in the light of accumu-
lated experience. At Charleston, as in Philadelphia[27] and in New
York,[28] the experiment of a school in town, free from the plantation
regime, and other distractions, had for its real object the training of
Negro teachers on a larger basis than the removal of young Negroes
to London for schooling could ever allow.

The close identification by the Society of island with continental
plantations[29] is seen in the reports of missionary trips to adjoining
islands, and in such instances as the proposal to send Andrew from
the Charleston school to Codrington, rather than to sell him. Andrew's
refusal to go is typical of the Negro's philosophical habit of making
the place where he lives his own. Further, it will be remembered that
Commissary Garden was appointed by the Bishop of London for the
Bahamas as well as for North and South Carolina. On the Codrington Estates in Barbados there was being conducted the century-long
experiment of the Society to show on its own property both humane
management and business profits. After periods of difficulty from
poor crops or absentee problems, it was, in brief, successful in both
aims. Missionaries, ordained and instructed in London, and often as
in the case of Le Jau with service periods in the Islands, of course
drew inspiration from the Codrington effort.

In the light of eventual emancipation this Anglo-colonial social
scene gives much information on race relationships, and suggests the
many factors which entered into the variable progress of American
antislavery opinion. The growth of industrialization and the rapid
development of machinery in the eighteenth and nineteenth centuries
were creating new problems for the Negroes as well as for the white
laborers. In Great Britain it made more jobs, in many instances, at

[27] See Edgar Legare Pennington, *Thomas Bray's Associates and Their Work
Among the Negroes* (Worcester: 1939). The Philadelphia school was a project
of the Bray Associates, but naturally of special interest to the S.P.G. Also see
Richard I. Shelling, "The Reverend William Sturgeon, Catechist to the Negroes
of Philadelphia, . . ." in *Historical Magazine of the Protestant Episcopal Church,*
VIII, No. 4 (December, 1939), pp. 388-401.
[28] The foundation for successful Negro education in New York was laid
by Elias Neau, S.P.G. catechist in New York, 1704-1722. See William Webb
Kemp, *Support of Schools in Colonial New York by the Society for the Propagation of the Gospel in Foreign Parts* (New York City: 1913), pp. 234-261; F. J.
Klingberg, "The S.P.G. Program for Negroes in Colonial New York," in *Historical Magazine of the Protestant Episcopal Church,* VIII, No. 4 (December,
1939), pp. 309-311.
[29] Samuel Gaillard Stoney, in *Charleston, Azaleas and Old Bricks,* p. 5, says,
"Almost until the time of the Revolution, the province was clearly allied by blood
and interest with the Antilles, so that it seems to have been regarded as a sort of
errant island that had got itself moored somehow to the North American continent."

least, than there were men to fill them, and hence produced long hours and intensified workers' hardships by increased speed and fatigue. So the cotton gin had an untoward effect on the Negro. The increased utility of the fibre called for speed of production in the fields, and for continued slave carrying from Africa. At the same time the industrial structure, due to the increasing mobility of capital, brought new problems of unemployment and retardation in areas where financial backing was suddenly withdrawn. The capitalist in London, for instance, was able to abandon his position in the West Indies and to transfer his money to Asia and to Africa. The Negroes, in large parts of the West Indies, were consequently left to their own fate, and humanitarian enterprises there had to function for some years in a collapsing regime, but with increasing population.[30]

Antislavery sentiment, under these circumstances, might well tend to lose ground. The British antislavery movement, as it migrated to the United States, concurrently with this West Indian decline, seemed to show loss in power. This temporary reversal was due, perhaps, to the split between Quakers and other elements in the antislavery group, or possibly caused by the lack of success in the cruiser suppression of the illicit slave trade. The mortality of sailors in the cruising patrol squadrons on the African Coast, had an unfavorable effect on public opinion. The antislavery forces had been caught between two periods: they had met with success and failure in the American world, and the opening up of Africa had not yet occurred, with the instant challenge to humanitarian forces to rearm. However, any specific evaluation of British antislavery strength points in the direction that it was not, on the whole, operating with diminished vigor, but cooperating with the American movements, and that setbacks were temporary and periods of discouragement short-lived. The new phenomenon was that antislavery men in other countries, the United States and France, sought out British antislavery support; additional centers of international agitation and opposition were founded in several countries. Lewis Tappan and William Lloyd Garrison are but two men who were active in schemes of cooperation.[31]

[30] See W. E. B. Du Bois, *Black Folk,* pp. 177-178, for a short statement of capitalistic mobility, taxation, salaries, investment returns, labor, etc., and for a pessimistic statement: "The labor of the islands, ignorant and degraded and exploited for centuries, was freed only in the sense that the importations of Africans ceased."
[31] For accounts of Tappan's and Garrison's cooperation, see Annie H. Abel and Frank J. Klingberg (eds.) *A Side-Light on Anglo-American Relations, 1839-1858. Furnished by the Correspondence of Lewis Tappan and Others with the British and Foreign Anti-slavery Society,* (Washington: 1927).

The flight of capital from Jamaica and the consequent economic retardation of the country has, moreover, a good deal in common with the course of events after the Civil War in the South. Gradual emancipation in the West Indies, a generation before the Civil War in America, was intended, in less than a decade, to transfer the Negro from slavery to peasant proprietorship, a process which took the white man centuries. There was legal emancipation in both cases, and in Jamaica at least partial compensation for the loss of the slaves, but, nevertheless, Jamaica suffered in that the compensation money went to the bankers and other holders of mortgages in Great Britain, and did not come in quantity into the islands. The uncertainty of apprenticed and emancipated labor under a wage system, and the competition of slave grown crops from Cuba, Brazil, and elsewhere, intensified by the adoption of free trade in Great Britain in 1846, contributed to making the freedman's lot difficult. He was legally free, but lived under static economic conditions, and therefore his possibilities for development were limited.[32] In an expanding environment, such as in New York, the Negro, though in minority, could benefit from business revival when it came after a Revolution or other crisis. But in the South after the Civil War, as in the West Indies, economic paralysis held the Negro, as well as the white man, in subjection to outside interests. Professor Toynbee, in his incisive comment on South Carolina suggests that South Carolina and Virginia particularly suffered a collapse as severe in depth as their previous supremacy had reached in height. The great planters, and therefore their areas, could not rebuild their estates as could the poorer, more resourceful small farmers of other states.[33]

[32] Lowell Joseph Ragatz (comp.), *A Guide for the Study of British Caribbean History, 1763-1834, including the Abolition and Emancipation Movements* 1932): William Law Mathieson, *British Slavery and Its Abolition 1823-1838* (London: 1926). These authors study the economic hazards of the Islands, and thereby have explained the loss of the West Indian interest in England, particularly in Parliament, quite an obvious by-product of the diminishing significance of the British West Indies in the world economy of the Empire.

[33] See Arnold J. Toynbee, *A Study of History*, Vol. IV (Oxford University Press: 1939), pp. 289-291. The "time machine" which destroyed British slavery, helped industrialization to gain a fresh hold, and worked more fortuitously than in the prevention of war, which, supported by both industry and democracy, further intrenched itself (pp. 137 156). In this connection, the part of the small farmer in the South is sometimes overlooked. Henry H. Simms, "A Critical Analysis of Abolition Literature, 1830-1840," in *The Journal of Southern History*, Vol. VI, No. 3 (August, 1940), points out that "500,000 farms in the eleven states which seceded, over half of which consisted of from 20 to 100 acres," were shown in the census of 1860, and concludes regarding the 306,272 slave holders listed: "After deductions for slaveholders who were not farmers, and allowances for duplication in farm ownership are made, it would seem that there were many small farmers, . . . who owned no slaves." (p. 377n)

To return to the eighteenth century scene, a fact of great significance is that at the time of the adoption of the American Constitution,
there was a general feeling, even among slaveholders, that slavery
was an evil, evidenced by Jefferson's declamations against slavery,
the provisions of Washington's will, the unopposed barring of slavery
from the Northwest Territory, and the fact that one man alone, in
1784, prevented the States in the Confederation Congress from
barring slavery in the entire West. In addition to economic explana-
tions, it must be remembered that the Southern planters were, to a
large extent, Anglicans;[34] that the Society for the Propagation of
the Gospel had sent missionaries over to them, who had an English
outlook on slavery, and that the Society, from the beginning, was
committed to the task of urging upon the masters the duty of allow-
ing their slaves to be Christianized, with all the social and economic
implications that were implicit in a thesis that the slave had religious
rights.[35] The fact that the South was early supplied with ministers
chosen and controlled by a Society with specific and distinct humanitarian aims, must be taken into account, to a considerable degree, as
a factor in the enlightened attitude of the better planters of the
1780's.[36]

[34] By way of comparison, see Nash Kerr Burger, "The Diocese of Mississippi
and the Confederacy," in *The Historical Magazine of the Protestant Episcopal
Church*, Vol. IX, No. 1 (March, 1940), pp. 52-77. Established as a Diocese in
1826, Mississippi experienced the same sudden wealth as had South Carolina
in the middle eighteenth century, "And since the Church, as generally in the
South, was strongest with the planter group, the diocese shared the general
good times." (p. 53)
[35] This point is discussed in F. J. Klingberg, "The S.P.G. Program for Negroes in Colonial New York," in *ibid.*, Vol. VIII, No. 4 (December, 1939), pp.
306-371.
[36] A striking example of recognition of Negro rights by the courts of South
Carolina in 1792 is the case of *"Guardian of Sally (a negro) v. Beaty*, I, Bay 260,
May, 1792" cited in Helen T. Catterall, *Judicial Cases concerning American
Slavery and the Negro*, II, p. 275, involving the purchase of one slave by another in order to set her free. Chief Justice Rutledge, in his charge to the jury,
commented, "if the wench chose to appropriate the savings of her extra labour
[allowed by her master] to the purchase of this girl . . . to set her free, would a
jury of the country say no? He trusted not. They were too humane and upright,
he hoped, to do such manifest violence to so singular and extraordinary an act
of benevolence. The jury, without retiring from their box, returned a verdict for
the plaintiff's ward, [Sally] and she was set at liberty." With the turn of the
century, evidence appears of a retreat from that liberal position, and in 1820 an
act was passed forbidding emancipation of slaves except by act of the legislature
(*cf.* 267). Judge O'Neall, in 1848, in advising the repeal of the act of 1820, urged
his fellows to "get back alongside of such men as C. J. Rutledge who, in the case
of Guardian of Sally . . . [gave] expression . . . [to] the benevolent feelings
which had been tried in the crucible of the revolution . . . the ruling . . . spoke
what, I think, always belongs to Carolina—a love of mercy, of right, and a
hatred of that which is mean or oppressive. Until fanaticism and folly drove us

To summarize briefly, it is, of course, true that the success or failure of educational and humanitarian programs is closely associated with the economic prosperity of communities. Thus, education of white men in Great Britain was possible, because of rapid increase in wealth and the use of labor saving devices of the machine age, which eventually freed the children for school; whereas in South Carolina this same machine age tied the Negroes to the fields, to produce more rice and cotton. In the West Indies the economic collapse made further advances difficult, if not impossible.

The records of the Society presented here throw new light on the means by which humanitarian and intellectual ideas migrated through the British-colonial world in the eighteenth century. The movement of men from area to area, the ordination of the Clergy in London, requiring a stay of some months in which the candidates were under instruction,[37] their close direction there and in the field by the Society itself, the careful study of their reports, the spending of immense amounts for the publication of books and tracts, were all managed by a corporation which used the precise and business-like methods of the eighteenth century trading companies. In fact, this was a business company trading in ideas, and demanding in business terms that all who made money in trade, in the shipping firms and towns, put up the funds for the Christianization of native peoples uprooted or affected, as were both Negroes and Indians, by the introduction of the white man's economic life and social customs.[38] Its educational

---

from that position; the law of our State had uniformly favored emancipation . . . with such limitations and guards as rendered the free negro, not a dangerous, but a useful member of the community."

[37] Instructions for the Clergy of the Society contained, among other directions, the following statements: "That till they can have a convenient passage, they employ their time usefully; in reading Prayers and Preaching, as they have Opportunity, in hearing others Read and Preach; or in such Studies as may tend to fit them for their Employment," and continued: "That they constantly attend the standing Committee of this Society, at *St. Paul's* Chapter-House, and observe their Directions; . . . That before their Departure, they wait upon his Grace the Lord Arch-Bishop of *Canterbury*, their Metropolitan, and upon the Lord Bishop of *London*, their Diocesan, to receive their Paternal Benediction and Instructions." See *Journal of S.P.G.* "Instructions for the Clergy Employ'd by the Society for the Propagation of the Gospel in Foreign Parts. (L.C. Photo.) I, Part II (Film page 612, printed page 1).

[38] The Bishops in their Annual Sermons often mentioned the duty of the shipping merchants to give money to the Society because of the wealth they received from the plantations. For example, Gilbert Burnet, 1704, said "our Colonies are so many Mines of Wealth to us, and . . . vast Numbers of Seamen are imployed in so many hundreds of Ships. . . . While we have so many Blessings coming home daily, shall we take no Care to secure those Blessings to us and to our Brethren in those Plantations. . . ." p. 20. (Huntington Library) William Dawes, Bishop of Chester, in 1709, did not ask for financial contributions, but

attempts emphasize the difficulties of a transition period in which the Negro was neither wholly free nor wholly slave. The Society laid bare the conflict between slavery, with its abrogation of legal and human rights, and the humanitarian regime, with its claim for black men or red.

Present from the earliest settlements, the Negro[39] is seen in the S.P.G. letters as resident in large numbers in the pioneer days of a virgin land, a contemporary with the tribal Indian. As a builder, with the white man of the very foundations of the colonial life, the suggestion occurs that he may yet have his own Societies of pre-Revolutionary service.[40] Not only did his skills set the hearthstones of the city of Charleston, but he labored upon the plantations, and eagerly spent his spare time in schooling himself.

Today, leaders of the race are calling upon the Negro to resume his role as a skilled worker in industry and as a businessman:[41] his capacities in crafts and on the land were demonstrated in the eighteenth century, and form a part of his American heritage. It is a curious fact that the agents of his Americanization were representatives of British ideology who, reinforced by the detachment of time and space lent by the home office in London, were able to see the

mentioned that captains could transport missionaries and recommend the work of missionaries to their agents.

[39] See Ralph Henry Gabriel, *The Course of American Democratic Thought,* pp. 7, 139. On page 7 Mr. Gabriel states, "The children of the imported Negro captives of the eighteenth and of the early nineteenth centuries, 'and their children's children, having no memory of African scenes or tribal ways or Negro languages, cheerfully made the plantation life their own. . . . A plantation . . . was a home of very diverse human beings . . . with a prospect of life-long relationship. . . . This pattern of life did not permit the masters to remain mere Englishmen or Frenchmen, any more than it permitted Negroes to remain Africans.'" However, just as the masters retained some traces of their English or French background as part of the new life, so, imbedded in the Gullah dialect are traces of the Negro's lingual history. African words, as well as 17th century English, and fragments from Spanish, Portuguese and French, still appear in the Gullah speech.

[40] Such an organization was the Century Fellowship Society in Charleston; a continuation of the Brown Fellowship Society organized by free Negroes in Charleston in 1790. "On the 117th anniversary of the organization, the president, in his annual address, epitomized the career of his caste in the following words: 'Fortunately there were the classes in society, and as our forefathers allied themselves with them, as a consequence they had their influence and protections and they had to be in accord with them and stood for what they stood for. If they stood for high incentive so did our fathers. *If they stood for slavery so did our fathers to a certain extent. But they sympathized with the oppressed,* for they had to endure some of it. . . .'" From E. Horace Fitchett, "The Traditions of the Free Negro in Charleston, South Carolina," in *Journal of Negro History,* Vol. XXV, No. 2, p. 150.

[41] See "The Story of the Exceptional Negro," in *The Negro History Bulletin,* Vol. III, No. 9 (June, 1940), pp. 129-130.

Negro not alone as a producer, but, more fundamentally, as a human being. In a plantation pattern which required slave labor, the missionaries functioned not only to guide the Negro into his new environmental adaptation but also intervened for him with the white masters, urging an acceptance of his right to a place in the church and in the school. Under the Society's observation, and with its assistance, the Negro in the United States began the slow process of winning his civil and religious rights and establishing his rightful role as an American. A common consciousness of this long story is important to both black man and white, for a race, like a nation, measures its expectancies of the future by its achievements in the past.

APPENDIX

THE MISSIONARY ROLL—PARISH BY PARISH

A PICTURE of the continuity of each parish, of the inter-change of personnel, and of the educational background of the missionaries in the South Carolina field is of value to the student. The following, compiled from C. F. Pascoe, *Two Hundred Years of the S.P.G.* (pp. 849-850), shows a total of 54 missionaries serving 14 central stations.

This list does not include such men as Commissary Alexander Garden, his successor, the Rev. Richard Clarke, and the Rev. Robert Smith, who, as rectors of St. Philip's, a parish which received little or no financial assistance from the Society, were, nevertheless, active supporters of the S.P.G. and trusted correspondents of the home office in London.

CHARLESTON and *ST. PHILIP'S* were used interchangeably in referring to this parish. The Charleston Church, the first in South Carolina, was established about 1681, but on November 4, 1704, when the parishes were established by law, Charleston and Charleston Neck became the Parish of St. Philip's.

1705-08 Thomas Hasell, M.A. Ordained deacon, 1705; priest, 1709. Also at St. Thomas' 1709-43. Died October 9, 1743-44.

1708-16 Gideon Johnston (ex-vicar of Castlemore, Ireland.) Commissary to Bp. Lon. Drowned April 23, 1716 off Charleston by upsetting of boat while taking leave of Gov. Craven.

1712-13 William Guy, M.A. Ordained deacon, 1712, priest, 1713. Also at St. Helen's, 1714-15; Charleston, 1716-17; St. Andrew's, 1719-51. Died 1751.

1714-16 John Whitehead. Died Nov. 8, 1716, "of an inward heat."

1716-17 (see Guy)

1722-27 Thomas Morritt. Ordained deacon 1717, priest, 1718. Also Winyaw, 1728-34; Christ Church, 1735-36. Resigned.

1727-29 John Lambert, M.A. Died August 14, 1729.

CUFFEETOWN (or Coffee Town)

1770-82/3 Samuel Frederic Lucius. Refugee in Charlestown and Congarees during Revolution.

CHRIST CHURCH

1713-21 Gilbert Jones, M.A. Resigned.

1722 Benjamin Pownall, M.A. Resigned.

1727-29 John Winteley, M.A. Connection dissolved by Society for neglect of duty or other unsatisfactory conduct.

1730-34 John Fulton, M.A. Ordained deacon and priest, 1730. Connection dissolved by Society.

1734-35 John Fullerton, M.A. Ordained deacon and priest, 1734. Died Sept. 4, 1735.

1735-36 Thomas Morritt. Ordained deacon, 1717, priest, 1718. Also served
         Charleston, 1722-27; Winyaw, etc. 1728-34. Resigned.
1738-39 Robert Small, M.A. Ordained deacon, 1737, priest, 1738. Died Sept. 28,
         1739.
1740-50 Levi Durand, M.A. Ordained deacon, 1738, priest, 1739. Also St.
         John's, 1750-65. Died 1765.

GOOSE CREEK

1702-06 Samuel Thomas (of Ballydon, Sudbury). Died Oct. 1706 of fever.
1706-17 Francis Le Jau, D.D. Trinity College Dublin; born Angiers, France,
         about 1665; (ex-Canon of St. Paul's London, and Missionary to
         St. Christopher's, W. Indies, 1700-01. Died Sept. 10, 1717.
1717   William Wye (an Irishman.) Appointment Aug. 1717 to Goose
         Creek cancelled Dec. 1717 because obtained by forged testimonials.
1721-22 Francis Merry, M.A. Also St. Helen's, 1720. Resigned.
1723-28 Richard Ludlam, M.A. Died Oct. 1728, bequeathed £2,000 to
         S.P.G.
1729   John Thomas, Apt. 1729 but drowned Sheerness while embarking.
1732-46 Timothy Millechamp, M.A. Ordained deacon, 1726, priest, 1729.
         Sick leave 1746-48. Resigned for Colesbourne, Glos.
1748-51 Robert Stone, M.A. Hert. Coll. Oxford, Died about Oct. 20, 1751
         "of a bloody flux."
1752-65 James Harrison, M.A. Queen's College. Oxford; Curate Battersea
         2 years; ordained deacon, 1749, priest, 1750.

PRINCE FREDERICK

1736-51 John Fordyce, M.A. Ordained deacon and priest, 1730. Died 1751.
1753-57 Michael Smith, M.A. Trinity College, Dublin, ordained deacon, 1740,
         priest, 1747. Left.

SANTE

1710   James Giguillet. Resigned.

ST. ANDREW'S

1707-10 Alexander Wood, M.A. Died.
1711-17 Ebenezer Taylor. Transferred to North Carolina.
1719-51 William Guy, M.A. Ordained deacon, 1712, priest, 1713. Also
         Charleston, 1712-13; St. Helen's 1714-15, Charleston, 1716-17.
1753-61 Charles Martyn, M.A. Balliol College, Oxford and curate in Devon;
         ordained deacon, 1746, priest, 1748. Resigned S.P.G. salary 1761
         and parish 1770.

ST. BARTHOLOMEW'S

1713-15 Nathaniel Osborne. Escaped to Charleston during Indian irruption
         but died July 13, 1715 "of a flux or feaver."
1735   Robert Gowie, M.A. Ordained deacon and priest, 1733. Died Nov. 7,
         1733.
1734-43 Thomas Thompson. Ordained deacon and priest 1730. Also St.
         George's 1744-46. Resigned.
1745-49 Charles Boschi ("formerly a Franciscan Fryer"). Resigned on
         appointment as Chaplain to the garrison established about that
         time in Ruatan, Bay of Honduras. His offer for services to con-
         vert the Indians there accepted by the Society, but in 1749 he died.
1749-52 William Langhorne (ex-curate, Pickering). Ordained deacon, 1747,
         priest, 1749. Also St. George's, 1752-59. Resigned, illness.
1753-64 Robert Baron, M.A. Died April 1764.

ST. GEORGE'S

1719-21 Peter Tustian, M.A. Resigned.

1723-36   Francis Varnod ("a foreigner"). Ordained deacon, 1722, priest, 1723. Died 1736.
1737-42   Stephen Roe, M.A. Ordained deacon, 1730, priest 1732. Transferred to New England.
1744-46   Thomas Thompson. Ordained deacon and priest 1730. Also St. Bartholomew's 1734-43. Resigned.
1746-47   Samuel Quincy, M.A. Transferred from Georgia to St. John's, S.C. then S.P.G. at St. George's. Resigned.
1747-52   William Cotes. Ordained deacon, 1746, priest, 1747. Died Sunday, July 19, 1752 after having performed service that day.
1752-9   William Langhorne (ex-Curate, Pickering) ; ordained deacon, 1747, priest, 1749. Also St. Bartholomew's, 1749-52. Resigned, ill.

ST. HELEN'S
1714-15   William Guy, M.A. Ordained deacon, 1712, priest, 1713. Also Charleston, 1712-13 and 1716-17; St. Andrew's, 1719-51. Died 1751.
1720   Francis Merry, M.A. Also Goose Creek, 1721-22. Resigned.
1725-44   Lewis Jones, M.A. Died Dec. 24, 1744. Bequeathed £100 to S.P.G.
1745-50   William Orr. M.A. ordained deacon and priest 1736. (Charleston, not S.P.G., 1737-41) Also St. Paul's 1741-44. Resigned. Died St. Paul's, 1755.
1747-50   Richard St. John, B.A. Transferred from Bahamas. Resigned.
1751-56   William Peaseley, M.A. (tr. from Newfoundland). Resigned, ill.

ST. JOHN'S
1707-17. Robert Maule, M.A. (Irish, recommended by archbishop of Dublin) born about 1680. Died of dysentery 1717. Bequeathed £750 to S.P.G.
1720   Moses Clark (or Clerk) Died 1720.
1723-26   Brian Hunt, M.A.
1729-48   Daniel Dwight, M.A. Yale College, Conn., ordained deacon and priest, 1729. Died March 28, 1748.
1749-50   Robert Cuming, M.A. Glasgow or Edinburgh. Ordained deacon and priest, 1748. Died 1750.
1750-65   Levi Durand, M.A. Ordained deacon, 1738, priest, 1739. Also Christ Church, 1740-50. Died 1765.

ST. PAUL'S
1706-07   William Dun (from Clogher Dio.) Born about 1677. Resigned.
1712-23   William Tredwell Bull, M.A. Bishop of London's Commissary in S.C. 1716-23. Resigned.
1724-28   David Standish, M.A. Died 1728.
1729-39   Andrew Leslie, M.A. Ordained deacon, 1727, priest, 1728. Resigned, ill, died 1740.
1741-44   William Orr, M.A. Ordained deacon and priest, 1736. (Charleston, not S.P.G. 1737-41). Also St. Helen's 1745-50. Resigned. Died (St. Paul's) 1755.

ST. THOMAS'
1709-43   Thomas Hasell, M.A. Ordained deacon, 1705, priest, 1709. Also Charleston, 1705-08. Died Oct. 9, 1743-44.
1744-65   Alexander Garden, M.A. (nephew of Comsy. Garden). Ordained deacon and priest, 1743.

WINYAW
1728-34   Thomas Morritt. Ordained deacon, 1717, priest, 1718. Also Charleston 1722-27; Christ Church, 1735-36. Resigned.

BIBLIOGRAPHICAL NOTE

THE sources used in the preparation of this volume are listed in the footnotes. These references indicate the documents used and give bibliographical information. The Index directs ready access to them.

The vast manuscript records of the S.P.G. in the Library of Congress, and the fine collection of Accounts, Collections, Digests, Annual Sermons, and Abstracts of the Proceedings of the Society in the Huntington Library have furnished the basic sources for this study. No attempt has been made to incorporate the extensive historical literature on South Carolina into this volume. Rather its purpose is to make new stores of material available and to present new aspects of colonial life.

The tremendous volume of letters, written by men in the field to the secretary in London, referred to in the footnotes as *S.P.G. MSS.*, are rich in the intimate detail of community life. In addition to their many general letters, the workers had to make factual reports semi-annually, based on the Society's carefully worked out questionnaires.

The *Journals* are the records of the home office in England. These minutes of the deliberations and decisions of the Society reveal that all possible sources of information were used to formulate policy and to determine activity. Supplementing the field reports, the *Journals* include materials from governmental officials at home, in the colonies, and from foreign observers. Sir William Johnson was but one of these notable men.

The *Abstracts* of the Proceedings, printed for distribution to the entire sustaining membership of the Society, especially in the home isles, are ably codified to show in summary, from Newfoundland to the Mosquito Shore, the year's work in factual and objective form. The *Annual Sermon*, a survey of achievement, a digest of contemporary thought, religious and philosophical, and a challenge to morale, was usually bound with the *Abstract* of Proceedings.

The Society published and distributed immense quantities of literature: prayer books, spelling books, Psalters, primers, Bibles, and theological tracts, all of which were greatly valued in the colonies and at home. Typical of the latter is Bishop Edmund Gibson's *Three*

Addresses on the Instruction of the Negroes (1727), which included an address to the Christians in England to promote Negro instruction, another to the masters and mistresses in the plantations, and one to the Society's missionaries.

For the specialist, a more extensive bibliography on S.P.G. materials is to be found in the Author's *Anglican Humanitarianism in Colonial New York.* Here it is only necessary to note that for South Carolina the Society's records are particularly rich on the white colonist as well as on the Negro. The many able writers responsible for these fine records included Richard Ludlam, Francis Varnod, Robert Maule, Francis Le Jau, and Alexander Garden.

Among many other works, vital in the preparation of this volume, the following are fundamental additions to the S.P.G. materials:

Andrews, Charles M., *The Colonial Period of American History* (4 vols., New Haven, 1934-1938).

Carroll, Bartholomew R., *Historical Collections of South Carolina* (2 vols., New York, 1836). This work is valuable for economic and social facts.

Catterall, Helen T., and Hayden, James J., *Judicial Cases Concerning American Slavery* (5 vols., Washington, 1926-1937).

Cross, Arthur L., *The Anglican Episcopate and the American Colonies* (New York, 1902 and Cambridge, Mass., 1924).

Dalcho, Frederick, *Historical Account of the Protestant Episcopal Church in South Carolina* (Charleston, 1820).

Donnan, Elizabeth, *Documents Illustrative of the History of the Slave Trade to America* (4 vols., Washington, 1930-1935).

Pascoe, Charles F., *Two Hundred Years of the S.P.G. An Historical Account of the Society for the Propagation of the Gospel in Foreign Parts, 1701-1900* (2 vols., London, 1901).

Powicke, F. M., Johnson, Charles, and Harte, W. J., *Handbook of British Chronology* (London, 1939).

Sykes, Norman, *Edmund Gibson, Bishop of London, 1669-1748, A Study in Politics and Religion in the Eighteenth Century* (London, 1926).

Sykes, Norman, *Church and State in England in the Eighteenth Century* (Cambridge, England, 1934).

GENERAL INDEX

The headings listed below are intended to guide the reader to specific materials as well as to ideas stated or implied, to give access to the store of information included in the text and footnotes, and to supplement the bibliographical note.

For this Index I am indebted to Helen E. Livingston.

toward, 14, 58; *see also* Courts, Human rights, Religious rights.

Civil Rights Act of 1875, 4n.

Clapp, Gilson, a slave owner, 59.

Clark (or Clerk), Moses, missionary in St. John's parish, 142.

Clarke, Richard, Commissary of Bishop of London and superintendent of the Charleston Negro school, 118-120, 140.

Clarke, Saml & Jonah, slave owners, 59.

Clay, C. C., Senator from Alabama, 50n.

Clement, Rufus E., "The Church School as a Factor in Negro Life," in *Journal of Negro History* (XII, 5-12), 122n.

Cincinnati, Ohio, riots in, 126n.

Civil war, American, 4, 46n, 103, 125, 130n, 135; government attempts to give aid to Negroes during, 8n.

Clergy, instructions to, 4n; missionaries cooperate with, 4; to superintend and act as Attorneys for the Charleston Negro school, 106; *see also* MISSIONARIES.

Clergy of South Carolina, correspond with S. P. G. regarding good example of certain masters, 44, 44n; in American Revolution, 120n, 128, 128n, 129, 129n; outline impediments to Negro instruction, 6-8, 124n.

Clergymen, grant for, by Colonial Legislature, 76, 98, 99, 100; Swiss, assisted by S. P. G. with passage, 99.

Climate produces illness, 93n.

Cline v. Caldwell, 33n.

Codrington Estates, in Barbados, 108n, 115, 115n, 133.

Collinson, Peter, 103n.

Colonies, American: close relation to Africa of, 2; "dearness" of living in, 83; need of missionaries in, 10n, 25; provision of missionaries for, 10n; rivalry of, 74n; tie with mother country, 3; trade of, 36, 37, *see also*

Trade; wealth of, 36, 37, 137n, *see also* Wealth.

Colonists:

— and S. P. G.: missionaries appointed by Society only on application of, 8n, 27, 27n; missionaries help form liberal opinions of, 27; not interested in Negro instruction, 37-38; opposition of, to Negro instruction by missionaries, 6, 7, 8, 8n, *see also* INSTRUCTION; request Church of England minister, 8n, 64, 98n-99n; seasonal attendance at church of, 98; subscribe toward building church, 78, 79; support Negro school, 113; urged to support Charleston Negro school, 112-113;

— attitudes of: desire of, for self-determination, 125; indifference of, 98; infidels, 7; interested in spiritual things, 98n-99n; irreligion of, 34, 98n; seek manifold advantages of British Constitution, 42; use Indians and Negroes as check on each other, 47; well-behaved, 64, 65, 84; wicked lives and scandalous behavior of, 30;

— living conditions of: driven to northern provinces by war, 96, 97; forty-five average life span of, 93; illness among, 93, 93n, 115n, 120, *see also* Diseases; Epidemics; Illness; poverty of, 11, 63, 87; threatened by French, 41n, 67, 102; threatened by Spanish, 41, 67, 75, 102; *see also* Frontier; Insurrections; Masters; Planters; Population; Wars; White settlers;

— migration of: extend into back country, 48, 48n, 67n; from coast to uplands, xi; remove to Cape Fear, 92; transient families, hired from year to year, 88;

— nationalities of: British, x, 2, 102; French, xi, 2, 10n, 28, 98n, 99, 99n, 102; German, x, 1, 2, 48n, 74n, 99, 102; Irish, 1, 48n; settlers from northern colonies, 48; Swiss, x, 2, 73n; West Indian, 102; Yankee, 102.

— Charity: for poor children, 91, 91n; for poor whites, Negroes, and Indians, 26; Ludlam legacy for, 50, 50n; missionaries urge need of, 91;

— for Negroes, 26, 101, 101n, 122n, 133; books used in, 26; closed, 39n; continued *sub rosa,* 128n; in evening for grown slaves, 116-117; no civil establishment for, 119; *see also* Bray Associates; Charleston Negro school; New York City, Negro school in.

Schoolmaster: for Negroes, 66; house built for, 77; needed for white children, 16, 25; Negro to be employed as, 106; Negro selected by S. P. G. for life-long service as, 106; salary for, 77; *see also* Catechists; Teachers.

Schoolhouse, in need of repair, 26; provided for Charleston Negro school, 112-113; to be provided by parishes, 109.

Scotch, as founders, 1n.

Scotch Covenanter, 71.

Scotland, Alexander Garden a native of, 103, 103n.

Sculptors, Negro, 45n.

Seamstresses, free Negroes as, 125n.

Secession, Reasons for, 4, 4n.

Secker, Thomas, Bishop of Oxford, sermon of, 37, 37n, 95, 95n, 123n.

Second Charter, granted by King Charles II, to Proprietors, 41.

Segregation, in churches, 72n; in schools, 126n.

Sermons, delivered at annual meeting of S. P. G.: advocate program for Negroes, 5, 35-37, 95, 95n, 123-124, 137n-138n; discuss theories regarding primitive man, 36; distributed, 27, 27n, 86, *see also* Literature; function of, 35, 143; ideas in, 123n; important role of, 35-37; *see also,* Philip Bearcroft; Martin Benson; George Berkeley; William Beveridge; Samuel Bradford; Gilbert Burnet; Joseph Butler; Edward

Chandler; Sir William Dawes; Robert Drummond; William Fleetwood; John Leng; Richard Newcome; Beilby Porteus; Jonathan Shipley; Thomas Secker; George Stanhope; William Warburton; John Williams; Richard Willis; Bishops; Deans.

Sevrier, Peter, a minister in Episcopal orders, 99n.

Sharecroppers, 88.

Sheep, 48n.

Shelling, Richard I., "Benjamin Franklin and the Dr. Bray Associates," in *Pennsylvania Magazine of History and Biography* (LXIII, 282-293), 44n, 101n; "The Rev. William Sturgeon, Catechist to the Negroes of Philadelphia, . . ." in *Historical Magazine of the Protestant Episcopal Church* (VIII, 388-401), 133n.

Shipbuilder, needed, 67n.

Shipley, Jonathan, Bishop of St. Asaph, 123, 123n.

Shoemakers, free Negroes as, 125n; needed, 73n, 92n; Negroes apprenticed to, 106n.

Shropshire, Denys W. T., *The Church and Primitive Peoples,* 57n.

Shute, John, a slave owner, 60.

Silk, culture of, tried, xi, 98n.

Simms, Henry H., "A Critical Analysis of Abolition Literature, 1830-1840," in *The Journal of Southern History* (VI, 372, 377n), 109n, 135n.

Simons, Rebecca, a slave owner, 59.

Sioussat, Dr. St. George L., xi.

Skene, Alexander, 40, 41-42, 43-44, 55n, 58, 58n, 110.

Slave, amount of rice produced by each, 90n.

—— Code of South Carolina, 69-70, 74, 76, 109; a threat more than an actuality, 109n.

—— labor, as applied to rice and indigo, 90n-91n; division of, 44n; excluded white artisans, 45; indigo added working hours to, 91; Irish

detachment of time and space of home office, 138; advice of, to missionaries regarding baptism of Negro children, 23-24; almanac project urging planters to instruct Negroes approved by, 39; clergy appointed to superintend the Charleston Negro school, 106; close direction of missionaries by, 137; colonists must request missionaries from, 8n, 27, 27n; committee of, considers proposal for Charleston Negro school, 107, 108; consent of, required for removal of missionaries from area to area, 137; instructions of, to clergy and catechists, 4n; instructions of, to missionaries owning slaves, 52-53; provide books for Charleston Negro school, 119, 120, 121n; publications of, 137, 143, *see also* Literature, Pastoral Letters; records of, 143; Secretary of, 9, 143;

— program of, for Negro education: accepted part of social order for footage to institute change, 105; assumed future of Negro identified with white man, 4; attempted to modify discipline of plantation, 124; committed to Christianization of slaves, 136; conciliatory rather than contentious in technique, 51; education program of, inseparable from Christianization, 5; effect of American Revolution on, 128; hostility of slave owners toward, would threaten liquidation, 124; in long-term perspective, 132-133; intervened for Negro instruction, 123; need for Negro instruction urged, 36-37; saw Negro not as a producer but as a human being, 138-139; sensible of the great importance and necessity of Negro instruction, 35, 101; strategy to enlist support for Negro instruction, 54, 119, *see also* INSTRUCTION, missionary techniques; stressed cooperation rather than segregation, 126; wide scope of, 123.

See also INSTRUCTION, MISSIONARIES, Planters, NEGROES, Slaves, White settlers.

South: non-slaveholders in, at time of Civil War, 126n; present living standards in, compared with Africa, 127, 127n; stock of, 2.

South America, 2.

South Sea Annuities, to be used by S. P. G. for Charleston Negro school, 108.

Southern Literary Messenger, The, 2n.

Spain, 115.

Spaniards, 2.

Spanish, in Florida, offer freedom to slaves, 68, 68n; threats of, 67, 75, 102.

Spanish garrison, Negroes desert to, 68, 68n.

—— land grants, x.

—— language, fragments of, in Gullah, 138n.

—— settlements, 102.

Spell, ability of Negro boy to, 68.

Spelling books, requested, 114, 117, 143; *see also* Literature.

Standish, David, missionary in St. Paul's parish, 142.

Stanhope, George, Dean of Canterbury, sermon of, 37, 37n.

State v. Green, 94n-95n.

State v. Hudnall, 46n.

Stealing, defense of Negro, 52n; Indians learn from whites, 57; of books, 92.

Stevens, Robert M., minister in Goose Creek, 9, 9n.

Stew, Abig., a slave owner, 60.

Steward, Dan, a citizen, 60.

Stiles, Debor., a citizen, 59.

—— Sam, a citizen, 59.

Stone, Robert, missionary in Goose Creek parish, 93-94, 141.

Stoney, Samuel Gaillard, *Charleston, Azaleas and Old Bricks* (plates by Bayard Wootten), 20n, 46n, 48n, 133n.

Stono Rebellion, 68, 68n, 69, 69n, 80.

Stowe, Harriet Beecher, 44n.

Traders: cause woman slave to be scalped, 19; garrison for, 82; Indians revolt against tyranny of, 41n; lewd and debauched characteristics of, 30; missionary should accompany, 56; opportunity of, to incline infidels to Christianity, 37; wars promoted by, to get slaves for profit, 11.

Tradesmen, encouraged to settle in colony, 91n.

Transient families hired from year to year, 88.

Tribal arts, preservation of Negro, 45n.

—— customs, of Negroes and Indians, 55-57.

Trinity college, Dublin, 10n.

Truancy, of slaves, 29, 29n.

Tryon, Thomas, treasurer of the S. P. G., 115.

Turpentine, shipments of, xi, 74n.

Tustian, Peter, missionary in St. George's parish, 141.

U

Uprisings, Indian, 55, 61n, 67n, 76; see also Frontier; Insurrections.

—— apprehension of Negro, 94, 94n-95n.

Union, New York legislature acts on discrimination against Negroes in, 126, 126n.

V

Varnod, Francis, missionary in St. George's parish, 55-61, 73, 74, 86, 142, 144.

Vaux, Meta, 45n.

Vesey, Denmark, conspiracy of, 69n.

Vestry, ministers to be members of, 10n; writes to Society, 61, 66.

Vibert, Faith, "The Society for the Propagation of the Gospel in Foreign Parts: Its Work for the Negroes of North America before 1783," in *Journal of Negro History* (XVIII, 171-212), 39n.

Vine, culture of, 98n.

Vintners, need for, 73n.

Virginia, 102, 125n; colonization societies in, 33; manumission forbidden in, 33; Negro population in, 2n; state church of, after Revolution, 128-129, 129n; use of Irish instead of slaves for dangerous work, in, 21n.

Virginia, A Guide to the Old Dominion, 33n.

Virginia Quarterly Review, 127n.

Voyageurs, the, 66n.

W

Wages, Negroes would work for, 36.

Walker, Rich., a property owner, 91n-92n.

Wallace, Wm., a slave owner, 60.

Wally, Th., a citizen, 59.

Walter, Ricd., a citizen, 112.

Warburton, William, Bishop of Gloucester, sermon of, 123, 123n.

Warring, Josh & Joseph, slave owners, 59.

—— Richard, a slave owner, 59.

—— Th., a slave owner, 59.

Wars, Indian, 41; Cherokee, 94, 97, 120; colonists driven north by, 96, 97; colony ravaged by Indians, 41; commotions and confusions of, 94; halt profitable Indian trade, 41; of Yamassees, 41, 41n, 55; promoted by traders to get slaves for profit, 11; with French, 78n; see also Insurrections.

Washington, Booker T., 18.

Washington, D. C., riots in, 126n.

Washington, George, provisions of will, 136.

Wassamsaw, S. C., 92, 96.

Way, Aaron, a slave owner, 60.

—— Ebenezer, a citizen, 59.

—— Mos., a slave owner, 59.

—— Sam, a citizen, 59.

—— Th., a slave owner, 60.

—— Wm., a slave owner, 59.

Wealth: frontier as source of, 67; increasing, 74, 74n, 90-91; of colonies, 36, 37, 137n; of London, 37;